A HISTORY OF EAST EUROPEAN JEWS

A HISTORY OF
EAST EUROPEAN JEWS

by

Heiko Haumann

CEU PRESS

Central European University Press
Budapest New York

©2002 by Heiko Haumann
Translation © by James Patterson

First published in German as *Geschichte der Ostjuden*
by Deutsche Taschenbuch Verlag GmbH & Co. KG, München,
in 1990
Second German edition published in 1998

English edition published in 2002 by
Central European University Press

An imprint of the
Central European University Share Company
Nádor utca 11, H-1015 Budapest, Hungary
Tel: +36-1-327-3138 or 327-3000
Fax: +36-1-327-3183
E-mail: ceupress@ceu.hu
Website: www.ceupress.com

400 West 59th Street, New York NY 10019, USA
Tel: +1-212-547-6932
Fax: +1-212-548-4607
E-mail: mgreenwald@sorosny.org

Translated by James Patterson

The photos included derive from a private collection.
Photographer and date are both unknown.
The photos can be dated at the time between the turn of the century and
World War One.

All rights reserved. No part of this publication may be reproduced,
stored in a retrieval system, or transmitted,
in any form or by any means, without the permission
of the Publisher.

ISBN 963 9241 37 7 Cloth
ISBN 963 9241 26 1 Paperback

Library of Congress Cataloging-in-Publication Data

Haumann, Heiko, 1945-
  [Geschichte der Ostjuden. English]
  A History of East European Jews / by Heiko Haumann.
      p. cm.
  Includes bibliographical references (p.) and index
  ISBN – ISBN
  1. Jews–Europe, Eastern–History. 2. Europe, Eastern–History. 3. Europe, Eastern–Ethnic relations. 1. Title
  DS135.E8 H3813 2002
  947'.004924–dc21
                                        2002000999

Printed in Hungary by
Akaprint

Dedicated to Gottfried Schramm

TABLE OF CONTENTS

List of Maps	xi
Author's Preface	xiii

PART I. POLAND AS A PLACE OF REFUGE FOR JEWS — 1

The Polish Princes' Offer of Protection from Persecution	3
The Opponents of the Jews	11
Economic Success	15
Social Structure and Self-administration of the Jews	18
Learning and Culture	22
The Jews as Intermediaries between Town and Country	27
A Golden Age for the Jews in Poland?	30

PART II. EAST EUROPEAN JEWRY AS A 'CULTURAL PATTERN OF LIFE' IN EASTERN EUROPE — 33

The Catastrophe of 1648	35
The Consequences of the Catastrophe	39
The Kabbala	42
The Messiah in Poland: Shabtai Tsevi and Jacob Frank	47
The Popular Piety of Hasidism	51
The Origins of the *Ostjuden*	56
The 'Shtetl'	58
Contacts between Jews and Non-Jews: Jewish Peddlers and Innkeepers	61
The Symbiosis Diminishes	63
Jews in the Partitions of Poland	68
The Reaction of the Jews to the New Political, Intellectual, and Religious Conditions	74
The Tsarist Empire and the Jews	78
East European Jews outside Tsarist Rule	91

PART III. THE CRISIS OF THE JEWS IN EASTERN EUROPE AND A NEW IDENTITY 99

Transformation of the Traditional Intermediary Function	101
'Expulsion' and 'Restructuring'	106
Luftmenshn	109
Transformation of the Occupational Structure and New Intermediary Activities	111
Competition to Oust Rivals from the Market and Anti-Semitism	117
Haskala: The Jewish Enlightenment	119
Assimilation and Acculturation	122
'Necktied' and 'Kaftaned' Jews	123
By Way of an Example: Jews in Warsaw and Łódź	125
The Jewish Family	133
Men and Women in Jewish Society	135
Jewish Upbringing	143
Everyday Religious Customs	146
Synagogue and Community Organizations	156
Increasing Conflicts with the Non-Jewish World	161
Socialism, Zionism, New Jewish Identity	162
Immigration as an Attempt to Find a New Homeland	175
A Center of East European Jewry: Galicia and Bukovina	181
A Positive Model with Contradictions: Hungary	190
Different Attitudes to the Emancipation of the Jews in Romania, Serbia, and Bulgaria	194
A 'Ritual Murder': The Case of Bohemia and Moravia	198

PART IV. ATTEMPTED ANNIHILATION AND NEW HOPE 205

The Jews in the Russian Revolution and in the Soviet Union	207
East European Jewish Nationality and New Waves of Anti-Semitism: The Jews in Poland between the Two World Wars	214
A Precarious Situation in Individual East European Countries	228
The Attempted Extermination of the Jews	233
The Jews in Postwar Poland: New Suffering and New Hope	239

AFTERWORD: THE SIGNIFICANCE OF MEMORY	**245**
NOTES	**251**
SELECTED BIBLIOGRAPHY	**263**
Bibliographies, Lexicons, and other Aids, Periodicals	263
General Overviews and Comprehensive Works	264
Bibliography to Part I: Poland as a Place of Refuge for Jews	266
Bibliography to Part II: The East European Jewry as a 'New Cultural Pattern of Life' in Eastern Europe	266
Bibliography to Part III: The Crisis of the Jews in Eastern Europe and a New Identity	267
Bibliography to Part IV: Attempted Annihilation and New Hope	269
INDEX	**271**

LIST OF MAPS

Map 1. The Khazar Empire (ca. 650–ca. 970)   8
Map 2. Poland–Lithuania (ca.1550)   16
Map 3. The Spread of Hasidism   53
Map 4. The Jewish Pale of Settlement in the Russian Empire   83

AUTHOR'S PREFACE

"I am an East European Jew [*Ostjude*], and our homeland lies wherever we have our dead." So speaks the millionaire Henry Bloomfield in Joseph Roth's novel *Hotel Savoy* as he visits the grave of his father, Jechiel Blumenfeld. This sentence encompasses the entire history of the 'East European Jews' (sometimes referred to simply as *Ostjuden*). They are not simply 'the Jews in Eastern Europe'—although they developed there as a characteristic type—because they are scattered throughout the world. They have left behind their dead in many countries. Often, memory remained their only homeland.

One of the roots of this remembering lies in the region in which the East European Jews originated in the eighteenth century and took shape in the nineteenth: old Poland. As a result, the history of Polish East European Jews—under different forms of governance after the Partitions of Poland between 1772 and 1815—stands at the center of my account. It is in relation to this that the history of the Jews in Eastern Europe as a whole is concisely and comparatively sketched: the prehistory of East European Jewry, its spread throughout the region, and its encounters with West European Jewry. In this way, its characteristic features and the structures of everyday life emerge more clearly. An account of the circumstances in emigration would have been beyond the scope of this volume. The fate of the East

European Jews in the twentieth century is likewise merely outlined. Knowledge of this topic can be readily assumed.

This book is intended as an introduction, the purpose of which is to reinforce remembrance of the history and way of life of the East European Jews—which are part of our own history . For English-language readers, many studies are available, at different levels of specialization, about the history of the Jews, and in particular of those who lived in central and eastern Europe. But there is still no general account of this kind. In addition, my studies have concentrated on the specific role of the Jews in the region as intermediaries between different strata of society and different economic structures. I present the development and change of this role across the centuries, albeit in mere outline. To this end, I describe cultural and religious issues in parallel with social and economic ones, without claiming to do more than summarize the results of work done by others. My goal was to arouse curiosity, and to stimulate more detailed engagement with the theme. In order to make this often 'alien' world more vivid, I also use literary sources, even when the poetic license taken in their creation means that they are rather indirect reflections of reality.

Some parts of this book may sound elementary and even superfluous to many readers. However, the basic characteristics of Jewish religion and family life (such as the *bar-mitzvah,* the rites of the Sabbath, and so on) are essentially unknown to most of the present generation of Germans. At the same time, in Britain and America, especially in the metropolitan areas, these are fairly well known, and many a Gentile will have attended an occasion of this kind. Authors who write about the Jewish life of the past, such as Isaac Bashevis Singer, are also much more likely to be known to English readers than to Germans. The presence in New York, London, or Toronto of observing Orthodox Jews, speaking Yiddish and retaining much of the ways of life of their places of origin—that is, eastern Europe—makes the subject-matter of this book much less 'exotic' there than for readers in post-Shoah Germany and Austria. The author apologizes to those who feel 'patronized' by these explanations; they are welcome to skip them.

A word of explanation concerning the German word *Ostjuden* which I chose to retain: it is a notion that would be poorly reflected in the plain geographical term 'East European Jews'. (Moreover, the concept of eastern Europe is very differently understood in, for example, Britain or the USA, and elsewhere.) A more precise explanation of this notion will be found in part two of this book.

Finally, a note on personal and place names, particularly on the territory of the historical Polish–Lithuanian Commonwealth. It is normal in German books to call the capital of Silesia—in Polish Wrocław—by its German name Breslau, as German burghers have done for centuries. However, the modern reader would not be able to find Breslau in a contemporary atlas. In order to avoid any connotation of political revanchism, to which people in the region are understandably sensitive, in this book the place names (and occasionally Slavic or other personal names) are given in the form presently used and represented on up-to-date maps or in the relevant scholarly literature. For clarity's sake, when names first appear in the text, I have added other well-known variants in parentheses.

I have to thank a number of institutions which have supported research projects on whose results I was able to draw: the Volkswagen Foundation (Volkswagen-Stiftung), the German Research Council (Deutsche Forschungsgemeinschaft), the Swiss National Fund for the Promotion of Scientific Research (Schweizerische Nationalfonds zur Förderung der wissenschaftlichen Forschung), the German Academic Exchange Service (der Deutsche Akademische Austauschdienst), and the Polish and the Czechoslovak Academies of Science. The staff of the archives and libraries of Warsaw, Łódź, Prague, Freiburg im Breisgau, and Basel were very helpful. The illustrations were made available by Joanna Brańska, and Catherine Schott helped with their procuring and selection. I have received valuable advice from many colleagues, including Dr. Jürgen Hensel, Prof. Jerzy Tomaszewski, und Prof. Feliks Tych, as well as my colleagues at the History Seminar of the University of Basel. This book is dedicated to Gottfried Schramm, whose questions concerning the history of the *Ostjuden* stimulated me greatly and who has followed my work with sympathy, advice, and criticism.

The first German edition of this book appeared in 1990. It has met with such a favorable response that the fifth impression appeared as early as 1999. It has already been translated into Italian, Japanese, Czech, and Polish. I am very pleased that, after some delay, an English-language edition is now being made available to interested readers. The idea of turning to Central European University Press was Larry Wolff's. János Bak has vigorously supported the realization of the project. In addition, like Heidemarie Petersen, he has given valuable advice concerning the reworking of the text. James Patterson has translated the text faithfully. My deepest thanks go to them and to everyone else who has lent their assistance.

Basel, January 2002

Part I
POLAND AS A PLACE OF REFUGE FOR JEWS

THE POLISH PRINCES' OFFER OF PROTECTION FROM PERSECUTION

Israel saw how its sufferings were constantly renewed, impositions increased, persecutions grew, servitude became more onerous, and the rule of evil led to disaster after disaster and heaped up expulsion after expulsion, so that it could no longer withstand those who hated it, and so it took its leave and sought and inquired concerning the paths of the world, with a view to discovering which way it should take to find peace. Then came a message from Heaven: go to Poland!

So they went to Poland and gave an entire mountain of gold to the king as a gift, and the king received them with great honor. And God adopted them as His own, and He caused them to find mercy in the eyes of the king and the princes ... But there are also grounds for supposing that Israel had dwelt in the land of Poland since time immemorial and had prospered there in wisdom and law. For when they came from the Kingdom of the Franks they found in Poland a forest whose trees were covered in writing—a treatise from the Talmud was carved into every tree. This is the Forest of Kawczyn, which leads to Lublin.

And there are those who believe that even the name of the land springs from a holy source: the language of Israel. For Israel, when it came there, said "po-lin", that is, "spend the night here!", by which it meant "we wish to spend our nights here until God gathers the scattered people of Israel once more."

This is what our fathers told us.[1]

This legend expresses the hope that the Jews put in Poland, a hope which for a long time seemed to have become a reality. It also contains the origin of the migration to the East, that is, persecution in Central Europe, as well as why the Polish princes were interested in the Jews: their money. Ever since the bloody riots which broke out as a result of the First Crusade, Jews from German and Bohemian cities had sought refuge in Poland, especially in Silesia. In 1264 the Prince of Great Poland, Bolesław the Pious (1221–1279) issued the Statute of Kalisz, which became the basis for all later protective decrees for the benefit of the Jews.

This Statute built on Emperor Frederick II's Privilege of 1236 and on subsequent Privileges. It declared the Jews the 'chamber servants' of the Prince (see p. 9), to whom they had to make payments and who in return promised to protect them and assure them freedom in their economic activities. Moreover, Bolesław granted them the right to form self-governing communities. Attacks of any kind against Jews, even accusations of ritual murder, were severely punished by the Prince. King Casimir III the Great (1310–1370) reaffirmed the Statute in 1334 and extended its validity beyond Great Poland to include the whole territory under his authority.

Casimir energetically encouraged the immigration of Jews as they fled Central Europe—and also from Silesia, which was now a Bohemian fiefdom. He may have seen an opportunity to use the Jews, who would necessarily feel indebted to him, to counterbalance the German burghers in the cities. The king also had a Jewish 'court banker' called Lewko, to whom tax farming and the administration of salt mining were entrusted. At this time, tax farming, die cutting, and the minting of coins were extensively practiced by Jews in Poland.

In 1364 and 1367 Casimir issued new decrees to regulate additional areas of Jewish life. In this way the Jews ceased to be subject to German law and came under the jurisdiction of the voivode—the representative of the king in individual regions. In cases involving capital offences they even came under the direct jurisdiction of the king. This was a more or less consistent measure given the Jews' status as servants of the king's chamber. Jews also acquired economic privileges, including the right to acquire land and houses, both in the city and in the countryside. All these privileges were confirmed by Casimir's successors. These documents constituted the basis of the Jews' legal standing until the Partitions of Poland at the end of the eighteenth century.

In Lithuania—which since 1386 had been linked to Poland by personal union—a similar role was played by the Privileges of Vytautas/Witold (cousin of King Władysław Jagiełło and also Grand Prince from 1392 to 1430), which were granted to the three Jewish communities in Trakai, Brest-Litovsk, and Grodno.

> We hereby allow them [the Jews—H.H.] to purchase goods of all kinds and to retail beverages of all kinds, whether brewed by themselves or purchased, in their houses, if they pay our house an annual tax. They shall be permitted, like the burghers, to engage in buying and selling, both in markets and in shops, and also in trades of all kinds. They shall be permitted, like the burghers, to acquire fields and grassland, insofar as they pay the necessary sums to our house.[2]

Basically, this entailed equality of rights between Jews and non-Jews, at least in the economic sphere. Opponents of this policy were not long in coming forward, however. Living conditions for Jews in Poland–Lithuania could by no means be desribed as idyllic.

Actually, the history of the Jews of Eastern Europe goes back to the history of their expulsion from Israel, their wanderings in many lands, and their renewed persecution. The most significant migrations of the Jews went on the one hand to the Iberian peninsula (Hebrew: *Sepharad*) and on the other hand to Central Europe, particularly what would later become Germany (Hebrew: Ashkenaz). The Sephardim and Ashkenazim were henceforth to play an important role in Eastern Europe. There is evidence of Jewish merchants from the West in Eastern Europe since the eighth century. Others came from the Byzantine Empire. Towards the end of the eighth century, the khagan of the Khazars, Obadia, and that part of the upper echelons of Khazar society which was close to him, converted to Judaism, an event which caused a sensation through Europe.

The polemic between representative of different religions which was supposed to have led to the khagan's decision in favor of Judaism was presented by the famous philosopher of religion Judah ha Levi (ca. 1075–1141) in his work *Sefer ha Kuzari* ('Book of the Khazar'). Foreign-policy considerations must have been decisive: Obadia wanted to underline the independence and parity of his khaganate with respect to the Christian Byzantine Empire and the Muslim Caliphate. Between the seventh and the tenth centuries the Khazars built up an enormous empire which stretched from the Aral Sea to the northwest of the Black Sea, and from the Caucasus far to the north. The adoption of Judaism by the greater part of the ruling circle did not mean that the different tribes of the empire gave up their religions. In fact, it appears that internal differences were sharpened. When Kievan Rus', the first Russian state, was formed after 860, the two states soon came into conflict. Between 964 and 968 the Kievan prince Svyatoslav finally defeated the Khazars who had already been weakened through civil wars and the raids of the Pechenegs. Apparently, part of the Khazar Jews remained in their areas of settlement because there is evidence of a messianic movement among the Jewish khazars of the Crimea. Others returned to the Caucasus and there augmented the Jews who had earlier immigrated from Persia. They formed the core of the

'Mountain Jews' who even today live in communities rich in tradition. Khazar Jews also settled in Kiev and other cities in Rus', as well as in Poland. In early medieval Kiev there was a 'Jewish Gate', and when unrest broke out in 1113 after the death of the unpopular prince Svyatopolk II, Jews were also the victims of popular anger. They had represented the prince in business transactions, and also owned the salt monopoly, which made them very unpopular. A patter of conflict is already discernible here.

The great thrust of Jewish immigrants into Eastern Europe was connected to changes in their situation in Western Europe. The Christians, among whom anti-Jewish notions arose relatively early as a result of religious rivalries, had at first forced the Jews into fields of economic activity—above all tax farming and money-lending at interest—which appeared closed to themselves on religious grounds. However, it subsequently became clear what sort of profits could be made in this way, and after they had acquired the requisite skills the Christians sought increasingly to narrow the range of opportunities available to the Jews. From the eleventh century onwards prohibitions accumulated, culminating in persecutions and expulsions. The Jews were no longer needed.

A great wave of persecutions swept over Germany and Central Europe as a result of the First Crusade in 1096, and again during the Second Crusade in 1146–1147. Later, the pogroms reached their peak in 1348–1349 as the Black Death stalked the land. In search of the causes of the epidemic, people made 'scapegoats of the Jews'—they were supposed to have poisoned the streams and the wells. Here too we find a pattern of argumentation which pervades later history and presents a fundamental problem for the analysis of minorities: actions and events which are not clearly understood tend to be attributed to strange or exotic persons whose beliefs are suspicious and whose actions are unpopular.

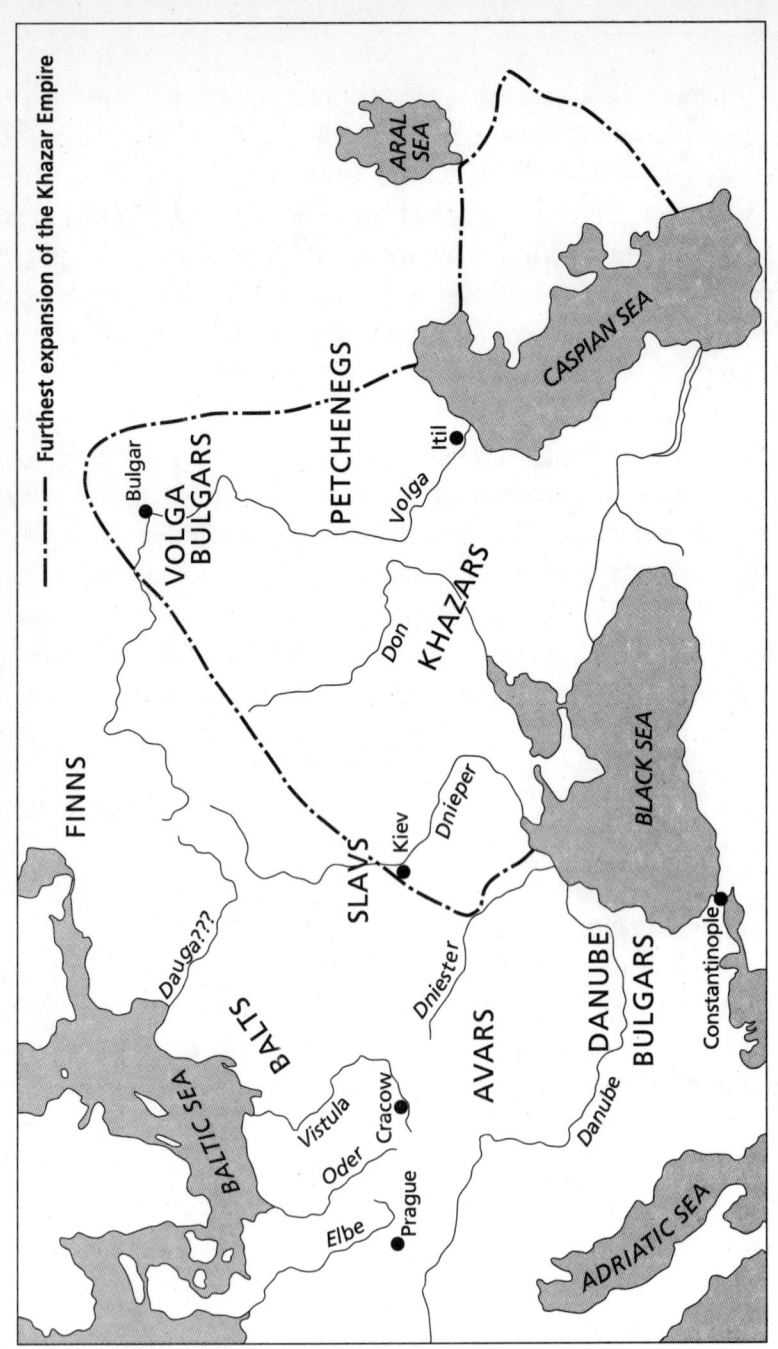

Map 1. The Khazar Empire (ca. 650–ca. 970)

Both the Jews' debtors and economic competitors benefited when, in 1389, the Christian population of Prague, stirred up by the accusation that the Jews had desecrated Easter and had attacked priests, burned down the Jewish ghetto in the Old Town, murdered a large part of the inhabitants, and looted their property. This was not to be the only attack on the Jews in the city. The Prague Jewish community at that time was one of the largest and most prosperous in Europe.

In the first half of the thirteenth century, accusations of ritual murder were increasingly brought forward as grounds for persecution. At Passover, Jews were alleged to slaughter Christian children in order to obtain the blood needed for ritual purposes. An investigation instigated by Emperor Frederick II in 1235 in the wake of an alleged ritual murder rejected the accusations. This was to little purpose, however; just as occasional papal decrees against accusations of this kind or against suspicions of poisoning streams had little effect. Belief in this legend continued until the recent past.

Frederick II, who was interested in the Jews primarily for economic reasons, declared them to be 'Servants of our Chamber' in 1236. This measure was intended to protect them—and at the same time to increase their service to the emperor, which augmented his treasury. As a result, Jews were subject to special laws, a development which had been coming for some time. With their subjection to special legal status the possibility arose of issuing an increasing number of extraordinary decrees. As a result, Jews were placed in circumstances of extreme uncertainty and dependency: many an emperor pawned, loaned, or sold his sovereign rights. Jews' 'lesser status' visibly forced them to the margins of society. They became a strongly delineated minority which was overwhelmingly looked down on by the majority.

Prominent among the special regulations to which Jews were subject were special taxes and clothing decrees, covering everything from pointed hats to the so-called '*Judenfleck*', a golden ring on the robe for men and a blue-striped veil for women. By these means it was made clear that the Jews stood outside the social order. Particularly important in this regard were the fourth Lateran Council of 1215, the Council of Basel in 1431, and—for Bohemia—the Prague Synod of 1349. The dress regulations for Jews were grounded not least on the fact that similar dress had hitherto mistakenly led to sexual relations between Christians and Jews.

These measures were accompanied by the increasing confinement of Jews to certain streets or quarters. Originally, this had frequently taken place of its own accord for commercial reasons—similarly to the streets inhabited by Christian artisans—to make religious life easier and to preserve their identity. Now, access to the Christian quarters was made more difficult, since 'Jewish streets' had to be closed off in the evenings. From the sixteenth century, after the Venetian model of 1516, the term 'ghetto' gained acceptance.

In most European countries people did not confine themselves to persecutions and special laws. Full-blown expulsions and deportations formed the—provisional—conclusion of this development. England and Southern Italy (excluding Sicily) began this process in 1290, and—after a number of different attempts—France (1394), Spain (1492), Portugal (1496–1497), Naples (1503), and, with some exceptions, the Papal States (1593), followed by other Italian states. The expelled Jews were once again scattered. Eastern Europe—for example, Walachia and Hungary—was the destination above all of the Sephardim.

German Jewry was spared such comprehensive expulsions. Political division into countless small territories helped: if the Jews were persecuted in one place, they could find shelter in a neighboring region. Even this was bad enough, however. Moreover, Jews—especially from the first half of the fifteenth century—could no longer obtain rights of citizenship in many cities. All this meant, incidentally, that retail trade between town and country remained the most important economic activity of the Jews and that they attained a central mediating role.

Although the history of the Jews in the European Middle Ages is by no means exclusively one of discrimination and persecution—there were numerous periods of peaceful coexistence with good mutual, even cultural relations—their situation was still precarious. In the event of social conflict, famine, or epidemics, accusations of ritual murder and bloody riots could occur at any time. Among ordinary people, belief in the potential guilt of the Jews was widespread, and as a rule this belief was strongly promoted by the church. As a result, it is not surprising that more and more Jews—Ashkenazim from Germany and neighboring territories—answered the call of the rulers of Poland, who promised them effective protection and privileges.

THE OPPONENTS OF THE JEWS

The Catholic Church was very much in the vanguard as far as anti-Jewish measures were concerned. On the model of the Lateran Council of 1215, the Council of Wrocław, then under the sway of one branch of the Piast dynasty, decided in 1267 that Jews should be compelled to reside in quarters separated from Christians and wear special insignia on their clothing. They would not be permitted to occupy any public office or obtain any position in which Christians would be their subordinates. It was also desired that Jews should be barred from the farming of taxes, duties, and minting, which would have deprived them of one of their most important sources of income.

However, although later Councils reiterated this decision, these measures met with little practical success. The Jews were much too important to the Polish rulers—above all for their Treasury—for the latter to agree to any significant reduction in their activities. As a result, it is not surprising that Jewish immigration to Poland continued. In the fourteenth and fifteenth centuries, we find increasing evidence of Jewish quarters in Polish cities: 1356 in Lviv (Lemberg), 1367 in Sandomierz, 1386 in Kazimierz near Cracow, and many others in Great Poland, Kujavia, Pomerelia, and Red Ruthenia.

Opposition to the Jews increased in proportion to their settlement and economic success. The Catholic Church was joined in its hostility above all by Christian merchants who felt threatened by Jewish competition. They demanded that Jews should be forbidden from lending money on real estate or letters of safe conduct, and generally that their activities should be restricted. It cannot be by chance that a series of accusations of ritual murder and crimes against the Host were made at this time. When in 1407 one priest preached from the pulpit of the Church of St Barbara in Cracow that the Jews had murdered a Christian child and used his blood for ritual purposes, the incensed crowd stormed Jewish houses, looted them, put them to the torch, murdered many of the inhabitants, and forcibly baptized countless Jewish children.

These campaigns reached their peak when the Franciscan monk John Capistran, endowed with inquisitorial powers, came to Poland in 1453. The reputation of this preacher—who clearly had great rhetorical gifts—as a 'scourge of the Hebrews' preceded him: he had already created havoc in Italy, Austria, Bavaria, and Silesia, and his rabble-rousing propaganda had had a devastating effect even in Bohemia and Moravia. He was able to win the support of the Polish cardinal Zbigniew Oleśnicki and to unite the demands of the clergy and the Christian burghers, as well as another ally, impoverished members of the minor nobility who were debtors of the Jews. King Casimir IV (1427–

1492), who had just reaffirmed the Privilege of the Jews, came under increasing pressure, especially when Capistran admonished him: "Take care that your neglect of my warnings does not bring the punishment of Heaven upon you!"[3] Casimir gave in and in 1454 declared that the Privilege could not conflict with divine law and the constitution.

The opponents of the Jews felt that their position had been strengthened by all of these events. In 1463 Poles who wanted to answer Pius II's call for a crusade once again looted the Jewish quarter of Cracow. In 1469 the Jewish quarter was moved in order to make room for the university. In 1564 in Poznań, a pogrom followed an outbreak of fire. In both cases, after the rioting the Jewish municipal authorities had to pay fines. The attempts of cities to obtain privileges *de non tolerandis Judaeis*—not to tolerate Jews—were of long-term significance. In many cities this could be achieved, although the prohibition was frequently circumvented. Bydgoszcz (Bromberg) set the ball rolling at the beginning of the fourteenth century. In 1483 the Jews were driven from Warsaw, and in 1494 the Jews of Cracow gave in to the constant pressure and moved to the suburb Kazimierz. Cracow remained closed to Jews as a place of residence, with a few exceptions, until 1867. At the end of the fifteenth century all Jews were expelled from Lithuania, although they were permitted to return on payment of a large fee: it seems that they still had their uses. The situation was particularly hard for the Jews in Royal Prussia—what later became West Prussia around Torún (Thorn), Gdańsk (Danzig), and Elbląg (Elbing)—a tradition which would continue during the Reformation among the Prussian Lutherans. The privileges which were granted to 20 cities in the sixteenth century developed out of individual expulsions. Interestingly enough in some quarters, suburbs, or even whole cities the Jews managed to obtain privileges *de non tolerandis Christianis:* for example, in 1568 in Kazimierz; in

1633 for the Jewish community in Poznań; in 1645 for all the Jewish communities in Lithuania. It is doubtful whether these measures provided particularly favorable conditions for peaceful coexistence between Jews and Christians.

In 1538 the Polish diet of Piotrków, under pressure from debt-laden members of the lower nobility, prohibited Jews from leasing public revenues. The Jews' highest organ of self-administration endorsed this measure in Lublin in 1581 and prohibited, on pain of excommunication the farming of salt-works, the minting of coins, duties on draught beer, customs duties, and tolls in Great and Little Poland, and in Mazovia. "People spurred on by a lust for profit and enrichment from numerous great leases—God forbid!—risk unleashing great danger on all [Jews]."[4]

They had learned from experience and wanted to take the wind out of their opponents' sails. At this time, by virtue of a heightened Counter-Reformation carried through by the Jesuits, an anti-Jewish mood had been stoked up once again. The causes of this included individual cases of conversion to Judaism, the accusation that the Jews had incited the Hussites to their heresies, and the Judaizers movement. This had come into being in the fifteenth century as a mixture of Judaism and Christian rationalism in Moscow and Novgorod, and in the sixteenth century had spread to Poland–Lithuania. There were further accusations that Jews had committed ritual murder or stolen consecrated communion wafers in order to obtain blood from them. For the Jews concerned, these accusations often meant death at the stake.

ECONOMIC SUCCESS

Despite all these anti-Jewish measures, the majority of Jews in the great kingdom of Poland could develop relatively freely. In 1565 a papal legate from Poland reported:

> In these territories there are great numbers of Jews who are not as despised as is elsewhere the case. They do not live in a state of degradation, and they are not restricted to despised professions. They own land, they engage in trade, and they study medicine and astronomy. They possess great wealth and are not only considered to be respectable people, but often wield authority over them. They bear no distinguishing insignia, and they are even permitted to bear arms. In short, they possess all civic rights."[5]

Even if this report is a little too extravagant in the positive picture it presents, it nevertheless makes some important points. In fact, there were Jews in Poland who were landowners and farmers—for the time being they had been spared restrictions of the kind familiar in Western Europe. Some rich Jews acted as organizers of settlements, founding villages. Others leased land and villages. In addition, many Jews practiced agriculture on the side, especially in the smaller towns, just like Christian townsmen who farmed a smallholding.

A larger group worked as tradesmen, supplying their co-religionists. This was necessary on the grounds of strict religious prescript alone, in accordance with which special butchers, bakers, and tailors were required. Different sources also speak of Christians commissioning Jewish craftsmen. That must have given rise to protests, particularly from the guilds, which were jealous of their monopoly. In many cities they were able to compel Jewish craftsmen to restrict their activities or at least to pay higher fees.

Map 2. Poland–Lithuania (ca. 1550)

But we should not overestimate the consequences of all this. Often, Jews were able to get round the prescriptions of the guilds—as a consequence, like Christian non-guild craftsmen, they were portrayed as *partacze* or bunglers, which can by no means be taken as an indication of the quality of their work. While Jews who lived in towns which belonged to the church had virtually no rights, the king protected them for the most part in his own towns, as did, increasingly, the upper nobility. He sought by this means to promote his own towns at the expense of the others. Until the middle of the sixteenth century Jews engaged in almost all forms of skilled trade. In Cracow, Lviv, and Przemyśl and other towns, Jews had their own guilds.

For the time being the attempts by Christian merchants to restrict the business activities of the Jews were relatively unsuccessful. In the wholesale trade Jews were supposed to restrict themselves to certain goods, while people wanted to keep them out of the retail trade altogether. Since the king and many of the higher nobility lent the Jews their support, however, they were always able to assert their rights. At the top were the wholesalers with their long-distance connections with Western Europe, but also with the East. Jews from Poland generally participated in the great fairs of the period: Venice, Florence, Leipzig, Hamburg, Frankfurt, Gdańsk. From the sixteenth century they established trading companies in order to have access to sufficient capital. Jews and Christians sometimes even combined to form one company. However, the majority of Jewish traders operated as small- or medium-scale shopkeepers or as grocers or peddlers. They often lived on the brink of subsistence.

The credit system was linked to trade for the purpose of securing financing. As money transactions increased this business became more and more important. Jewish lenders were centered in the economic focal points of Cracow, Poznań, and Kalisz, and only gradually penetrated the economically less developed regions. Not only did the king and the higher nobility profit from the skills of Jewish bankers, but also small merchants and craftsmen needed credit in order to open shops and workshops, while farmers often had to bridge the gap until the next harvest. To be sure, debts could not always be repaid. This insecurity explains, why between the thirteenth and the fifteenth centuries the rate of interest permitted to Jews—not only in Poland—was at times one hundred percent a year, or even more. Only later was it significantly reduced. Members of the lesser nobility and of the petit bourgeoisie in the towns were particularly badly hit by the burden of debt. It goes without saying that, as a result, the Jews were deeply unpopular. In many cases they invested their profits—as far as possible—in the farming of taxes, customs duties, and road tolls, and the leasing of salt mines, mills, distilleries, breweries, taverns, and estates, which they then partly subleased to poorer family members. In this way, however, they came into conflict with the peasants.

SOCIAL STRUCTURE AND SELF-ADMINISTRATION OF THE JEWS

Alongside a small upper stratum of rich merchants, financiers, and leaseholders; a relatively wide middle stratum of small traders, money lenders, brokers, craftsmen, and employees of the community had also come into being. The lower stratum was very diverse: its members ranged from journeymen, small shopkeepers, and shop assistants, through carters, porters, and servants, to hawkers and peddlers.

Mobility was greater within Jewish society than in its Christian counterpart. For all that, however, the hurdles which stood in the way of Jews ascending to the burgher class or to the nobility were virtually insurmountable. After the Counter-Reformation it became well-nigh impossible to overcome this 'apartheid' without converting to Catholicism. In Lithuania the fact that former Jews could subsequently be ennobled without further formalities was an inducement to conversion. Every now and then there were exceptions: for example, in 1525 the Lithuanian tax collector Michel Ezofowicz obtained a title of nobility without having to convert. Only in the eighteenth century did the Lithuanian nobility once more close its ranks.

Despite this high mobility there were also social tensions among the Jews. There are reports from the middle of the sixteenth century onwards concerning struggles between Jewish craftsmen and Jews who had invested their capital in the leather, textile, and clothing trades and as a result threatened not only the craftsmen's independence, but also their way of life. Popular rabbis lambasted the rich for exploiting the poor and attacked those rabbis who ingratiated themselves with the rich.

Sometimes non-guild Christian and Jewish craftsmen found themselves taking common action against guild elders. Jewish and Christian burghers also made common cause against the nobility. For example, in 1589 Jews reached an agreement with the municipal authorities in a place called Kamionka Strumiłowa, something which also shows that harmonious coexistence was perfectly possible between Jews and Christians. The councilors, according to this document, "have admitted the Jews into all their rights, into all their freedoms, and they shall bear all of them as burghers." The Jews undertook to participate in work for the benefit of the town, to post watches, and to do their share alongside the Christians during floods and similar eventualities. In return the Christians undertook to "protect the Jews as our neighbors from persecution and violence, from the nobility as well as from soldiers, to defend them and not to allow injustice to befall them … since they are our neighbors."[6]

But it was not only with Christians that spontaneous, loose organizations or firm arrangements were formed. Since the first Privileges were issued, Jews had had the right to regulate their own internal disputes in accordance with their own principles and to administer themselves. Until the sixteenth century this self-administration developed in a way the like of which could not be found anywhere else in Europe. Each community (*kehilla*) had its own *kahal*, its administrative organ, which combined both political and religious powers. The *kahal* elders were chosen from the most respected—and usually also the richest—members of the community. It was their task to oversee peace and security, cleanliness, and the observance of religious prescriptions. They therefore had to supervise the bathhouses, the utilization of meat, burials, and the school system. In addition, they were responsible for charitable works. Last but not least, they had to determine each individual household's share of the taxes which the community had to pay, and then collect them.

The need to fill the coffers of the state induced the governments of many countries, for example Russia, Poland, and Germany, to allow organs of self-administration to be set up. Even in the early modern period, when intrusion into the daily lives of citizens was increasing, such bodies were more effective tax-collecting agents than state authorities.

It was for this reason that King Sigismund I 'the Old' (1467–1548) decided to extend the self-administration of the Jews beyond the sphere of their communities. Between 1518 and 1522 he established four Jewish 'provinces' which could choose their own elders and tax collectors. In order to resolve disputes between Jews from the individual provinces, in 1530 the king ordered the creation of a standing tribunal of arbitration with its seat in Lublin. After the poll tax for Jews was introduced in 1549, Stephen Báthory (1533–1586), who had been crowned king of Poland three years previously, appointed a representative body for the Jewish population in the whole of the Kingdom of Poland–Lithuania. This 'Council of the Four Lands' (in Hebrew, *Va'ad Arba' Aratsot*), the 'Jewish parliament', met for the first time in Lublin in 1581. It was to sit at least once a year and elect a council, from its ranks, the 'Generality of the Jews': a marshal-general, a rabbi-general, a scribe-general, and a treasurer-general.

The Jews now had an unprecedented institution at their disposal. Other 'Jewish state parliaments' and similar organs were permitted elsewhere, but they never achieved the same significance as the one in Poland–Lithuania. In 1623 separate Jewish parliaments were established for the two parts of the kingdom to make tax collection easier. They remained in existence until 1764, and were revived shortly before the destruction of the Polish state.

The *Va'ad* by no means confined itself to matters of taxation, even though this was its main task in the eyes of the state. It organized charitable donations, regulated leases, and made recommendations concerning economic activity. In addition, it responded, as already mentioned, to anti-Jewish opinions and envy. For example, the Lithuanian *Va'ad* ordered that modest clothing should be worn and that even at weddings no conspicuous gifts should be given. The number of Christian servants also had to be reduced in order to counter criticisms. Young girls who had passed their fifteenth year and were still not married could obtain support to improve their marriage prospects. Care of orphan boys, including their food and clothing, was distributed among the community.

> Those boys who through God's mercy are gifted with understanding and whose education would be advantageous shall be sent to school for the purpose of learning Torah. Those boys whose understanding

would not suffice for study of Torah shall be employed as servants or set to learn a craft. Every effort should be made to ensure that they do not devote themselves to idleness.

Similar care was taken of refugees from other lands.[7]

In other words, the decisions of the *Va'ad* covered every aspect of Jewish life. Furthermore, the *Va'ad* negotiated with the state authorities and with the Polish regional and state parliaments. It was supported by the 'advocate' or *shtadlan*, who was required to reside at the seat of the Polish Sejm, the diet, and to represent the interests of the Jews through lobbying and gifts. This was a traditional and widespread method—not confined to Poland—of protecting oneself against persecution or further restrictions.

Besides taxation, the participation of Jews in civic construction work or defense also had to be dealt with. Included in this were agreements for the construction of fortified synagogues. If cities were attacked by enemies of the kingdom, Jews often stood shoulder to shoulder with Christians on the walls in the common fight. From the beginning of the sixteenth century they had to form their own militia units; though they could usually have this obligation commuted to the payment of a sum of money. Only after 1648 was greater pressure put on them in this regard. Religious prescriptions made common military service between Jews and Christians difficult, though isolated cases have come down to us from the sixteenth and seventeenth centuries.

LEARNING AND CULTURE

The relatively favorable circumstances of the Jews in Poland also fostered scholarly and cultural achievements. These reached their peak in the sixteenth and seventeenth centuries, although they continued to have an effect thereafter. In the foreground stood a preoccupation with religion and its practice. The invention of printing contributed to the rapid spread of literature. In 1534 the first Hebrew printing office in Cracow was founded, only a little later than the one in Prague, then the intellectual center of Judaism. Books were published in Hebrew for the educated reader. At the same time, many works were published in Yiddish in order to reach the mass of the people. At that time, Yiddish was little different in Eastern and in Western Europe, so the exchange was relatively straightforward. Particularly popular were biblical legends and simple explanations of the Talmud, as well as tales and chivalric romances. Although Jewish women as a rule were not particularly well educated, one of the most important authors of that period was a Jewess: Rebecca, daughter of Rabbi Meir Tiktiner from Tykocin (in the province of Białystok, in northeastern Poland), wrote not only religious songs, but also a book of advice for Jewish women. It was published in 1618 after her death and enjoyed great popularity.

Rabbinical literature, which consisted in the study and interpretation of the Talmud, represented the acme of Jewish learning. Fundamental questions of religious understanding were discussed, but the interpretation of the Talmud also had relevance for everyday life.

Within the rabbinical literature of Polish Jewry two methods of interpretation stood in opposition. The Cracow rabbi Jacob Pollak (1460–1541) was instrumental in establishing the so-called *pilpul* method. This method—the name of which means 'pepper'—amounts to a dialectical game with thesis, antithesis, and synthesis, and is used to address controversial problems. In a way, *pilpul* expresses the fact that the Jewish religion does not know dogmatism—attempts in that direction ultimately did not succeed—but is an open system oriented towards discussion and dialogue. Using this method one attempts to do justice to each of the great teachers and to follow his utterances, even in the case of teachers who opposed each other. In many cases this method was used merely as an exercise, using arbitrary themes, or what were in fact only apparently disputed questions. In such cases it was simply a matter of 'wit.' Of course, this could easily lead to hairsplitting. As a result, many rabbis—such as Lubliner Salomon Luria (1510–1573)—turned against *pilpul* and in its place approved a rational method, strictly oriented towards the object of discussion. Nevertheless, *pilpul* remained predominant for a long time.

Of the great scholars of that period mention should certainly be made of Moses Isserles (1520–1572). He led the Yeshiva, the school of Talmudic learning, founded by Jacob Pollak in Cracow and wrote many important works on religion, philosophy, and as well as secular fields of study. His *Mappa* ('The tablecloth'), a commentary on one of the main works of Talmudic literature, the *Shulhan 'arukh* ('The prepared table' or 'The well-laid table'), made a particular impressian on his contemporaries. The *Shulhan 'arukh* is a long authoritative work of Jewish law, written by the rabbi of Adrianopole and Safed in Galilee, Joseph Caro (1488–1575). Moses Isserles adapted it to the needs of the Jews of Central and Eastern Europe and made it a companion to draw upon in all vital questions.

In the period of the Reformation and the Counter-Reformation, commentaries on the Talmud began to represent Judaism in a favorable light in comparison to the Christian faith. This followed on from earlier polemical tracts, particularly those of Yom Tov Lipman of Mühlhausen, who had lived in Cracow between 1400 and 1425. His most important work was published in 1644. Particularly well known were the polemics of Isaac of Trokai (1533–1594). He pointed out contradictions in the Christian religion, but he was most concerned with contradictions between Catholicism and how Catholics conducted themselves. This triggered violent discussions which continued after his death. The French *encyclopédistes*, and particularly Voltaire, praised his pointed argumentation and took him as an example in their critique of Christianity.

The fact that such Jewish polemics could appear at all, and that even public disputations between Jews and Christians could take place, is another indication of the tolerance enjoyed by the Jews in Poland. In Western Europe this would not have been possible at that time. Only after the intensification of the Counter-Reformation did this situation change.

A body of early enlightenment thought may be found in the rabbinical literature. It is therefore not surprising that Jews also played an important role in the secular sciences grounded in reason and sought to bring them into harmony with faith. The Jewish community in Poland yielded a number of important figures, particularly in mathematics, mechanics, astronomy, and medicine. Historiography also reached a pinnacle with Natan Hanower from Zasław (died 1683). It was his task, in his chronicle *Yavein metsula* ('Deep swamp'), published in Venice in 1653, to pass on to posterity the sufferings of the Polish Jews during the Cossack pogroms of 1648 (see below).

Jewish learning was by no means confined to a narrow upper stratum. From the sixteenth century onwards, Jews were obliged to send their sons between the ages of four and eight to the *qahal* school. There they studied Hebrew, read the Bible, learned the four basic arithmetical operations and were introduced to them principles of morality. In the secondary schools, which were attended by boys between the ages of eight and thirteen, study of the Talmud and its commentaries began. The basis of education was learning by rote. Girls were not admitted to these schools and received their education at home, in richer families with the help of a tutor. The most important thing for girls was preparation for their later household duties, not study.

For men, however, scholarship often brought considerable prestige. To marry his daughter to a learned young man, however poor he might be, was the highest aim of every Jewish father. Many young men looked upon learning and study of the Talmud as their life work. As a result, they had to be supported in some way by their family or by the community. This study took place in *yeshivot* (plural of *yeshiva*), schools for talmudic study. Here the young men sat all day long in the community of students, chanting passages from the Talmud, rocking back and forth in order to aid their concentration. They discussed difficult passages in groups, usually employing the *pilpul* method.

The educational level of the Jews in Poland was higher in the sixteenth century than in the eighteenth. There was a *yeshiva* in all the larger towns, and the Polish *yeshivot* were highly respected throughout the Jewish world. Natan Hanower wrote:

> Nowhere among the scattered Israelites was there so much learning as in Poland. There was a *yeshiva* in every community and the rector of that yeshiva was always well rewarded so that he could work without cares and make teaching his vocation ... Every community supported young people and granted them a weekly allowance so that they could study with the rabbis of the *yeshiva*.[8]

With the onset of wars and devastation from the middle of the seventeenth century, the situation changed drastically. Before then few rich Jews sent their sons to secular schools rather than to *kahal* schools.

Despite the strict adherence to religion, the culture of the Jews in Poland was still not sharply separated from that of their surroundings. Jews met with Christians, celebrated with them, and dressed like them. The prescriptions of the Catholic Church concerning clothing were scarcely observed for a long time. We may assume that a characteristic Jewish garb gradually developed from the sixteenth century onwards, including the kaftan and black cap, supplemented by the long beard and the side- or temple locks, the *peyes*. The construction of their dwellings was similar to that of Christians, apart from some peculiarities related to religion, just as they were characterized by different practices and celebrations. There was as yet no thoroughgoing separation of Jews in Western and in Eastern Europe.

Material culture found expression primarily in the construction of synagogues and in the fashioning of sacred artifacts. Ornamentation with animal and plant symbols has particular significance, since Jews are forbidden to depict people. The oldest monument of Jewish architecture in Poland is the Old Synagogue in Kazimierz, the suburb of Cracow. It was constructed at the end of the fourteenth century after models in Worms, Regensburg, and Prague, and renovated in 1570. In the eastern regions of Poland–Lithuania synagogues as big as fortresses were built. Also widespread, although predominantly only from the eighteenth century onwards, were wooden synagogues with wonderful murals. The carvings on synagogue doors and gravestones reached a high level of artistry. Here, as in a wide range of artistic crafts, close interrelations with non-Jewish art in Poland and with Central and Western Europe may be discerned.

THE JEWS AS INTERMEDIARIES BETWEEN TOWN AND COUNTRY

By the seventeenth century the Jews had managed to obtain for themselves a unique position in Poland not only in culture, but also in the economic and social spheres. They took up the role of intermediary between town and countryside. To be sure, this function also fell to Jews of other lands: it was "the characteristic quality or trait of the Jews in European history."[9] In Poland, however, they exercised a virtual monopoly, and even its concrete expression marked out its exceptional nature. As already mentioned, the richer Jews often invested their profits in leases, which they then subleased to poorer family members: taxes, customs duties, road tolls, milling, distilleries, breweries, and taverns, even estates. They entered into a virtual symbiosis with the higher nobility which was in terms of economic function and relation to the rest of the society so close that the latter protected the Jews from their enemies. Later still it was said: "My grandfather on my mother's side, who no longer 'possessed a piece of land', always said that 'you can't be a proper Polish nobleman without a Jew!' My grandfather on my father's side, on the other hand, who still 'possessed a piece of land', was of the opinion that 'one is even more noble if one has both a piece of land and a Jew!'"[10]

As lessees or administrators of the property of the nobility, the Jews came into direct contact with the peasantry, for example, in mills and above all in taverns. Since they were at the same time connected to Jewish merchants they were soon organizing economic activity as a whole. As administrators and lessees they gave instructions concerning the running of the manor and production. As taverners they sold the products of the manor—not only spirits—to the peasants or provided a 'trading center' for many business negotiations. The hawkers or 'village walkers' and the grocers satisfied the requirements of the peasants for goods from the town, but also purchased their products. Jewish taverners and small traders alike often acquired the trust of the peasants and then helped them with their affairs, and not only commercial matters. As a rule, it was also Jewish traders who bought the surplus products of the noble estates and sold them in the towns. In the other direction, they supplied goods from the towns, which they often obtained from Jewish craftsmen there.

In this way an economic circulatory system operated between town and countryside within the Jewish community and generally within Polish society—peasants, nobles, and town-dwellers were all linked together by the Jews. This central position was certainly not free of conflict. Apart from the attacks of the Catholic Church, the indebted lesser nobility, and the rival Christian burghers, relations with the peasantry were particularly complex. Even when peasants trusted 'their' Jews, and entrusted the arrangement of their affairs to them, two different ways of life collided here. The 'moral economy' (E. P. Thompson) of peasants was determined by definite ideas about 'honor' and production which had been handed down to them by their forefathers. At the forefront in this regard was the requirement to secure one's daily necessities and livelihood, not an orientation towards profit. The profit motive, however, characterized the economic activity of the Jews. Because they were predominantly involved in financial transactions they were considered to be 'greedy for money' or generally avaricious. As 'pioneers' or even as 'colonizers of progress' the Jews entered the peasant world as aliens.

Furthermore, the Jews, when they collected taxes or served schnapps, were readily regarded as instruments of the lord of the manor. In this way they became involved in the social tensions which existed between the peasants and the feudal lords. When Catholic priests fanned the flames of religious conflict, pilloried Jewish inns as the refuge of the Devil, or even seized upon accusations of ritual murder—reproaches which hit their target because Jewish religious practice seemed secretive to the outsider—the otherwise good relations between peasants and Jews could quickly turn into aggression and violence. As a result, the intermediary function at the same time embroiled Jews in social conflicts.

A GOLDEN AGE FOR THE JEWS IN POLAND?

All in all, the Jews in Poland constituted a flourishing community. Moses Isserles wrote: "Better a morsel of dry bread in peace, as in these regions [around Cracow], in which their hatred does not descend upon us as it does in the German lands".[11] In the opinion of Natan Hanower: "What is generally known does not require proof: never was there so much Torah in the whole of the Diaspora as in the land of Poland."[12] It was often said, in comparison with other lands and with later periods, that the Jews lived in a 'golden age.' From the sixteenth century comes the proverb: 'The Republic of Poland is hell for the peasant, purgatory for the town-dweller, heaven for the nobleman, and paradise for the Jew.'[13] One example of the respect in which the Jews were held is the story that Rabbi Saul (Shaul) Wahl (ca. 1545–1617), a customs duties and tax farmer, became the councilor of the great persons of the kingdom. According to one common legend, in 1587, when two kings were elected at the same time by different electors—Sigismund III Vasa ultimately defeated Maximilian of Austria, the Habsburg candidate—Saul even became king for a night.[14]

Although this 'paradise' was often fairly wretched, Poland remained extremely attractive to Jews, a fact which also found expression in a growing population. In 1500 there were around 18,000 Jews in Poland and 6,000 in Lithuania—less than one percent of the total population—while in 1648 the number had increased to 500,000, five percent of the population. The bulk of the immigrants still came from the German empire. Some Sephardic Jews had in the meantime settled in Zamość, southeast of Lublin. From one-quarter to one-fifth of the Jews lived in the countryside, the majority in the towns. Preeminent in this respect in the seventeenth century was Red Ruthenia, where thirty to forty percent of its Jewish population living in towns, followed by Little Poland with ten to fifteen percent, and Great Poland with ten percent. In Mazovia, despite extensive prohibition, ten percent of the Jewish population was urban.

At this time the economic activities of the Jews were also at a highpoint. In the Union of Lublin of 1569 the different regions of the kingdom were redistributed between Poland and Lithuania. Southern White Russia and Ukraine, Podlasia, Volhynia, and Podolia went to Poland. The magnates began immediately with the colonization of these regions which were economically or politically underdeveloped. For this they needed the Jews, either as financiers or as lessees or sublessees. It was precisely here that *arenda*, leasing, was particularly characteristic. A large-scale Jewish migration eastwards began. In a number of towns the Jews made up the majority of the population. The existing peasant population was forced to become part of the Polish feudal system, a process in which the Jews were involved as "the instruments of manorial oppression."[15] In Ukraine the Jews became entangled in a conflict which was even more pronounced than in the regions further to the west because social problems were compounded with religious and nationalistic ones: Jews were caught between lords of the manor and peasants, between Catholics, Orthodox, and Uniates, and between Poles and Ukrainians. They appear to have been well aware of their dangerous situation. Many sources speak of their weapons or of their fortified synagogues. And then came the great catastrophe.

Part II
EAST EUROPEAN JEWRY AS A 'CULTURAL PATTERN OF LIFE' IN EASTERN EUROPE

THE CATASTROPHE OF 1648

In April 1648 a torrent of Cossacks from the lower reaches of the Dnieper poured into Ukraine attacked Poland from the east and annihilated the Polish army which was stationed there. Encouraged by this victory, Ukrainian peasants rebelled and joined forces with the Cossacks. The Crimean Tatars, vassals of the Turks who had long been in conflict with the Poles, also supported the rebels. In campaigns of unprecedented cruelty which lasted over many years, with short breaks and varying success, the Cossacks and their allies plundered large parts of what was then Poland and Lithuania: Ukraine, White Russia, and Polissya, Volhynia, Podolia, and regions of Red Ruthenia. Kiev, Minsk, and Brest-Litovsk were captured. The armies advanced as far as Lviv. As the armies advanced and in the captured towns and cities unimaginable butcheries took place among the Polish and especially the Jewish population. Estimates of the number of Jews who lost their lives vary from tens of thousands to well over 100,000.

Jews in the kingdom of Poland were now subjected to pogroms of hitherto unknown violence. The suffering and the shock continued to afflict the survivors for a long time afterwards. Long accumulated tensions were released in this bloody massacre. The Cossacks, ethnically mixed, warlike mounted nomads, had probably settled from the fifteenth century in different regions of southern Russia, control over which was still not fully established. In the sixteenth century they were strongly Slavicized and considered themselves to be Russian Orthodox in matters of religion. Russian peasants ('runaways') who were fleeing from being bound to the land—a precondition of serfdom—in the Principality of Moscow, came to join them. Many inaccessible settlements were established in the marsh- and riverside forests of the great rivers. Men capable of bearing arms elected a Hetman as leader and decisions were taken on all important matters at general assemblies. In the seventeenth and eighteenth centuries, the Cossacks formed the nucleus of the great revolts against serfdom or the extension of state power.

From this standpoint, the Dnieper or Zaporozhian Cossacks—the land 'beyond the rapids' in the bend of the Dnieper before its mouth in the Black Sea was called Zaporozhye—were defending themselves against the attempts of the Polish magnates to colonize Ukraine. Neither they nor the absconded peasants wished to become the serfs of Polish seigneurs and perhaps also be forcibly converted to Catholicism. For the moment a compromise was reached: whoever cultivated the empty steppe should be registered and thereby regarded as free (also from taxes). Nevertheless, the Poles attempted to keep the number of 'registered Cossacks' low and maintain Cossack loyalty to Poland in order to drive a wedge between the contending parties. Furthermore, no one wanted to lose the services of the Cossacks in the wars against Russia, Turkey, or the khanate of the Crimean Tatars.

Anger over the excessively low number of 'registered Cossacks' found release from time to time in unrest and uprisings. This problem also played a catalytic role in 1648. The Cossacks had at their disposal a particularly capable hetman, Bohdan Khmelnytsky (ca. 1595–1657), who gave up his secure life as a lord of the manor, probably for personal reasons, and placed himself at the head of the uprising. It was said that he had employed a Jew on his estate to run a schnapps enterprise for him, so enabling him to boost his revenues. That did not prevent Khmelnytsky from giving free rein to the hatred which many peasants and Cossacks felt for the Jews: they had suffered too much at the hands of the latter in their role as the instruments of the Polish nobility in the form of tax collectors, traders, estate stewards, lessees, or innkeepers. The Jews were regarded as the henchmen of all evil, as a result of which—reinforced by religious rabble-rousing—the general bitterness was directed against them. Naturally many people were promised a share of the booty.

In 1654 the Cossacks swore an oath of allegiance to Alexis, the tsar of Russia, in Pereyaslavl' (the so-called Pereyaslavl' Agreement), and submitted to Russian autocracy. Khmelnytsky had hoped, through the uprising and his diplomatic maneuvers between the powers involved, to obtain an autonomous Cossack republic, federated with Russia and bound in personal union to the tsar as overlord. The only thing that came of this was a letter of clemency which to a large extent reaffirmed for the Cossacks the rights and privileges which they had earlier enjoyed under the Polish king and conceded a larger number of 'registered Cossacks.' It denied them autonomy in the sphere of external affairs and made the election of the hetman dependent upon the confirmation of the tsar. The incorporation of the Cossacks in the Russian state and the subjugation of the peasants under serfdom was now only a matter of time.

The wars—and with them the sufferings of the inhabitants of all regions—by no means came to an end in 1654. The tsar took this opportunity to move against Poland with the help of the Cossacks. In 1655 Sweden also entered the conflict; Swedish involvement which continued until 1660. From 1659 armed clashes took place with 'renegade Cossacks' who had no intention of bowing to tsarist authority. In 1667 Russia and Poland finally agreed a truce as a result of which Ukraine was divided along the Dnieper River. With this the "wars of bloody inundation" came to an end.[1] They were effectively continued, however, in successive conflicts for supremacy in Eastern Europe, which came to a head in the Northern War during the time of Peter the Great, and even found expression in the Partitions of Poland at the end of the eighteenth century.

The uprising of 1648 marked the start of the military and political decline of the Polish "republic of nobles with a monarchical head" (Engels). At the same time, the region which was most heavily populated by Jews became a theater of war for more than a century. The pattern of 1648 was repeated again and again: social and confessional tensions discharged themselves on the Jews. Things came to a new climax with the uprising of the Haidamaks—the 'irregulars'—in 1768, when, in connection with the Polish–Russian conflict, Orthodox Ukrainian peasants rose up against Catholic Polish nobles and Jewish intermediaries. Once again, many Jews lost their lives.

On the other hand, the relative intellectual and religious tolerance enjoyed by the Jews came to an end. The terrible events caused people's religious feelings to become fanatically inflamed. This found expression, for example, in the fact that, after the defense of the monastery of the order of St Paul in Częstochowa against Swedish forces, which was regarded as a miracle, the King of Poland, John II Casimir, declared the Virgin Mary to be the Queen of Poland (in 1656). In this climate people found it difficult to tolerate those of a different faith. The Catholic Church attacked the Jews ever more fiercely and declared them to be responsible for many of the unfathomable occurrences characteristic of those troubled times. The Jesuits and the Inquisition of the Dominicans were particularly prominent in this. There are many reports of accusations of ritual murder and desecration of the Host.

THE CONSEQUENCES OF THE CATASTROPHE

The Jews who survived in Poland somehow had to cope with the shock of the pogroms. Apart from that, they were forced to realize that, while one part of Poland had stood up for them—it had defended them or had fought alongside them—another had deserted them and offered them up for sacrifice. The attacks of the Catholic Church were increasingly striking a chord among the faithful. How should the Jews react? The former institutions had been laid low; the flower of learning had been cut down. A great number of schools and colleges had been destroyed by the insurgents, as had many important book collections. In spite of the greatest efforts the education system could not be reestablished at its previous high level. The *kahal* was also badly affected, although, at least at first glance, it seems to have been able to reorganize the communities. In this connection we come across the astonishing phenomenon that many nobles, even priests, entrusted their money to the Jewish community organizations as a result of the disappearance of many banking and credit houses during the troubles. The *kahal* at times became a 'bank' and so the mediating function of the Jews was utilized in a new way.

Since the *kehillot* were increasingly financing themselves through banking, they often became dependent on their financial backers. The need to make a profit came to the fore and favored those who actually carried out the financial transactions. A *kahal* oligarchy came into being which no longer allowed the whole community, and the growing number of poor Jews, to share in their prosperity, as had earlier been the case. The new oligarchy even knew how to take advantage of the allocation of tax and duty obligations. The kahal degenerated into an "instrument of internal Jewish exploitation."[2]

The fact that the supraregional organs of self-administration, particularly the Jewish parliament, had lost significance, both in

Poland and in Lithuania, also contributed to this development. During the troubles and the wars the king and the nobles, even the Sejm itself, paid less and less attention to the *Va'ad*, which was now seldom consulted in most decision-making. In 1764 it was formally dissolved. Only during the final phase of the Polish state, in 1788, would it again play a role, if only for a short time.

The previous situation was not reestablished in the economic or social spheres either. Superficially, the Jews in Poland experienced a rapid 'consolidation.' In 1764 there were 750,000 Jews in the kingdom of Poland—around seven percent of the population. The human losses caused by the troubles were 'made up' through a high birth rate, and partly through immigration. This is all the more remarkable because some of the surviving Jews left their homeland and fled, even to the West. Many 'Jewish villages' in Germany had their origin in this process or at least their Jewish population grew considerably. The immigration of Jews from the West to the East began to reverse itself. More Jews—one-third—had now settled in the countryside than in the first half of the seventeenth century. They found employment on those noble estates which had been smitten by the hand of war. More than ever before nobles were now bringing in Jews as lessees and administrators. But even in the towns, not least in the 'private towns' of the nobility, the Jews once again played an important economic role. The symbiosis which existed within the framework of the Jews' intermediary-function seemed to reassert itself, even to become deeper.

> Szybuscz is an old town and has been inhabited by Jews since the beginning of the migration; in the year 1648, when destruction came upon the town, the great synagogue was burned down and everyone in the town was murdered. Prince Potozky had had it rebuilt and had brought back the Jews and freed them from taxes, duties, and other

obligations for twelve years for the maintenance of the lord's household. Thenceforth every Jewish householder paid him an annual sum of one thaler for his house and half a thaler for each chimney. One Jew was put in charge of the houses as assessor and had to decide what a 'house' meant for tax purposes. The Jewish butchers did not need to slaughter any of their pigs but every week, on the day before the Sabbath, brought to the princely authorities a basket of fat and to the representative of the *starosta* brought a great dish of meat. People bought houses, purified salt, brewed beer, and made wine, traded in their own way, and were not subject to the jurisdiction of the city authorities, but rather to the judges of the prince's court. Rabbis and community representatives were appointed in accordance with Jewish custom and law.[3]

As in the case of the reorganization of the *kahal*, there were few who ever really recovered from the catastrophe in the economic sphere. Even when Jews could obtain a controlling position in domestic trade, business was mostly on a small scale. In comparison with how things had been before there were fewer Jews with sufficient capital. The gulf between rich and poor became greater.

All these changes did not leave the Jews' way of life untouched. Added to the shock produced by the massacres and the increasing hostility of their surroundings came uncertainty because the world as it was now was quite different from what it had been before. The internal social conflicts came to a head, and tried and tested institutions lost their authority. Even the answers of the rabbis, especially their sometimes hairsplitting *pilpul* interpretation of the Talmud, were in many cases no longer satisfying as people sought the meaning of events, and an appropriate response to new and unusual situations. Many began to seek new paths.

THE KABBALA

Kabbalistic learning, which was very popular in Poland, was a considerable aid in the search for answers to the circumstances which now prevailed. It was nourished by traditions which incorporated different lines from Germany, Spain, and Palestine. The Kabbala (Hebrew for 'tradition') had been active in Judaism for a long time and can by no means, as is usually the case, be described as a purely mystical movement. In its strict relationship to religion and religious laws, and in its particular kind of philosophy, thoroughly rationalistic elements are discernible which are bound up with mystical influences.

The Kabbala received its first systematization in the Middle Ages, above all in German Hasidism. The Hasidim (from Hebrew *hasid*, 'pious one'), took the "religious values and ideals" of the people further.[4] Philosophy was part of Jewish folk culture.

The teachings which were developed primarily between 1150 and 1250—the most famous were those of Judah the Hasid (died 1217)—primarily concerned the secrets of creation. For example, it was a matter of dispute among the Hasidim whether an end of time could be calculated on the basis of indications contained in the Bible. This question stirred people's emotions, and Christians were also concerned with considerations of this kind. High moral demands were made of the 'pious': he should ascetically turn aside from the world, observe religious prescriptions, and practice love and the fear of God. Those who erred should not be despised but treated with humanity.

According to the Bible, "in the beginning was the Word." The Torah was considered to be divine in nature: no letter or full stop could be changed or left out. On this basis, attempts were made to discover the power of the secret name of God with combinations of a certain number of words and letters. Some thought that in this way the Golem, an artificial man, could be brought into being. In a late form such Kabbalistic ideas and experiments appeared in Poland from around 1600 and revolved around Rabbi Elia of Chełm who had died in 1583. He bore the epithet 'ba'al shem'—which goes back at least to the eleventh century—'master of the name'. This expressed the idea that he knew the true names of living creatures and things and had magical powers. He was supposed to have created a man out of clay and brought him to life with the help of the divine name. On his forehead he wrote the word 'emet,' that is, 'truth.' The golem performed all kinds of services, but grew to such a height that the rabbi could no longer reach his forehead in order to erase the first letter 'e', so that the word 'met'—that is, 'death'—would remain and the artificial man would be destroyed. When the golem became too dangerous the rabbi hit upon a cunning plan: he got the golem to take off his boots and was then able to reach his forehead. Unfortunately the collapsing clay crushed the rabbi to death (or badly injured him, according to another version of the story).

This legend was probably passed on from Poland to the famous Rabbi Judah Löw ben Betsalel of Prague (ca. 1520–1609). The artificial creature also became dangerous here when the Rabbi forgot to remove the paper bearing the name of God from its mouth before the Sabbath. Just in the nick of time—the community had already sung the Sabbath psalm, but the Sabbath itself had not yet begun—Rabbi Löw was able to take the name of God out of the golem's mouth. The practice of singing the Sabbath psalm twice in the Prague 'Altneushul' is attributed to this. There have been a number of different literary treatments of this legend. A number of attempts have been made to find the remains of the golem on the roof or in a secret room in the synagogue. The report by the "raging reporter" Egon Erwin Kisch has become famous.[5]

A continuation and partial transformation of the Kabbala took place in Spain in the thirteenth century. Two forms must be fundamentally distinguished. Abraham Abulafia (ca.1240–1291) strove "to unseal the soul, untie the knots which bind it".[6] In fervent and at the same time rational expositions he prescribed how, with the help of letters of the alphabet or combinations of them, one could meditate and achieve a state of ecstasy so as to immerse oneself in the name of God. This was supposed to contribute towards man's liberation.

In contrast Moses de León (died 1305) rejected the path of meditation. One should concentrate entirely on the words of Holy Scripture, the Torah, in order to examine the "secret contents of the world of the divine itself." By this means one may enter into a direct relationship with God, with whose hidden life one can—as a mystery—become one. Moses wanted to retain "naïve folk belief," notwithstanding the complexity of his symbolism.[7] Something quite new was his idea that, with the divine queen, the Shekhina, the feminine element in God had separated itself from the element of the masculine and that only by redemption will complete oneness in God be restored.

This teaching is reflected in one of Isaac Bashevis Singer's stories:

> He [Reb Yomtov], a talmudic scholar, who was responsible for removing the impure fat and veins from kosher meat, had the soul of a female. When he prayed he called not so much to the Almighty as to the Shekhina, the female complement of God. According to the Kabbala human virtues bring about the unification of God with the Shekhina, and also that of the angels, cherubim, seraphim, and holy souls in heaven. However, total merging in heaven will take place only after the Redemption, the coming of the Messiah.[8]

By the way, this notion also had an influence on the Jewish conception of love and marriage. Whoever attains communion with God in constant love (*devekut*–Hebrew: 'attachment') is a *tsadik* (Hebrew: 'righteous man'). Moses set down his teachings, which were to become the most comprehensive collection of the elements of kabbalism, in the *Sefer ha-Zohar* ('Book of splendor'). This book soon became, alongside the Bible and the Talmud, a canonical text of Judaism, despite the fact that it was not taught in 'normal' Jewish schools and only the most gifted students were initiated into this 'secret' knowledge.

After the expulsion of the Jews from Spain the Kabbala proved its great vitality among the Jews who had to come to terms with this event psychologically and spiritually. Expectations that the last days were nigh, appeared realistic—particularly since in earlier kabbalistic writings 1492 had often been calculated as the year of the apocalypse. The messianic and apocalyptic elements of Judaism combined in the Kabbala, particularly the Spanish version.

The messianic movement of David Reubeni represented something of a climactic moment for the Kabbala in the wider world. Reubeni claimed to be a prince descended from the tribe of Reuben and for a time was even able to win the trust of Pope Clement VII. The Portuguese Marrano (a Jew forcibly baptized) Solomon Molcho spread the teaching of the Redemption which was expected to take place in 1533. Arrested on the instructions of the Emperor Charles V, Molcho died at the stake in 1532, while David Reubeni disappeared in the dungeons of the Inquisition.

Safed in Upper Galilee (now Zefat, Israel), where Isaac Luria (1534–1572) taught, became a new center of the Kabbala. He tried to understand "creation from nothing." According to him, God had set free part of his being, had withdrawn from it, in order to make room for the creation. Harmony was disturbed by evil, however. When the divine light streamed into the universe not all of the vessels which were supposed to catch it could hold onto it and a *shevirat ha-kelim* ('breaking of the vessels') took place. As a result, evil was in a position to unfold itself, but at the same time the possibility was made available to man to restore the original harmony, by means of *tikkun* ('restoration') which involved a radical inwardness, prayer, and compliance with religious law. Isaac Luria taught what was virtually a 'magic of inwardness', an

> ecstasy of quiet merging, of a descent of the human will into an encounter with the divine will, in which the words of prayer serve as a banister. The person in prayer holds fast to this banister so as not to be caught unprepared or suddenly to be caught up in an ecstasy, in which the holy waters would close over his consciousness.[9]

Let it be mentioned in passing that this amounts to an examination of the question with which the most diverse trends within Judaism are concerned: How can one come to terms with the fact that man possesses both good and evil passions, that both are created by God, and both must be brought into harmony if one is to be able to love God?

The Kabbala was widespread in Poland in all its different forms. In the seventeenth century they were introduced to the Jews by Yeshaya Horowitz (1632–1689) from Kazimierz near Cracow. To be sure, his practical conclusions were less well received: "the hair shirt, fasting, weeping, and sorrow" led to God; man should live in "trembling, fear, shame, and purity," and not "follow the temptations of the flesh, but the voice of the spirit."[10] In a time of pogroms and ruin this was never likely to meet with widespread approval. People sought real hope. As a result, teachings concerning the imminent coming of the Messiah, of imminent salvation, were very popular.

THE MESSIAH IN POLAND: SHABTAI TSEVI AND JACOB FRANK

Shortly after the devastating wave of murder and looting which followed in the wake of the Cossack uprising of 1648, rumors were rife among the Jews of Poland that the day of salvation was nigh and that the messiah already walked the earth. His name was Shabtai Tsevi. Full of expectations, many people hoped that the end of their misery was in sight.

Shabtai Tsevi was born in Smyrna in 1626 and had received a wide-ranging education, including the teachings of the Kabbala. It appears that he suffered from manic depression. After he declared himself to be the messiah he was banished by his community and wandered throughout Asia Minor. In 1664 he married a Polish woman. One year later he met the twenty-year-old Kabbalist Nathan of Gaza (1644–1680), who persuaded him that he really was the Messiah and became his propagandist. Shabtai Tsevi named twelve apostles, returned to Smyrna, and set 18 June 1666 as the Day of Salvation. He described himself as a messianic king, occupied the temple, and did many things against Jewish doctrine. At the beginning of 1666, he traveled to Constantinople in order to await the redemption there. The Ottoman authorities had him arrested and presented him with a choice: either to convert to Islam or suffer execution. He chose conversion, possibly to protect his followers. In 1672 Shabtai Tsevi was denounced for practicing Judaism secretly and sexual libertinism, rearrested, and banished to Albania, where he died in 1676.

The Shabtaian teaching was disseminated primarily by Nathan. His point of departure was the Lurian Kabbala, particularly its ideas on creation. The Messiah takes it upon himself through eternal sufferings to restore to the earth its original harmony. He surrenders to evil in order to overcome it from within, that is, insofar as he himself is 'impure' he is able to purify the impure. As a result, he is not under the authority of the Torah and he can do what is forbidden. Even the renunciation of religious faith, apostasy, forms part of the process of redemption.

In Poland, this teaching spread quickly. It seems that many Jews felt that this doctrine was tailor-made for the situation in which they found themselves, while orthodox Judaism could no longer furnish convincing, comprehensive answers to the events and problems of the time. The Shabtaian movement has a number of complex features: mystical hopes related to justifications of a sinful way of life; and, at the same time, a breaking away from traditional teachings and methods—such as *pilpul*—which also opened up the way to enlightened thinking. This was a popular movement with thoroughgoing emancipatory elements, which at the same time sought to secede from the hegemony of the rabbinical upper stratum and the oligarchy of the *kahal*. It was, in common with comparable Christian movements of the seventeenth and eighteenth centuries, part of the "dialectic of enlightenment" (Horkheimer and Adorno).

Since the messiah failed to appear, and even Shabtai Tsevi did not appear again, the movement became more radical—insofar as it remained in existence at all—though for a while continued to win new adherents. In a way, it also became vulgarized, becoming a "religious myth of nihilism." Building on Nathan's, teaching, ideas of what was called 'sacred sin' emerged. Whoever sins is good and honest in the eyes of God, and impurity attracts the spirit of holiness. Even more extremely, it was held that Shabtai Tsevi had already sublimated evil and now everything was pure; nothing was blameworthy any longer.[11]

This strain of salvation theory culminated in the movement of Jacob Frank. Frank, born in 1726 in the border region of Podolia and Bukovina, had studied many kabbalistic books and in 1755 presented himself in Poland as the new messiah and the successor to Shabtai Tsevi. He soon had many fanatical followers. He taught that contact with God was possible through the joy of living and heightened ecstasy. Sexual ecstasy in particular was supposed to pave the way to religious ecstasy: one could enter the "halls of holiness" through the "gate of licentiousness."[12] Humanity was thoroughly degraded in the many orgiastic celebrations of the Frankists, "for he who had descended into the deepest depths appeared best able to see the light."[13]

Apostasy was a component part of 'the way' for the Frankists, too. Rabbis denounced Frank for his apostasy from Judaism and riotous life and forced him to to flee. He is supposed to have converted to Islam in Salonika. After his return to Poland in 1755, he engaged in disputations with rabbis and Christian clergymen. After a long hiatus, the tradition of public religious debate was resumed, at which Jews were able to present their point of view. The strength of Frank's personality and the extent of his influence can be measured by the fact that King August III was present—perhaps even as Frank's godfather—when he converted to Catholicism in 1759. However, shortly afterwards he was denounced for secretly practicing Judaism, arrested, and imprisoned.

After the first Partition of Poland the Russians released him from prison. Passing through Bohemia and Moravia he went to Germany, where he, at the latest from 1788, lived with around 400 followers in the castle of the Count of Isenburg at Offenbach and in the surrounding area. He died there in 1791. His daughter Eve, whom rumor claimed to be the illegitimate daughter of the Russian Empress Elizabeth, led the movement for a while longer. The sect deteriorated rapidly. A number of Frank's disciples surfaced in later reform movements. The most famous was Junius Frey, a relative of Frank, who was condemned to the guillotine together with Danton in 1794.

Here once again the twofold character of such movements becomes clear. It vaguely became apparent that in Frankism the ultimate goal was really liberation from all forms of authority, first from those of religion and doctrine, and then from those of the spiritual and political worlds in general. The demand for emancipation would no longer be satisfied by mere legal equality, and people did not want to have to wait for salvation at some unspecified time in the future. It was not without reason that the Frankists on many occasions demanded their own territory. In this way the traditional Jewish and non-Jewish order was challenged. The Frankist teaching radicalized an already existing trend in Judaism which centered on freeing oneself from the fetters of tradition through one's own power instead of waiting passively for solutions—or even the coming of the messiah—or rather brought these things about through one's own efforts and so actively fostered the process of salvation. The particular significance of Frankism lies in this 'turn towards activism.'

The messianic movements mirrored the crisis of the Jews—concretely in their living conditions, but also in their religious forms and the rule of the rabbis, and in the fragility of traditional Jewish society. Hope of salvation, and readiness for positive action, and the power which could be obtained in this way, remained alive among the Jews of Poland, and even influenced the thought of non-Jewish circles of Polish society. After the failure of the 1830 Polish Uprising against tsarist overlordship, the view became widespread that the history of Poland was the 'way of the cross' which would redeem all mankind. The best known representative of this standpoint was the poet Adam Mickiewicz (1798–1855). He declared that Jewish messianism had influenced Polish messianism: "Not for nothing did this people choose Poland as their homeland ... this belief has had some influence on the character of Polish messianism."[14]

Mickiewicz therefore demanded equal rights for the Jews in the conservation of their culture. The utopia of a Polish–Jewish synthesis was envisaged, but of course not carried through. The after-effects of messianic movements of the seventeenth and eighteenth centuries may be found in the participation of many Jews in the Polish uprisings between 1794 and 1863, in the Jewish enlightenment, in tendencies towards assimilation, and in the turning away from religion towards socialism and Zionism. Furthermore, these after-effects made room for a certain rethinking among the Jews in which many kabbalistic and messianic ideas were influential.

THE POPULAR PIETY OF HASIDISM

A little earlier than Jacob Frank, Israel ben Eliezer, who was born in Podolia (West Ukraine) in 1700, came on the scene. He founded a mass movement which was much bigger that anything seen before. For several years he traveled and worked in a number of different trades until, from 1736, he became known as a pious miracle worker with magical powers. Many legends came into circulation about him. He took up residence in the small Podolian town of Międzybóż. A new Hasidism developed through him and his followers, a movement of the pious—including, by the way, many former Shabtaians—which proved to be momentous in its effects. In this revivalist movement, lay piety found expression. The Hasidim soon organized themselves into local brotherhoods against the rabbinical oligarchy. In this way, they attained a degree of power which outstripped everything which had come before it.

Israel ben Eliezer, who bore the byname Ba'al Shem Tov—Master of the Good Name, of the Name of God—with the acronym Besh"t, died in 1760. He left virtually no written works. His teaching was subsequently assembled by his disciples. The Besh"t represented the kabbalistic trend of meditation on letters of the alphabet. In his view there was no room for evil—there was simply false knowledge or a lack of understanding of the divine; evil had become a "throne for lords."[15] Whoever recognizes the divine in evil, however, shall bring it to good. As a result, everyone may hope for personal reformation. No one should be afraid of sin; they will not be damned. But the Besh"t did not want to wipe out evil with evil—in contrast to Shabtai Tsevi and Jacob Frank—except through endeavoring to do good. Man should, in mystical fashion, hold fast to God and commune with him in love (*devekut*), even—or especially—in everyday life. "Man is the language of God", as one of his followers put it.[16] One should therefore take pleasure in God; not by turning aside from the world but by means of earthly things. The Hasidic piety of the Besh"t was life-affirming. Dancing, singing, and celebration were part and parcel of this. Finding and knowing oneself in harmony with one's surroundings, history, and God were highly valued. Everyone is himself a messiah in a manner of speaking; redemption may be found in every Jew who lives in harmony in this way.

The successor of the Besh"t and leader of the Hasidim until 1772 was his disciple the Maggid ('preacher') Rabbi Dov Baer of Międzyrzecz (1704–1772). Baer basically founded the Hasidic movement. To be sure, his teaching differed from that of the Besh"t in many respects: it was strongly grounded in the Lurian tradition. For him, evil existed alongside the good, as divine multiplicity, which must be brought into harmony again. For this purpose, great piety and conscious quietism were necessary in order to come to terms with the sufferings of the world. Not everyone was capable of this, however, only the righteous one: the *tsaddik*. The figure of the *tsaddik* here underwent something of a transformation with regard to traditional conceptions. Originally, the *tsaddik* was "the ideal of the norm," whereas the Hasid was the "ideal of the exception." The way having been prepared by vari-

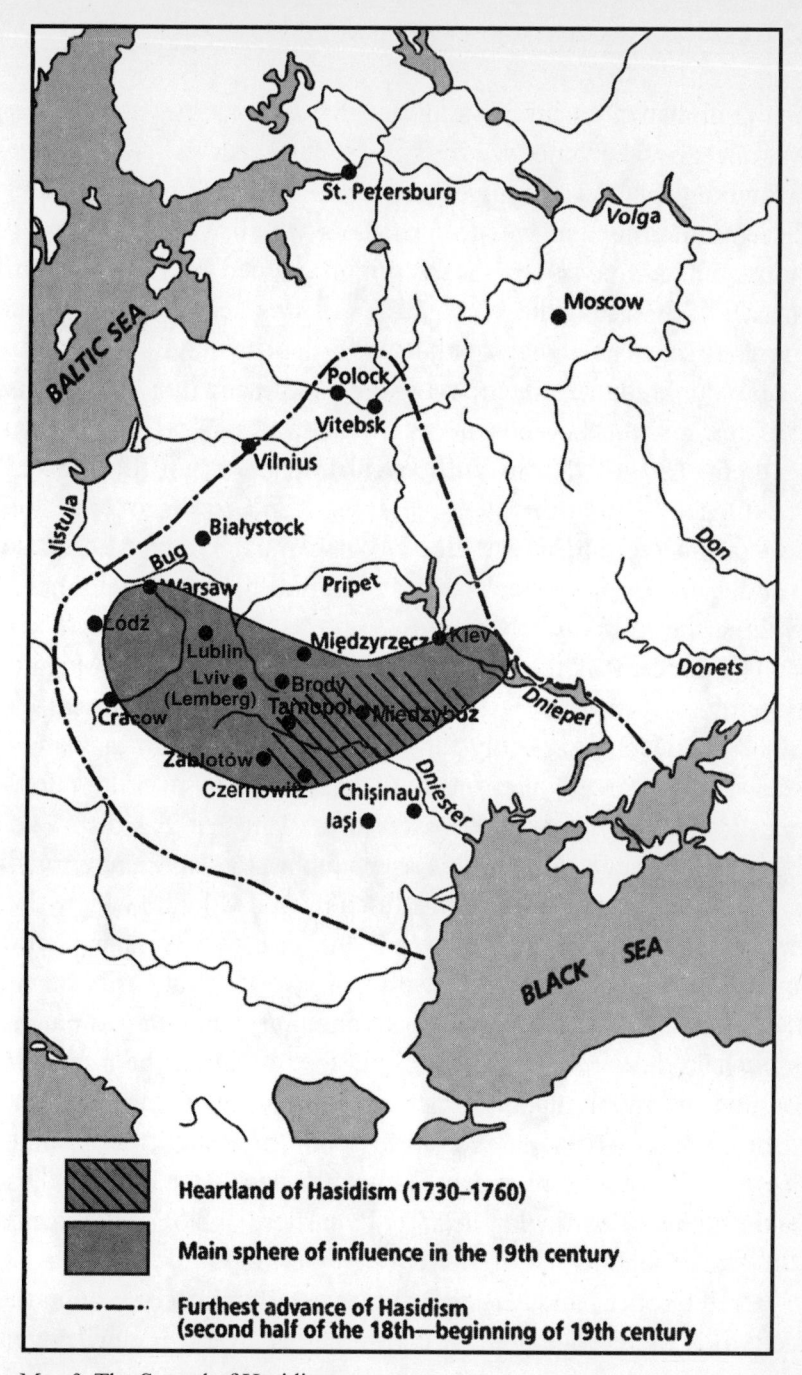

Map 3. The Spread of Hasidism

ous kabbalistic teachings and also hints from the Besh"t, the *tsaddik* now became a kind of 'super-Hasid.' The 'hidden righteous ones' were something of a special case. A widely disseminated legend was told of them which went back to old roots, but was now particularly highly valued by the Hasidim: in each generation there are 36 *tsaddikim* upon whose merits the continued existence of the world depends. As a rule, they remain unknown; indeed, they themselves do not know that they are among the chosen. As a result, all vanity is unknown to them. One of the 36 will reveal himself when the time of redemption has come: the messiah. If he is discovered too soon, however, he must die. No one must know who these 'hidden righteous ones' are. It "could be your neighbor," whether he lives piously or not.[17]

The concept of the *tsaddik,* as it was taught by the Maggid, certainly involved the public sphere: An elite mysticism was established which—probably through the influence of Frankism—was also linked with elements of a claim to power over its followers. Both these things contributed to the fact that Hasidism later became inflexible. The *tsaddik* or the rebbe stood as an intermediary between man and God. This fitted in well with the widely disseminated view that one had to put one's trust in 'wonder-rabbis' in order to come into contact with God, but it could easily hinder the liberating power of faith. The community, the Maggid taught, must help the *tsaddik*; it should hold fast to him, as he holds fast to God. Material support was important in this regard, as were dancing and merriment, even to the point of ecstasy, from which the *tsaddik* could draw power. This often degenerated into the establishment of particular '*tsaddik*-dynasties,' which later formed full-blown schools.

On the other hand, mysticism was communalized through the activities of the Hasidim in communities. Another new development in this connection was that women could now participate. The knowledge of the Torah which, according to received opinion, must remain closed to them was not necessary for the piety of the Hasidim. As a result, their position in public–communal life was able to improve. At least in early Hasidism, women also took part in communal dancing. Later, however it appears that, the traditional separation of men and women was reestablished, even intensified though this varied in different communities and *tsaddik* circles. In any case, it is astonishing that it is reported of numerous individual women—mostly widows or daughters of *tsaddikim*—who on account of their spiritual powers were honored as *tsaddikim*. As far as sources are concerned these stories often cannot be established accurately. One of these was the legendary 'Virgin of Lubomir', Hanna Rachel Werbermacher (1805/15–1892/95). Oral testimony has it that she observed religious rituals like the men and was highly educated, even in kabbalistic literature. Many attributed magical powers to her and were attracted to her 'circle,' where she had established a *bet ha-midrash* or 'house of study.' The local *tsaddikim*, of course, regarded this development with misgivings and took the view that she should get married in order to fulfill her obligations as a woman. When she finally gave in to this demand and later on married twice—neither marriage is supposed to have been consummated—her following dwindled. She spent her later life in Jerusalem in the study of Jewish mysticism. It is possible that a number of different trends in Hasidism found expression in the reactions to the 'Virgin of Lubomir.' The assertion that "Jewish women achieved complete equality of rights in religious life in Beshtian Hasidism" is too sweeping, but it does point to changes which would be worth further investigation.[18]

Hasidism had extraordinary resonance because it was concerned with everyday life, and did not require asceticism or sorrow—not to mention constant sin or personal degradation (compare Shabtaianism and Frankism)—but rather happiness and piety, fraternity and love. In the difficult circumstances of the time, in the crisis of the Jews, in which the old values no longer possessed unqualified validity, this was extraordinarily important. "The marvel was that Jews suddenly had the desire and the strength to sing while the sky was bedecked with blood-red clouds, and danger showed itself ever more clearly and drew nigh ever more quickly."[19] To be sure, Orthodoxy fiercely resisted this challenge. In many Jewish communities fissures opened up which could never be closed.

THE ORIGINS OF THE *OSTJUDEN*

Many historians have seen Hasidism merely as an instrument of popular stultification or of the oppression of religious Jews. This is true in a number of cases, but on the other hand this teaching, both in its original form and in later attempts at reform, contained strong emancipatory elements without threatening people's way of life. When someone asked a *tsaddik* "Why do you not live in the same way as your teacher?" he replied: "On the contrary, I am emulating him completely: just as he renounced his teacher, so I have renounced him."[20] To break free from tradition was also part of the tradition, of the Kabbala. The Maggid, too, pursued a different path from the Besh"t. Even criticism of God was possible.

In this religious search for meaning between messianic apocalypticism and pious, life-affirming coping with the world as it is; in this tightrope walk between the conservation of a way of life, together with a simultaneous liberation from norms which were felt to be meaningless; and an often stifling flight into mysticism, ruled by powerful wonder-rabbis, the type of the 'Eastern Jew' as a "self-contained cultural personality"[21] was formed in the eighteenth century. This concept, which first arose in the nineteenth century, and gradually became accepted in the twentieth, therefore designates more than a geographical classification, particularly because increasingly there were East European Jews [*Ostjuden*] outside Eastern Europe.

An *Ostjude* is someone who consciously declares him/herself to be Jewish, the understanding of which has been disclosed through arduous struggle. Tradition and memory exercised a formative influence in this, although without the *Ostjude* necessarily being conservative minded. In fact, the East European Jew as a rule dressed in his own garb and lived his or her life in accordance with strictly observed religious laws, customs and rituals which have been handed down. Exceptions, of course, are common. In any case, the Yiddish language belongs to the East European Jews [*Ostjuden*], who have also produced their own literary and artistic creations, as well as legal norms in it. *Ostjuden* used Yiddish in their daily dealings with one another, Hebrew remained the language of religious ritual and scholarship. In encounters with non-Jews, many Jews were in a position to use the relevant national language. Quite a few also had a command of German—not least because of its proximity to Yiddish—which was often the language of education.

The development of Eastern Yiddish into a thoroughgoing language in its own right had already taken place in the eighteenth century. The conclusion of Moses Mendelssohn (1729–1786), the great German–Jewish philosopher of the Enlightenment, that Yiddish was a mere mishmash of different languages and that as a Jew one should speak the relevant national language, had considerable influence over Enlightenment-oriented Jews in the East, especially in Lithuania, but it could not win general acceptance. Yiddish became the mother-tongue, the *mameloshen* of the East European Jews.[22] At the same time, regional differences emerged, most clearly between

Northeastern Yiddish in Lithuania and Belarus and Southeastern–Mideastern Yiddish in Poland, Galicia, and Ukraine, which were themselves further subdivided. Correspondingly, all communities had their own regional characteristics in dress and customs.

The development of the East European Jews was made easier by the fact that the traditional role of the Jews as an intermediary between town and countryside, experienced a resurgence. In the period of reconstruction in the wake of the numerous wars and devastation, Jews in Poland were indispensable as traders between nobility, peasants, and town-dwellers; as 'village-walkers' [*Dorfgeher*]—that is, peddlers—as money-lenders and agents for nobles and peasants alike, and as tenants for the taverns of nobles. This intermediary function characterized the lives of Jews even in their own communities, but it soon turned out that things had already changed as far as the whole basis of this role was concerned.

THE 'SHTETL'

The following sketches, which relate to a later time, can only hint at the reality, but can at least give us a taste of the atmosphere.

> Wooden houses in total disorder huddle around a market place ... as overpopulated as the slums of the big cities ... The streets are as tortuous as an argument from the Talmud. They are bent in a question mark and put in parentheses. They end in blind alleys like a theory which is refuted by reality; they lose themselves in courtyard entrances, backyards, or country roads ... [In the center] lies the market place with its shops, stalls, tables, and slaughter blocks. Every day, except in winter, the peasant men and women come in from many miles around and bring their animals and their vegetables, their fish

and their game, their wagonloads of grain, melons, parsley, and garlic. As a sideline they sell products from the city which the Jews bring in. Hats, shoes, boots, lamps, oil, spades, axes, and shirts. The tumult of the market place ... is one of the wonders of the world.[23]

Listen also to the words of Mendele Moykher Sforim (Mokher Seforim, 1836–1917) in *Fischke der Lahme* [Fischke the cripple] (1869/88):

> Briefly I stand still, look around me, and study the yearly market. It is seething, the crowd is huge, Jews do business with abandon—they just live. That's a Jew for you: at the yearly market he is like a fish in water. That's where life is, the yearly market! ... It is truly written, as the Jews say: it's a yearly market in heaven! What that really means is that paradise for Jews is a yearly market! Now, whether it is written or not, the Jews 'do the yearly market,' run, trade, and do not stand still for a second ... It's a seething hullabaloo. Over there, I can see, a Jew is running, a second, a third. In twos, very sweaty, their caps shoved back on their heads, someone taps them on the shoulder, then someone else, a gesture here with the hand, a gesture there, a turn of the thumb, and a chewing of the beard—a good idea, it seems. They run their souls out of their bodies: middlemen, marriage brokers, junk dealers, swindlers, chicken thieves, Jewesses with baskets and Jews with sacks, and others with nothing but their five fingers, young masters with their walking sticks, town dwellers with their bellies. All their faces are ablaze, no one has time, every minute costs one silver ruble.[24]

"Tales and myths hung in the air, we breathed them in,"[25] yet at the same time terrible poverty frequently held sway, which increased as time went by. The shtetls were Jewish centers in a non-Jewish, mostly rural environment. The rich Jews in the larger towns often looked with contempt on the 'outsiders' who lived cheek by jowl with the peasants. As with the disagreements between poor Jews and the *kahal* oligarchy, there are hints here of deeper social conflicts within Jewish society, which we will encounter in a different form later on.

The Jews in the shtetl lived in full consciousness of their Jewishness. Even when they were poor, because trade between town and countryside in the wake of general economic development yielded ever smaller profits; even when they lived crammed into narrow rooms, had hardly anything to wear, and often had to go hungry; they were proud of their Jewishness, and they felt at home where they lived. Not without reason particularly respected communities were given honorifics: for example, Berdichev, the 'Jerusalem of Volhynia,' or Rzeszów, the 'Jerusalem of Galicia.'

> Yes, it was an immeasurable, grotesque poverty, almost to the point of absurdity, but on the other hand not a wretchedness, because the people of Zablotow not only believed but knew that the situation was only temporary and that soon everything would change, even if the lean times had lasted for decades, if not centuries—in fact, since the victory of the Cossack hetman Bohdan Khmelnytsky in the year 1648. God—their God, naturally—always intervened. Late, very late, but never too late. Apart from that, at every moment one could count on the coming of the messiah, that is, with ultimate redemption ... They stood in the temple, lit by candles, the low monotonous singing with which, here and there, young men accompanied their study of the Talmud disturbed the enthusiastic debaters as little as the noise of playing children which was all the more patiently endured because many of them had recently lost either a father or a mother ... Singsong and the noise of children and not infrequently a loud dispute—none of that disturbed anyone, because everyone was busy with discussing everything, whether it be their own affairs or those of the wide world ... If I think back to these Jews, as I saw them up until my tenth year, in the streets, in the market place, in temples and studyrooms, I am reminded of two particular sounds: sighing, much sighing and groaning, but also laughter, good-humored or mocking, but always loud laughter, in which even those who had been sighing and groaning soon joined.[26]

CONTACTS BETWEEN JEWS AND NON-JEWS: JEWISH PEDDLERS AND INNKEEPERS

Outside the shtetl the 'village walkers,' Jewish peddlers, and innkeepers had the closest contacts with non-Jews. The peddlers offered their wares for sale to the peasants, and to some extent in the towns, and often took on additional tasks for their clients which had to be carried out in the next community or with the authorities in the district town. Their mediation services, therefore, went far beyond the merely economic. Nor should one underestimate the fact that the peddlers were often the first to acquaint the peasants with new developments in agriculture, tell them about cultural life in the towns and in general bring them news from the wider world. On the other hand, in the towns they told people about life in the village. It would be well worth investigating the extent to which the urban view of the peasants and rural conditions was formed by Jewish peddlers, and also whether village influences permeated urban customs—such as, ceremonies or festivals—in this way. In any case, the peddlers had a significant role as cultural mediators between town and countryside.

The Jewish innkeeper is perhaps *the* typical manifestation of this mediating function in a network of relations between nobility, peasants, and town-dwellers. Over one-quarter of the Jewish population of Poland–Lithuania belonged to this class in the eighteenth century. According to one methodical, though problematic, evaluation in 1813, up 61 percent of those employed in the production and sale of alcohol were Jewish. In the East, particularly in the countryside, this figure may have been significantly higher. Heinrich Heine, himself of Jewish origin, wrote in an account of a journey to Poland in 1822:

> In Poland, the Jews stand between the peasant and the nobleman ... With a few exceptions all the inns in Poland are in the hands of the Jews and their many distilleries are very harmful to the country because the peasants are thereby stimulated to excess [a favorite reproach against the Jews at that time – author's note] ... Every nobleman has a Jew in the village or in the town whom he appoints as a factor and who carries out all his commissions, purchases and sales, inquiries, and so on.[27]

For a later period, Joseph Roth described the dominant position of a Jewish innkeeper in eastern Galicia, on the border of the Russian Empire, in his novel *Das falsche Gewicht* (The false weight):

> In the village of Szwaby, which belonged to the Zlotograd district, Leibusch Jadlowker was more powerful than the sergeant of the gendarmerie himself. You should know who Leibusch Jadlowker was: of unknown origin. It was rumored that, years before, he had come from Odessa and that Jadlowker was actually not his real name. He owned the so-called border-inn, and no one even knew how it had come into his possession. In a mysterious manner, which had never been investigated, the previous owner, an old, silver-bearded Jew, had died ... his border-inn was the gathering place of all good-for-nothings and criminals. Three times a week the notorious Russian agent for the American Line dumped deserters from the Russian army in Jadlowker's border-inn so that they could go from there to Holland, Canada, or South America.
>
> As I have already mentioned, good-for-nothings and criminals frequented Jadlowker's border-inn: he gave shelter to vagrants, beggars, thieves, and robbers. And he was so cunning that the law could never get the better of him. His papers and those of his guests were always in order. The official informers, who swarmed around the border like flies, could not report anything prejudicial, anything immoral about his way of life ...
>
> Jadlowker had not only obtained his concession for the border-inn in a doubtful fashion, but also one for a shop for 'exotic delicacies'. And by 'exotic delicacies' he seemed to understand something quite

special. For not only did he sell flour, oats, sugar, tobacco, spirits, beer, caramels, chocolate, thread, soap, buttons, and string, but also he traded in girls and in men. He manufactured false weights and sold them to traders in the area; and many people were interested in the fact that he also produced forged money, silver, gold, and paper.[28]

In the period in which Roth's story is set, the significance of the Jewish innkeeper had already begun to diminish. He obviously continued to have an effect as a stock figure, however, and was certainly still very much alive in many cases. Often he served as a negative symbol of the cunning, avaricious *Ostjude* who tempted the peasants to drink, talked them into buying things they did not need, and was responsible for their indebtedness. In the eighteenth century, Catholic priests still liked to describe Jewish inns as the abode of the Devil.

THE SYMBIOSIS DIMINISHES

Attitudes to innkeepers indicated that the basis for the Jews' intermediary function was much more uncertain than it had been before 1648. Many peasants saw the Jews, much more strongly than before, as representatives of an alien world, which, particularly in times of radical social and economic change, was felt to be threatening. Furthermore, the Catholic Church stirred up religious antagonism in the course of heightened, more intolerant counter-reformation efforts, which could easily spark off riots.

The Church assemblies of the eighteenth century on many occasions again brought into force the anti-Jewish ecclesiastical council decisions of the Middle Ages. Synods forbade the Jews from being seen in public when there was a procession, or from keeping Christian servants. The construction and renovation of synagogues were hindered; for example, it was said that synagogues should not overshadow Christian houses. Bishops now and again demanded payment of substantial ransoms for not closing synagogues or for reopening them. Needless to say, accusations of ritual murder reared their heads once more. Many clergymen stirred up hatred of the Jews among the Polish population by this means. In a number of cases it resulted in convictions and executions. The persecutions reached such a height that finally even Pope Clement XIII (1693–1769) and King August III (1696–1763), on the entreaties of Jewish delegations, condemned these blood libels in 1763. However, the prejudices which had become established in the meantime could not be rooted out so easily.

Tough economic competition between Jews and Christians explains why clergymen's malicious sermons and pseudo-theological treatises from the towns fell on such fruitful soil. Pupils from Jesuit schools took the liberty of assaulting and maltreating Jews and looting Jewish houses. Christian guilds stopped accepting Jews as members and prohibited Jewish craftsmen from taking orders from Christians. Jewish traders were significantly impeded in the pursuit of their profession by the municipal authorities. In many towns Jews could only exercise the rights which had been granted to them in the royal and noble Privileges through the payment of large bribes.

The ambivalence of the circumstances was noted by, for example, the Jewish philosopher of the Enlightenment from Lithuania Salomon Maimon (1753–1800), a friend of Moses Mendelssohn:

> There is perhaps no country apart from Poland where religious freedom and religious hatred can be found in such equal measure. The Jews enjoy completely free practice of their religion there and of all other civic freedoms; they even have their own jurisdiction. On the other hand, however, religious hatred is so intense that the very name of Jew is becoming repugnant ...[29]

Apart from the weakened position of the king, the stance of the nobility, was decisive for the deterioration of Jewish living conditions in Poland. Earlier on, at least insofar as it benefited them economically, the noble landowners had protected the Jews against the alliance of Catholic Church, town-dwellers, and impoverished minor nobility. Now they were less willing to do so. The Church had obtained more and more power over them in the course of the Counter-Reformation and its warnings concerning the Jews ultimately had their effect. It is true that the landowners still employed Jews as factors because they were extraordinarily useful to them from an economic standpoint, but, influenced by the hatred which had afflicted the Jews in the unrest since 1648, landowners were now quite willing to let them go if their value to them was no longer sufficient. With the widely propagated image of the Jews now before their eyes they feared that they would be cheated by their stewards or lessees and therefore attempted, particularly in times of economic difficulty, to get rid of them.

Furthermore, the nobility now saw the Jews as unwelcome competition in respect of their own advancement. In the eighteenth century, therefore, the nobility saw to it that Jews were no longer taken into state service nor permitted to administer royal domains. It also supervised more strictly than before compliance with restrictions on residence and profession which had been imposed earlier. The extent to which the relationship between nobility and Jews was no longer one of symbiosis but of increasing conflict, and how the community of interests could turn into a clash of interests, can be illustrated by the following diary entry of a Volhynian landowner in 1774:

> The lessee Hershko still owes me the 91 thalers already due and I felt myself compelled to have recourse to legal action. As a consequence of a contractual provision I have the right, in case of failure to pay, to keep him, together with his wife and children, locked up until the debt is paid.

Yesterday, therefore, I ordered that he be put into fetters and placed in a pigsty, whereas I gave his wife and the *bahuren* (the young ones) permission to remain in the inn. Only the youngest son, Leiser, did I have brought to the estate and ordered that he be instructed in the catechism and our prayers. The boy is in fact very gifted and I would like to have him baptized. I have already written to the bishop about this and he promised to come to me for the baptism ceremony in order to escort the boy's soul [to the true faith]. At first Leiser was unwilling to cross himself and to learn our prayers by heart; after Strelezki, the estate steward, had punished him, however, he even ate pork. The priest of our church, Boniface, an outstanding member of the monastic order Minorum de observantia, had to struggle with the sweat of his brow to overcome the child's stubbornness and to win him for our faith.

Only three weeks later were Jewish neighbors able to pay the family's debt.[30]

However, the Jews in Poland still lived in favorable circumstances in comparison with the Jews in western European states. Salomon Maimon, who in his youth had himself experienced how the noble landowners had effected something of an about-turn regarding 'their Jews', wrote in his memoirs:

> The Polish Jews, who have always been permitted to engage in all forms of employment, and who are not, unlike in other states, restricted to sharp practice and usury, seldom hear the reproach of deception. They remain true to the land where they live and support themselves in an honest fashion.[31]

The Jews now found themselves in a contradictory position. Despite the manifold possibilities for development which certainly existed for them, their situation had become more insecure. Protection from the king and the higher nobility had become weaker, and so their existence was continually under threat. In response to the conditions of the time they developed their own characteristic way of life: the type of the *Ostjude* or East European Jew was formed. This was now very much grist to the mill of their opponents, who accused them of consciously cutting themselves off from society. The feeling of alienation towards them grew stronger and all of the negative prejudices which were in circulation about them seemed to be confirmed. In his travel journal of 1822 (see above) Heinrich Heine gave his impressions:

> The outward appearance of the Polish Jews is terrible ... However, disgust soon gave way to pity after I observed the situation of these people at close quarters and saw the pigsty-like holes in which they live, talk Yiddish, pray, horsetrade, and — are wretched. Their speech is a kind of German interwoven with Hebrew and shaped by Polish ... they are not advanced in European culture and their spiritual world has degenerated into an unedifying superstition, which a hairsplitting scholasticism crushes into thousands of wonderful forms. However, despite the barbaric fur cap which covers his head and the even more barbaric ideas which fill it, I value the Polish Jew far more highly than so many German Jews who wear their Bolivars [a fashionable hat of the period—H.H.] on their heads and carry their Jean Paul [a widely read romancer of the time—H.H.] in their heads. In its stark isolation the character of the Polish Jew has become a whole; through breathing in an air of tolerance this character obtained the stamp of freedom ... The Polish Jew, smelling of garlic, with his dirty furs, [lice-]crowded beard, and scheming, is to me still preferable to many a [German Jew] in all his splendor, underpinned by official papers as it is.[32]

Here it becomes clear how the Polish Jew had in the meantime become different from the German Jew: in his outward appearance, in his speech, in culture, and in his ways of thinking and behaving. Heine evaluated positively stereotypes which, as a rule, were directed against the Jews negatively. He saw how the centuries-long traditions in Poland had had an advantageous outcome for the Jews there. His observations and judgments express the diversity of conditions in exemplary fashion. At the time of this journey, however, a new turn for the worse was looming.

JEWS IN THE PARTITIONS OF POLAND

In the years 1772, 1793, and 1795, the Great Empire of Poland–Lithuania was divided up, piece by piece, between Prussia, Austria, and Russia. There would be no independent Polish state again until the end of the First World War. The Congress of Vienna in 1815 consolidated the final partition borders: Prussia obtained West Prussia and the province of Poznań, Austria got Galicia and Cracow (though Cracow at first remained a free city under the common overlordship of the partitioning powers) and Russia received Lithuania, as well as east and central Poland. The tsarist autocracy annexed the territory from Lithuania through Belarus and Ukraine to the Black Sea, but with the rest of old Poland it formed a kingdom linked with the tsar in personal union, which, in an allusion to its origin, was also known as Congress Poland.

In the course of the process of partition the 'Jewish question' played an increasingly important role, without, however, ever being 'solved.' The Great Sejm which sat from 1788 and represented the last attempt at thoroughgoing reform by the free Polish rump state, revived the Va'ad, the 'Generality of the Jewish nation.' Many Jews had not been able to pay the increased taxes and as a result the communities which were liable for these payments, the *kehillot*, had fallen into debt. A redistribution of income proved to be absolutely necessary, but a satisfactory settlement was not reached.

The parliament was immediately confronted with the precarious situation of the Jews. In Warsaw the earlier residence restrictions were still in force; the Jews could reside there only when the Sejm was sitting, although they sought ways of getting around this. The nobles had recognized that an interesting source of income could be developed here, and allowed the Jews, on payment of the requisite fees, to settle permanently on their estates outside the city walls. As a result, 'New Jerusalem' came into being with a large number of inhabitants. In 1775, however, the citizens of Warsaw had been able to have the Jews expelled. When the Great Sejm sat in 1788, thousands of Jews again poured into Warsaw and remained there because the parliament was in session for longer than usual in order to push through the intended reforms. In the end, the Christian inhabitants could no longer stand the feared Jewish competition and in March 1790 managed to have Jewish craftsmen and street traders expelled. Only merchants with places of business—that is, rich Jews—could stay. As those who had been expelled returned home, excitement mounted and the tiniest incident proved enough to trigger off a veritable storm of looting upon the dwellings and shops of Jews in Warsaw, which was only brought to an end through military intervention.

The Sejm now debated the situation thoroughly. In essence, there were three possible positions, which also had followers outside the Sejm: those who took a strongly Catholic line, such as the big landowner Zamoyski, wanted to restrict the rights and opportunities of the Jews even further. The extreme counter-position was represented by, for example, Jacek Jezierski (1722–1805) who suggested that the Jews should be supported, since they were very useful for the economy of the kingdom. In between stood opinions of various shades which wanted to afford the Jews civic rights, tolerance, and far-reaching freedom of trade, on the condition that they 'modernize' and assimilate. If they were not ready to do so of their own volition, then compulsion should be used. The representatives of this line—for example, the historian and financial expert Tadeusz Czacki (1765–1813)—thought that in this way they could prohibit early marriages, restrict the civic rights of uneducated Jews, censor Jewish literature, get rid of Jewish garb, abolish 'harmful' religious practices, reduce *kahal* autonomy, require the use of Polish rather than Yiddish, at least in official correspondence, and restrict the activities of the Jews to crafts, agriculture, and 'honest' trades, which excluded inn-keeping.

Equality was to be purchased at the expense of their own traditions and culture—a trend visible in many countries at that time. Although endorsed by many—and even King Stanisław II August Poniatowski (1732–1798), his goodwill possibly obtained by means of financial inducements, intervened in favor of more rights for the Jews—a resolution was prevented by the anti-Jewish side. The constitution of May 1791, the first in the whole of Europe, ignored this problem. It had become clear that the high nobility no longer stood behind the Jews, and indeed counted them among their adversaries.

In any case, the second and third Partitions of Poland made any more far-reaching endeavors futile. Evidence of Polish patriotism among the Jews was not lacking. Many Jews participated in the uprising of 1794 under Tadeusz Kościuszko (1746–1817), even in the defense of Warsaw. In the end, a Jewish legion was even formed under the leadership of Berek Joselewicz. It was hoped that this participation in the liberation struggle would persuade the Poles that they could live alongside Jews and grant them equal rights. After the suppression of the uprising by the Russians, the remnants of the Jewish legion managed to reach France after extraordinary adventures, where they joined the Polish legion and, under Napoleon, participated in the creation of the Duchy of Warsaw. In 1809 Joselewicz, now a colonel in the Polish army, fell in the war against Austria. The Duke of Warsaw, who was also the King of Saxony, graciously allowed Joselewicz's widow and children to settle in streets of Warsaw where Jews were not permitted to reside, and also, should the situation arise, to "sell schnapps."[33]

This was a notable concession. At first, the Jews nursed great hopes concerning the *Code Napoléon*. The adoption of the *Code civil* had provided them with equal rights. It also appeared that Napoleon wished to work with an official representation of the Jews—the 'Great Sanhedrin' on the model of the ancient Jewish supreme legislative and judicial court—but as early as March 1808 Napoleon suspended emancipation in France for ten years. The Polish adversaries of the Jews immediately sought to take advantage of this and in October 1808 pushed through a corresponding decree. Exceptions were still permitted, however—under the severest conditions. In 1809 it was decreed in Warsaw that the Jews had to move out of the smarter areas of the city: on 16 March 1809 the Warsaw Ghetto was established, which was soon taken by other cities as a model for similar institutions.

As early as 1808, compulsory military service had been imposed on the Jews: just as their rights were being taken away, more duties were being imposed on them. This measure was particularly painful for religious Jews because it meant that religious observance was no longer possible. Many leaders of the Hasidim petitioned the government for the withdrawal of compulsory military service and in return offered to renounce civic rights and to pay a high financial penalty. Since, at the same time, many Jews engaged in passive resistance and there was constant trouble, in 1812 the compulsory military service obligation was removed and instead the Jews had to pay a high defense tax.

When, in 1815, the Kingdom of Poland subsequently came under Russian rule, new debates were held concerning the 'Jewish question' in connection with the constitutional discussions. They were once more ignored by the constitution itself. At the same time, the regulations in articles eleven and twelve, proclaiming that the Israelite faith should not be regarded as being on an equal footing with Christianity and that religious and secular authorities should be separated from one another, constituted substantial intrusions into Jewish life. On the Polish side the standpoints already discussed reemerged. The leading politician of the day, Prince Adam Jerzy Czartoryski (1770–1861), made assimilation—except in religion—the precondition of equality. The Jews were an 'alien people,' and one should liberate them from 'intellectual immaturity' and oppression, but full civic rights could not be granted them. Jewish inns should be prohibited because the consumption of alcohol "has such disastrous consequences for the lower classes."[34] The Jews were alleged to entice the peasants to drink and ruin them, both financially and physically; Christians were simply incapable of such things.

Others were much more radical. The Catholic clergyman Stanisław Staszic (1755–1826), who already in the discussions during the final phase of the free Polish state had described the Jews as a "plague of locusts which strikes the land both in summer and in winter" and as "a load of parasites," remained true to his opinions and abused the Jews as "hobos and idlers," with whom one simply could not get along. Stereotypes which continued to form the image of the Jew until the twentieth century now appeared more and more frequently. Kajetan Koźmian (1771–1856) went further than most in 1817:

> It would be an error to believe that the Talmud alone keeps them Jewish; their way of life also contributes to it ... They are superstitious, ignorant, wastrels, traders, money-changers, and generally do their best to avoid working themselves, to live off others, and to pay for a comfortable life through cunning and deception.

Indeed, he said, Jews are not Poles since they have "no Polish blood" in them. Although he personally believed that what he regarded as negative Jewish mediation activities could take a positive form, and that total assimilation and integration were still possible, his position sowed the seeds of a racist exclusion of the Jews.

The violent attacks on the Jews were directed particularly against the efforts—not envisaged in the constitution—of the representative for Poland appointed by the Tsar, Senator Count Nikolai Nikolaievich Novosiltsev (1761–1836). In Russia, he had already been a member of a 'Committee for the Wellbeing of the Jews', which had prepared a law passed in 1804 concerning Jews in the tsarist empire. He did everything he could to achieve a lasting solution. To be sure, he did not wish to go as far as the Russian statesman Count Mikhail Mikhailovich Speransky (1772–1839) in 1803, who, though still very influential at that time, certainly would not have been able to have his ideas adopted:

> The reforms which have been introduced by the power of the state are in general not lasting and cannot be relied upon in cases in which the government has to struggle against centuries-old customs. Therefore it would seem more appropriate and more reliable to help the Jews to perfect themselves, restricting oneself merely to opening up for them the ways to their own advantage, overseeing their movements only from a distance, and removing everything which could cause them to stray from this path, without thereby applying any force or creating any special institutions, in order, instead of working for them, to help them to develop. A minimum amount of prohibition, a maximum amount of freedom, these are the basic elements of every social arrangement.

Novosiltsev at first blocked decrees which were disadvantageous to the Jews and finally, in 1817, proposed his own 'Comprehensive regulations for the Jews living in the Kingdom of Poland.' Educated and well-to-do Jews would receive full civil rights: they could therefore hold public office and organize politically. Others would be granted more limited civil rights, particularly in respect of economic activity. In place of the *kahal* there would be a Directorate with a strong rabbi at its head. He wanted to bring the Hasidim and other 'sects' under control. The

Jewish community would continue to be responsible for payment of taxes and quotas of recruits. On top of that, he foresaw granting no new innkeeping licenses to Jews and prohibiting trade on credit and trade in kind, including peddling, in the countryside. He himself wanted to be appointed 'Royal Procurator' of the Jewish question in order to get the details of his regulations approved by the noble landowners, but also of course to extend his own power.

But success was denied even to the representative of the tsar. The Polish nobility, like the Polish burghers, was not ready to sacrifice its interests. The Jews had in the meantime become economic competitors of both groups, and they were no longer mediators, even for the nobility. In addition, there was the influence of conservative forces in Russia which knew how to prevent pro-Jewish reform.

THE REACTION OF THE JEWS TO THE NEW POLITICAL, INTELLECTUAL, AND RELIGIOUS CONDITIONS

The utterances of the Jews themselves in these discussions are interesting. I have already mentioned that the Hasidim were ready to renounce civic rights in exchange for their traditions, culture, and way of life. Many of them were not concerned with politics anyway: "The Russians, Prussians, and Austrians had partitioned Poland between themselves, but the Russian Hasidim visited Austrian rabbis and the Austrian Hasidim visited their rabbis in Russia."[35] Even the orthodox Jews and the *kahal* oligarchy did not particularly trouble themselves with improving their living conditions. They were afraid that full equality would harm their political and social position. In this they sometimes even hoped for the assistance of Tsar Alexander I (1777–1825).

On the other hand, opponents of the rigid structures of the community wanted to abolish the *kahal* and become integrated into the Polish civil administration. Now and again, Enlightenment ideas came to the fore. For example, Mendel Satanower (also khown as Mendel Levin, 1750–1823), who had made contacts with Mendelssohn and Maimon in Berlin, and then became tutor in the household of Prince Adam Czartoryski, supported radical educational reform and material improvements for the Jewish masses. He fought strongly against the Hasidim who, in his opinion, kept the people in ignorance. 'Enlightened' Jews who favored assimilation—the *maskilim*, the 'thinkers'—who were to be found in the well-to-do stratum of society, threw in their lot with the Polish Reform Party, not least Prince Czartoryski. At the end of 1815 they presented their ideas to the tsar and thereafter exercised some influence over his representative, Novochilchev. The *maskilim* took as their point of departure the existing prejudices in non-Jewish society and were ready to accept a two-class legal system. The "distinguished Israelites"— that is, themselves—would receive full equality of rights, while the masses, who "retain their garb and their customs," would obtain only the "usual civic rights," because "their circumstances and knowledge are restricted".[36]

The attitudes of the Jews varied between desiring equal rights, even at the expense of cultural loss, and renouncing such rights and economic support in order to live in the manner to which they had become accustomed. This divergence mirrored the religious divide which had come into being in the eighteenth century. The Hasidim had their triumphal march primarily in south and southeastern Poland, in what was now Austrian Galicia and Ukraine. Everywhere there were intense struggles with the rabbinical trend, the orthodox Misnagdim (*Mitnaggedim*)—the 'opponents'. The Hasidim, who wished to see "the secret of God which is to be found in simple things," reproached the Misnagdim with overlooking the "true roots" in "excessive study."[37] They excluded one another from communities and many bloody clashes took place. These bitter disputes contributed to the fact that the originally even the liberating approach of Hasidism frequently became rigidified in extremely hierarchical forms and established schools with *tsaddik* dynasties and 'wonder-working rabbis.' Again and again there was criticism of the excrescences of *tsaddikism*, for example, from the great-grandson of the Besh"t, Rabbi Nahman of Braclaw (1772–1810), who with his learning and his allegorical tales wanted to inaugurate a return to closeness to the people and inner piety. At the same time, in the urgent search for God and in attempts to accelerate salvation—undoubtendy, influenced by Shabtaianism and Frankism—doubts were expressed in religious teaching which led many people to go over to the progressives.

The conflict between the Hasidim and the Misnagdim in Belarus and Lithuania took a particularly violent form, above all in Vilna (now Vilnius, Lithuania), the 'Jerusalem of Lithuania.' Vilna was a stronghold of scholarly rabbinism, but also of the German-influenced Jewish Enlightenment, the Haskala. All pious trends of Judaism, however much they opposed one another, fought against this development as a "fiend from Hell." Its adherents were abused as 'Berliners.' As a result, their influence in these areas was, for the time being, restricted before the turn of the century. The undisputed authority of rabbinism was Elijah ben Solomon (1720–1797), the *gaon* or (spiritual) 'excellency' of Vilna, who attacked Hasidism from the very beginning: in Hasidism feeling predominates, whereas religion should be built on compliance with the "laws." These laws are to be discovered through study of the Talmud, but once found they should be followed with blind obedience. In place of the traditional, often confusing *pilpul* method, Elijah developed an objective method of analysis for Talmud interpretation.

His chief opponent, Rabbi Shneur Zalman (1748–1813) was a reformer, too. Zalman attempted to renew Hasidism, teaching that one should not only surrender oneself to one's feelings, but also put them under conscious control. The study of the Torah was necessary for this, not for the sake of following the laws blindly, but rather to come closer to God through the Word. Everyone should comply with the three aspects—wisdom (*hokhama*), understanding (*binna*), and knowledge (*da'at*)—of the divine soul. After the initial letters of the three Hebrew words for the three concepts this trend was known as Habad Hasidism. Shneur Zalman belonged to a group of reformers who abjured excessive cultic and magical tendencies and strove for a return to simple teachings and popular faith, next to which the tsaddik could be no more than a champion of the faithful.

In May 1796, shortly after the third Partition of Poland, when the Hasidim were once more on the offensive, Elijah Gaon renewed and strengthened his earlier excommunication of the 'heretics.' He saw the unity of the faith as being under threat. He brusquely dismissed a request for disputation from Shneur Zalman. In many communities, there were bloody clashes. One year later the Gaon died and the Vilna Hasidim insisted on celebrating his death. Overflowing with deep feelings of revenge, the Vilna *kahal* reiterated the excommunication and denounced the Hasidic leaders to the tsarist authorities, saying that they would set in motion forces hostile to the state. There was now little trace of religions teachings in this quarrel. In 1798, a number of Hasidim were arrested, but they managed to persuade the authorities of their innocence. Even Tsar Paul I (1754–1801) took an interest in the case. After their release, the Hasidim plotted revenge on their own account. By means of bribery and accusations of embezzlement, they managed to have the *kahal* elders dismissed and to have Hasidim or their sympathizers elected in their place. The community split and mutual denunciations of the worst kind were traded back and forth. Shneur Zalman was again arrested, and was only released after the palace coup of 1801 which brought Alexander I to power. The 1804 law on Russian Jews was also a reaction to these struggles: the Hasidim could now have their own synagogues and rabbis, but at the same time the *kahal* administration remained in place.

THE TSARIST EMPIRE AND THE JEWS

Before the Partitions of Poland, the 'Jewish question' was artificially suppressed in the Russian Empire. Originally, in Kievan Rus', there was no particular hostility against the Jews. Jewish traders could be encountered everywhere, and Jews apparently lived in settlements too. This was connected with the conquest of the Khazar state. We have already mentioned the Kievan Khazar community, which professed its faith in rabbinical Judaism, and the conflicts there in 1113. The stronger the Orthodox Church became, however, more and more anti-Jewish tendencies unfolded. But in contrast to Germany or Poland, ideas of a crusade or legends of ritual murder did not find much resonance in Russia.

In the 'Muscovite Russia' of the late Middle Ages and early modernity, state-sponsored anti-Semitism intensified. In the sources there are numerous reports that after Mongolian rule had been shaken off and the new state began to expand, the Jews in conquered lands had to convert or be murdered. These brutalities reached their height under Tsar Ivan IV (1530–1584), who permitted no Jewish trade, since he feared a watering down of Russian Orthodoxy through the alien religion. The close relationship between tsarist autocracy and the Russian Orthodox Church played an important role here. Towards the end of the fifteenth century the heretical movement of Judaizers had spread from Novgorod. The significance of this movement is disputed, but it could be used as the occasion or justification for the anti-Semitic stance of Orthodoxy and the Russian state. To be sure, internal church power struggles at that time also played a role. The Judaizers' movement was brutally suppressed. Around the middle of the sixteenth century, similar heretical utterances were made in Lithuania, by the monk Feodosii Kosoy, who had fled from Russia. Perhaps this influenced Ivan IV directly. Although in Poland the Judaizers, together with the militant Counter-Reformation, provided a foundation for anti-Semitic slogans, in Russia people frequently identified the Jews with the Poles with whom they had often been at war.

This intensified during the Time of Troubles at the beginning of the seventeenth century. At times, Polish troops occupied Moscow and in 1610 the Polish prince Władysław (1595–1648) was even elected tsar, although he was never able to ascend to the throne. The claimants to the throne, who on several occasions falsely portrayed themselves as sons of the tsar, were occasionally described as 'Jewish'-born in order to discredit them. On the other hand, there were always small Jewish communities in Russia, primarily in the big cities. Traders were the first to set up in business here.

From the middle of the seventeenth century the tables were turned. The Russian Empire rose to become a great power at the expense of Poland and incorporated more and more Polish–Lithuanian territory as a result of numerous wars. Under Peter the Great (1672–1725) there was no particular anti-Semitism; he reigned as a typical, religiously tolerant man of the Enlightenment. This changed under his successors. The policy in the eighteenth century fluctuated between attempts to have the Jews expelled from the previously Polish, now Russian territories—for the first time in 1727—and measures to have those expulsions reversed, mainly on economic grounds. The strongest expulsion order was issued by Tsarina Elizabeth (1709–1762) in 1742. When the merchants of Riga lodged a complaint in the senate, pointing to the economic disadvantages which had resulted when the Jewish middlemen ceased to be involved in trade with Poland, and the senate adopted this standpoint itself in a petition, she answered: "I do not want profits from the enemies of Christ."[38] In 1744 she even prohibited Jews from visiting Russia.

This exclusion of the Jews also had its positive aspects. Because there were relatively few Jews, anti-Semitic stereotypes of the kind which were widespread in Poland could not develop so easily in Russia. This made things easier for the enlightened and pro-Jewish policies of Tsarina Catherine II (1729–1796). In 1763, one year after she came to power, she had at first renewed the earlier prohibition. Because of the shady circumstances of her coup d'etat, in which her husband, Peter III (1728–1762), was murdered, she needed the support of the Church and could not pick a fight with it. After the first Partition of Poland in 1772 Jews became inhabitants of the Russian Empire on a massive scale, and the problem could no longer be put to one side. The 'Jewish Question' had to be addressed with something other than prohibitions and expulsions.

In 1772, within the framework of her colonization policy, Catherine allowed Jews into Russia without particular restrictions. Her political and economic pragmatism was significantly strengthened by the influence of Enlightenment thought. The philosophers of the Enlightenment had no religious prejudices against Jews; they wanted to make good citizens of them with the same rights and duties as everyone else—although at the price of destroying Jewish autonomy and culture. We have already encountered these two sides of the Enlightenment among the Polish reformers. People must be liberated from the darkness of superstition and prejudice, but this liberation from "self-incurred immaturity" (As Kant wrote as the first sentence of his essay, 'An Answer to the Question: What Is Enlightenment?') could also mean that 'civilization' was imposed, and that existing ways of life were "colonized" (Habermas). Enlightened monarchs such as Frederick II of Prussia (1712–1786) or the Habsburg Joseph II (1741–1790) began to prohibit trades which were considered to be 'unproductive'—such as hawking, innkeeping, and distilling—to remove rights of autonomy, and to regulate all areas of their subjects' lives.

Furthermore, Catherine brought to Russia ideas about sharply delineated social strata—nobility, clergy, burghers, free peasants, serfs—which simply did not apply. For example, the difference between town and countryside was much less marked than in the West, and the boundary between town-dwellers and peasants remained in flux. When Catherine now founded numerous towns anew, gave existing small market towns town charters, and established guilds by decree in hopes of creating an organized civic community, she was going against Russian traditions. Most measures therefore soon petered out. For the Jews, however, they had radical consequences. According to Catherine's view of society, Jews, on the basis of their predominantly economic activities, were assigned to the stratum of burghers as merchants (*kuptsy*) or lower-class townsmen (*meshchane*). However, Jews for the most part lived in the countryside. What was intended to be emancipatory ended up being highly injurious.

Another sign of enlightenment was the fact that Jews were now referred to in Russian documents as 'Hebrews' (*evrei*), that is, as a religious community, while the term 'Jew' (*zhid*), with which national characteristics were connected, was subsequently used colloquially or pejoratively. In any case, after the first Partition of Poland, tsarist policy at first made the Jews equal with all other population groups. The fact that the Jews were to retain their *kahal*-autonomy was related—similarly to the right of the *obshchina* or peasant commune to govern itself, within limits—to the need to ensure tax collection and a certain social control, for which the bureaucracy was still not adequate. For a brief period, Russia was far ahead of all other European countries in respect to the equal treatment of the Jews.

However, equal treatment also brought with it regulation. For example, in 1782 it was ordered for the first time that "townspeople"—and this expressly included the Jews—had to live in towns. This provided an opportunity to drive the Jews from the countryside. One year later, the right to distil alcohol was given exclusively to the large landowners. At first, landowners could still sublease these rights to Jews, but they could also use the new regulations to force Jews out of business. Soon people were trying to circumvent the rights which had been granted to the Jews. At first, these attempts met with little success, but over time, particularly after the second and third Partitions of Poland, as ever larger numbers of Jews came under tsarist rule, there were greater retrograde steps. For example, from 1794 the Jews in certain provinces—in common with other religious minorities—had to pay double the amount of tax in order to help consolidate the state finances after the numerous wars.

In response to the complaints of Moscow merchants that the Jewish competition now streaming in made things extremely difficult for them; Catherine II declared on 23 December 1791 that Jews could not settle in Russia proper. They had to confine themselves to the areas newly annexed from Poland and to 'new Russia,' areas of the Black Sea littoral annexed from Turkey and now to be colonized. This move has long been considered to constitute the beginning of a consciously anti-Jewish policy. However, in all likelihood the measure was rather intended more to protect the Moscow merchants than to discriminate against

Map 4. The Jewish Pale of Settlement in the Russian Empire

Jews. Jews were not kept away from Moscow as Jews, but rather as unnecessary competition. Moreover, freedom of movement was restricted for most population groups in the Russian Empire. Nevertheless, with her decree Catherine had laid the foundations of the so-called 'Pale of Settlement,' which Jews, with some exceptions, were unable to leave until the First World War.

The Pale was formally established in Russia by the long-prepared 'Statue on the Jews' (*polozhenie dlya evreev*), adopted in 1804. This law gave expression to the view, which in the meantime had become the dominant among the Russian elites that the Jews must first be 'improved' and assimilated before they could be granted emancipation. For example, after a six-year period the Jews should keep their accounts only in a non-Jewish 'standard language,' and office-holders should no longer dress in a Jewish manner. The Jews were granted freedom of trade and employment, with the exception of inn-keeping and similar mediatory activities which allegedly corrupted the peasants. In compensation, the law offered Jews the opportunity to colonize land with state assistance, primarily in 'new Russia.' In fact, a corresponding initiative was launched in the province of Kherson. Several thousand Jews moved there, but found such chaotic circumstances and inadequate preparations on the part of the authorities that the project had to be abandoned in 1810.

Moreover, the enlightened–absolutistic policy of Tsar Alexander I took up the idea of Catherine II that the Jews must leave the villages in which they lived side by side with Christian peasants. Alexander justified his action on the grounds of protecting the peasants from Jewish 'exploitation'. Twice—in 1808 and 1823—the state initiated forced resettlement, although in each case it proved unenforceable. This hung over village-dwelling Jews as a constant threat, however, and was attempted for individual regions in later times.

The negative clichés and stereotypes of Jews which were widespread in Poland now increasingly began to manifest themselves in Russia. They found expression in the figure of the greedy, deceitful inn-keeper and 'village Jew,' which characterized the statute of 1804 and influenced the thinking of many politicians and writers. The Jews were supposed to be backward and their religion dangerous. Out of ignorance, people were taken in by untruths concerning the Talmud and Jewish religious laws; the strangeness of the Jews in particular promoted prejudice. One of the few early literary testimonies which, despite the many stereotypes, showed a measure of sympathy for the Jews, was Nikolai Karamzin's *Letters of a Russian Traveler, 1789–90* (1791–1797) in its portrayal of the Jewish ghetto in Frankfurt.

Even the groups of conspirators which made up the reform-friendly and Enlightenment-influenced Decembrists—so-called because of their uprising in December 1825—were in the grip of the prevailing view of the Jews. Pavel Pestel' (1793–1826) took an interest in the Jews within the framework of his projects for reform of the state. He regarded the Jews as an obstacle to a progressive state because the loyalty of the Jews was primarily to one another rather than to the state, because the rabbis had too much power over the Jews and kept all enlightened and integration-oriented elements at arm's length, and finally because the Jews considered themselves to be a chosen people superior to all others. He saw two possible solutions: either to obtain an agreement from the rabbis and other Jewish leaders to work together with the government, or to expel the Jews, if possible to Asia Minor, where they would then be able to establish an independent state. Pestel' was not the first to develop the idea of a Jewish state, but from now on this possibility inspired by the most diverse intentions and in several variants, would play an ever greater role.

The outlines of state policy towards the Jews as it had been formed under Alexander I for the Russian Empire, and from 1815 for Poland, remained in force under Nicholas I (1796–1855). The interference in the way of life of the Jews, however, increased markedly, although it was no longer only inspired by the desire to 'educate' or 'improve.' More and more obligations were imposed on the Jews without any more rights being granted them. For example, from 1835 they also had to serve as conscripts, an obligation from which they could free themselves only with the greatest difficulty. Even boys between the ages of twelve and eighteen were enlisted for compulsory pre-military training. Since service of this kind was scarcely in accord with their religious practices, many Jews engaged in passive resistance, went into hiding, fled from their homeland, or even maimed themselves, after protests and attempts at bribery had failed.

> Those who had no money, maimed themselves ... Their [the East European Jews'] clever reasoning calculated that it is better to live lame than to die healthy. This view of things was underpinned by their piety. It was not only stupid to die for an emperor, for a tsar, it was also a sin to live at odds with the Torah and against its commandments. It was a sin to eat pork; to bear arms on the Sabbath; to exercise; and to raise one's hand, never mind a sword, against an innocent stranger.[39]

As early as 1821, 'synagogal supervision' was introduced in Poland and as a result the *kahal* was abolished as a community organization one year later. In the same year Jewish organizations or societies—to begin with, the *hevra kaddisha* (holy society), responsible for burials—were prohibited. In 1844 Tsar Nicholas extended these regulations to the whole of the Russian Empire. He intended to dismantle all autonomous Jewish organizations, but was not successful, however. In the face of considerable difficulties, most organizations continued to operate illegally—with or without the acquiescence of local authorities. The Jews asserted themselves through their independent organizations and widely maintained the representation of their rights in their communities. The same held for getting around clothing ordinances which widely prohibited the wearing of characteristic Jewish garb on an everyday basis. This high level of autonomy, defended under very difficult circumstances, contributed substantially to the solidarity and self-consciousness which—in all conflicts—characterized the Jewish way of life in Eastern Europe into the twentieth century.

The communal tax—the *korobka*—on ritual foodstuffs and utensils, such as kosher meat and candles, was not abolished, which hit the poorest members of the community particularly hard. It was converted into a state tax. A temporary turn for the better came in 1856 with the reform age of Alexander II (1818–1881), which envisaged step-by-step, 'selective' emancipation for the Jews and in many respects looked back to the period of Alexander I.[40] For example, permits granted between 1859 and 1879, enabling Jews to leave the Pale of Settlement, were made available to the 'better circles' of Russian Jewry: merchants of the First Guild, the holders of academic degrees, guild craftsmen, and finally anyone who had attended a university or similar educational institution. When in 1867 discharged common soldiers, most of whom had served twenty years or more, were granted freedom of movement, it amounted to no more than a modest breakthrough for the lower classes.

There was some relief for Jews in the countryside. Under certain circumstances they were permitted to sell alcohol again. They were also permitted to participate without restriction in the *zemtsva*, organs of local self-government introduced in 1864. There was no discrimination either in the 1864 reform of the justice system or in the universal military service law of 1874. It was different in the case of the urban reform of 1870: Jews could only make up one-third of the representatives, even when they constituted the majority of the population, and could not be appointed head of the town.

The reform-euphoria of the period inspired the Jews in Russia to hope that there would be an improvement in their situation. Attendance of state educational institutions was substantially greater than before. Attempts at assimilation were discernible everywhere. In the tsarist bureaucracy, however, there were counter tendencies. For example, an imperial chancellery circular of April 1880 demanded that all governors in Congress Poland gather information on Jewish capitalists, who, it was common knowledge, "are part of the international *kahal*, which was founded with clearly anti-Christian intentions." It was alleged that Jews paid contributions to this organization and backed a revolutionary party.[41]

The assassination of Alexander II in March 1881 brought all expectations to a sudden end. The fact that in many places Russian peasants and petit bourgeoisie could easily be provoked by saying that the Jews were behind the terror attack, and that a new wave of pogroms inundated the country, made it lastingly clear that there had never really been any possibility of assimilation or even of integration. Subsequent investigations of the riots found in familiar fashion that the Jews themselves were responsible: they had provoked this response with their "religious fanaticism" and their usurious–sly exploitation of the non-Jewish population. From 1882 the rights of the Jews began to be drastically curtailed once again. New settlements and lease contracts in the countryside were prohibited. In state educational institutions the proportion of Jews could not exceed a certain, low percentage. A legal career remained barred to Jews. The right to vote for the organs of self-government of regions and towns was taken away from them. In the 1890s Jewish soldiers, craftsmen, and merchants, with few exceptions, even had to leave the city and province of Moscow and return to the Pale of Settlement.

This humiliating discrimination remained in place until the revolution of 1917. Within the apparatus of government there were certainly those who, for humanitarian or pragmatic—that is, economic—reasons, wished for at least a gradual rescinding of the extraordinary laws. Finance ministers in particular wanted a relaxation of the regulations. They knew that the Jews could be an important economic factor in the Empire and also feared that a continuation of anti-Semitic policies could have detrimental effects in the international sphere, due to the influence of Jewish bankers abroad. Instructive in this regard is a conversation between the distinguished finance minister Sergei Witte (1849–1915) and Tsar Alexander III (1845–1894). The latter asked Witte if he sympathized with the Jews. Witte asked in return whether it would be possible to drown all of the Jews in the Black Sea, and went on to say that if not, then the Jews must somehow be able to 'live.' This meant that ultimately they should be granted the same rights as all the other subjects of the tsar.[42]

Substantial improvements could not be carried through. However, as a consequence of the Revolution of 1905, Jews at least received the right to vote in the elections for the first elected parliament, the Duma, in 1906. In practical politics there were some relaxations. On the other hand, anti-Semitism strengthened within conservative circles in reaction to the perceived threat of capitalism and social reform efforts. This went so far that some elements with extreme views, which also had some representation in the ranks of the authorities, demanded pogroms against the Jews or organized them themselves. Particularly shocking were the pogroms in Kishinev in 1903 and during the Revolution of 1905, as was the trial of Mendel Beilis (1874–1934), who was accused of the ritual murder of a Christian boy, but ultimately acquitted in 1913.

In the First World War the Pale of Settlement was abolished—but not in response to the handicaps which it imposed on the Jews, but out of fear that Jews would collaborate with the enemy. A large part of the area settled by the Jews formed the center of military action. Hundreds of thousands fled before the fighting, looting, and requisitions. Anti-Semitic circles among the Polish National Democrats and the Russian General Staff spread the accusation, generalizing from actual individual cases, that Jews were spying for Germany and Austria–Hungary. As a consequence, pogroms broke out in a number of places. Increasingly, the tsarist military government took the view that the Jews should be expelled to those parts of the Pale of Settlement not touched by the war. Since conditions there were unendurable, in August 1915 the government abolished the Pale of Settlement and allowed Jews to settle also in other regions, indeed almost anywhere (although not entirely freely) in the Empire. The expulsions and deportations were conducted with their fair share of violence. Sometimes the Jews were even driven into enemy territory, towards the front. Those who were later able to return often found their homes already occupied by non-Jews.

Jewish soldiers in the tsarist army had to endure many forms of discrimination. In addition, in the hinterland and in the big cities rumors were spread concerning Jewish 'war profiteers', so diverting attention from those really responsible for the economic difficulties.[43] The successful revolution in February/March 1917 at last brought an end to all restrictions: the Jews were now citizens of Russia with equal rights.

By and large, Russian imperial legislation also applied to the Jews in the Kingdom of Poland, with a few differences in individual regulations. For a brief period, Poland was able to follow its own path: in May 1862 all substantive discrimination against the Jews in respect of civil rights was lifted and equality of rights decreed. This was not unrelated to Poland's resistance against its incorporation in the Russian Empire; during the time of the Partitions of Poland, many Jews had participated in the uprisings against the tsarist regime. In the futile uprising of 1830 many of them had been involved in the fighting. In the democratic trend of the 'Great Emigration,' the historian Joachim Lelewel (1786–1861), took up the cause of Jewish rights. In the upper echelons of government it was deemed expedient to work against this association. The last straw in this respect was the 'alliance' between the Warsaw Jews and Polish freedom fighters on the occasion of the commemoration of those who fell at an anti-Russian demonstration on 27 February 1861.

In view of the growing unrest among the population, the tsarist and Polish authorities tried to appease at least some of the malcontents and so to weaken the protest movement. As the course of the uprising of 1863 showed, this effort was partly successful. The attitude of the circles around Count Aleksander Wielopolski (1803–1877), commissioner of culture and later head of the civil government in Poland, also led to the concessions towards the Jews, persuading Tsar Alexander II of the benefits of such measures: They wanted to strengthen the assimilation efforts within the Jewish population and give free rein to the activities of Jewish entrepreneurs and bankers. Twenty years later, with the May Laws of 1882, which were extended to cover Russian Poland, consideration for the legal interests of the Jews was already a thing of the past.

EAST EUROPEAN JEWS OUTSIDE TSARIST RULE

While in Poland the consequences of the catastrophe of 1648 weakened the mediating function of the Jews between town and countryside, the repercussions of the Thirty Years War in Bohemia and Moravia only led to its full development. The higher nobility, which now was increasingly active economically, brought in Jewish merchants, who bought up the agricultural and commercial products of landed estates and exchanged them for products from the towns. Jews—from wholesalers through craftsmen to peddlers or 'village walkers'—became, as in Poland, the center of an economic circulation system which linked peasants, nobles, and town-dwellers, not least the guilds (including the Jewish guilds in Prague). Furthermore, the nobility increasingly 'farmed out' their distilleries and other businesses to Jews until the latter had a monopoly.

As their economic fortunes improved, Jews in the countryside, particularly in Bohemia, began organizing themselves better; Moravian Jews had had a regional organization since the sixteenth century. The Bohemian Jewish communities were subordinate to the one in Prague. The Jewish community in Bohemia felt particularly disadvantaged in respect to the allocation of the tax burden and finally decided in 1654 that they too would be granted a similar regional organization. This body, completed in 1659, was responsible for tax administration and other important decisions outside Prague.

However, Prague remained a Jewish metropolis. During the eighteenth century, of the estimated 40,000 Jews in Bohemia—there were around 25,000 in Moravia—around 10,000, perhaps more, lived in the capital. They therefore made up around one-third of the population and constituted the largest urban Jewish community. In comparison, in Frankfurt in the middle of the seventeenth century there were 2,000 Jews, in Vienna 3,000, and in Berlin just under 4,000. Only towards the end of the eighteenth century did the Jewish settlements in Polish (including Galicia) towns begin to grow. Reputed rabbinical authorities taught in Prague and it was considered particularly desirable among the Ashkenasim to study at one of the many Prague *yeshivot*. The honorary title of the Prague 'Jewish city' at this time was still 'Mother of Israel.' The well-to-do Jewish upper stratum strove from early on to emulate the lifestyle of Christian burghers. When the city was rebuilt after the devastating fire of 1754, the magnificent baroque houses of rich Jews made the contrast with the miserable quarters of the poor particularly glaring.

The brilliance of Prague and the outstanding economic functions of the Jews in the countryside—the 'outsiders', as they were somewhat condescendingly known among Praguers—could not hide the fact that the legal situation had by no means improved. Under pressure from economic interest groups in 1726/1727 the Habsburg Emperor Charles VI (1685–1740) passed the infamous 'familiant law': in Bohemia the number of Jewish families would not be permitted to rise above 8,541, while in Moravia 5,106 families were permitted. Only after the death of the holder of a 'family number' could a new marriage permit be issued. Since, this rule meant that only one son could get married and take up residence the other sons had either to remain single or to go abroad. Many other restrictions followed.

In tandem with this the Jews living in the countryside, and their organizations, underwent a decline. The Jews of course tried every means possible to get around the 'familiant' regulations, but for many, if they had no wish to emigrate or did not have enough money for a special exemption, the only way out was to marry secretly in accordance with Jewish law. These marriages [*chassenes*] were known as *Bodenhassenes* because they were performed in the attic [*Boden*]. Children from such marriages were considered to be illegitimate by the authorities. The distress which these conditions caused can be imagined.

Even after the enactment of the 'familiant law' voices demanding a further reduction of the Jewish population, or even its wholesale expulsion—as had been tried several times in the Middle Ages—did not die down. Not least due to the persuasion of church representatives Maria Theresa (1717–1780) finally decided to expel all Jews from Bohemia. In December 1744, regardless of the time of year, their state of health, or age first the Jews of Prague had to leave the city. However, for many people this was going too far. Even the adversaries of the Jews in the Old Town changed their minds. The economic disadvantages of this measure quickly became apparent, particularly because the Christian merchants were not in a position to take the place of the Jews. In 1748 Maria Theresa gave in to representations both domestic and foreign—even from the Pope—and allowed the Prague Jews to return home, though to their homes which had long since been looted. For an initial period of ten years she allowed them to stay in the territories of the Bohemian crown, subject to the payment of a handsome sum of money.

The 'Edict of Tolerance' introduced by Emperor Joseph II for the Jews of Bohemia and Moravia in 1781/1782, mainly on economic and foreign-policy grounds, had a contradictory character. It is true that many essentially discriminatory provisions and restrictions were abolished, and economic activity was promoted. However, this primarily benefited the well-to-do social strata which was ready to assimilate and indeed—just like the Jewish philosophers of the Enlightenment—overwhelmingly welcomed the reforms. They profited, moreover, from the economic situation. In 1807, of 58 textile factories 15 were in Jewish hands.

The mass of Jews, however, still suffered under oppressive taxes, the 'familiant law', the only slightly relaxed ban on freedom of movement, and above all the provision which stated that after a certain period only the German language could be used in official and business correspondence. Similarly, from 1787, both a first name and a family name had to be adopted in the German form. The compulsory military service introduced in 1788/1789 led to much unrest. During military service the Sabbath was profaned and the food laws and other ritual stipulations could not be observed. 'Going underground,' flight, and even self-maiming were the order of the day among poorer Jews who had no chance of buying themselves out.

It was probably on the occasion of a 'journey' abroad in order to avoid compulsory military service that two followers of Jacob Frank, the sons of rich Prague Jews, visited Offenbach and discovered the charlatanry of his daughter Eva Frank, who he had given out to be the divinity incarnate. The Frankists had many followers in Bohemia and Moravia. In Prague they hoped that the end of the world would come in 1800. When this did not come to pass disturbances broke out, apparently because of the annoyance orthodox Jews felt over the fact that the Frankists would not be converted even now.

All in all, developments in the eighteenth century led to the gradual dissolution of traditional Jewish society. The majority of the educated and of the economic upper stratum became integrated in the German cultural sphere, albeit with their own characteristic features. East European Jews [*Ostjuden*] played a subordinate role in Bohemia and Moravia, although Polish Jews had fled here after 1648. The Jews of these territories occupied a special position between West and East.

The type of the East European Jew had taken shape in the Kingdom of Poland–Lithuania after 1648. In the middle of the eighteenth century around 750,000 Jews lived here, around 7 percent of the population. With the Partitions of Poland they also found themselves living in different political territories. Outside the Russian sphere of influence most East European Jews now lived in the Habsburg Monarchy, mostly in Galicia. They were made very conscious of what tolerance towards the Jews meant in the enlightened–absolutist sense: they must renounce their 'peculiarities,' 'improve' themselves, and make themselves 'useful.' Earlier than in Russian Poland or in Russia itself, Jews in the Habsburg Monarchy had to contend with comprehensive legislative measures which interfered profoundly in their everyday lives. From 1773 marriages had to be approved by the Austrian governor. Only a male descendent could marry and so become a 'familiant,' just like in Bohemia and Moravia. Furthermore, in 1785 marriage licenses were linked to a certain level of German education. As early as 1776, inn-keeping and the holding in lease of landed estates were forbidden to Jews. In 1789 Joseph II passed his 'Edict of Tolerance' which reduced the scope of *kahal* self-administration, tightened up economic prohibitions, imposed settlement restrictions, made the adoption of a family name obligatory, and confirmed the strict marriage policy. The Enlightenment came once more in the form of a mission and was forcibly imposed on traditional culture.

Galician Hasidim and orthodox Jews fought strenuously against all enlightened tendencies, even within Jewry. The government became involved and in 1797, at the suggestion of Jewish progressives, imposed a 'lighting up' tax on Sabbath and holiday candles which remained in fore until 1848. This represented a heavy burden for the poorer members of the community. The Jews already had to pay higher taxes than the rest of the population. They were also subject to military conscription; only the richer Jews could buy themselves out of it. Many Jews reacted by fleeing abroad. In this way the Jewish population of Galicia shrank, according to different, though disputed estimates, from 225,000 (1773) to 145,000 (1777). Later on, it started to grow again, not least because of the territorial increase due to the third Partition of Poland, and by 1803 had reached around 400,000. Many Jews also married secretly and avoided military service illegally.

The new organization of the state brought economic benefits for the Jews. They now profited from the growing trade between Russia and the Habsburg Monarchy. Above all, the border town of Brody became a key place of exchange for goods and the "real Jewish capital" of Galicia.[44]

In principle, similar circumstances were to be found in Bukovina, which the Turks ceded to Austria in 1775 and since then had belonged to Galicia. The small number of Jews—the estimates range from 1,000 to 3,000—now began to increase rapidly.

In Hungary there were almost no *Ostjuden*. The conditions and settlements there in the Middle Ages can readily be compared with those in Poland. In 1251 King Béla IV (1206–1270) issued a charter of privileges for Jews in order to help repopulate the land again after the Mongol assault. Although the king subsequently by and large protected the Jews against the church, because they were good taxpayers and provided the crown with much needed money, the relationship was not free of conflict. In 1360 the Jews were even driven out of Hungary for a short period after an attempt by King Lajos (1326–1382) to convert them to Christianity had failed. The attacks of the Church did not fail to have an effect on the general population, however. Countless riots are recorded. And after Hungary's defeat by the Turks at the Battle of Mohács in 1526, many gave free rein to their fury in the Jewish quarters of the towns. A large part of the inhabitants were driven out. In 1785 there were only around 80,000 Jews in Hungary.

The situation of the Jews was most favorable in the Princedom of Transylvania. Many interesting religious trends appeared here; for example, Sabbathism, a mixture of Christianity and Judaism, in which the Jewish Sabbath (that is, Saturday) rather than Sunday was sacred. All in all, however, no "characteristic cultural personality" comparable with that of the East European Jews in Poland was formed. From the eighteenth century, little by little, Jews immigrated, primarily from Galicia. The policy of the Habsburgs, who had ruled the land since the driving back of the Turks at the end of the seventeenth century, was not particularly friendly towards the Jews. In the period of absolutistic 'tolerance' the conflict, as elsewhere, was primarily about compulsory military service and the Jews' freedom of trade.

In the whole territory of the Habsburg Monarchy, the number of Jewish inhabitants rose from less than 400,000 in 1785 to around one million in 1803. The type of the 'Western Jew' was still predominant.

Meanwhile, colonies of East European Jews developed from the end of the eighteenth century in Walachia and Moldavia. These Romanian princedoms then stood under Turkish overlordship. Originally, mainly Sephardim had immigrated via the Mediterranean region and Salonika. The princes and the noble lords of the manor, the boyars, now brought in Jews for the colonization of sparsely populated areas as had happened previously in Poland. These came especially from Galicia and Ukraine. Contributory factors in this emigration were the Haidamak uprisings and the new situation in Galicia after the first Partition of Poland. Most of the settlers were Hasidim. The Jewish population grew in a few years from 30,000 to 50,000, and then to 80,000 people. Most settled in Moldavia, principally in Iași, and a few in Walachia, around Bucharest. Their hope of finding a more peaceful homeland was not fulfilled, however. The Jews were also caught up in military conflicts here, this time between Russians and Turks.

There was an interesting development in Prussian Poland: under the influence of new circumstances, particularly the contact with German Jews and the economic opportunities which favored tendencies towards assimilation, the East European Jews there gradually turned into 'Western Jews.' Their faith remained overwhelmingly orthodox, however, and they sustained manifold contacts with the Jews in the other territories of partitioned Poland.

Part III
THE CRISIS OF THE JEWS IN EASTERN EUROPE AND A NEW IDENTITY

TRANSFORMATION OF THE TRADITIONAL INTERMEDIARY FUNCTION

The role of intermediary between town and countryside had been the central economic function of Jews in Eastern Europe. As inn-keepers, small shopkeepers, traders, peddlers, lessees, and administrators they linked together noble landowners, peasants, country or urban craftsmen, big merchants, and entrepreneurs in an economic circulation system. As a result, they were caught up in the social conflicts between the nobility and the peasants. In the seventeenth and eighteenth century the symbiosis between the Jews and the nobility had begun to come apart. Time and again from the end of the eighteenth century, one encounters among legislative measures attempts to force the Jews out of the inn-keeping trade or even out of the villages altogether. We must now look at the background to this development, which resumed with renewed force in the nineteenth century. Once again, Poland stands at the center of things.

At the beginning of the nineteenth century Central Europe was in the grip of a regional agricultural crisis. The grain monoculture of the manorial lords was directed towards export due to sluggish urban demand. Production prompted by high wheat prices in the export regions led to speculation and risky credit transactions at the turn of the century. The Napoleonic wars caused a devastating sales and financial crisis, the effects of which were repeated in 1819, triggered by British protective tariffs. When in 1823 the Prussian government also substantially raised the tariff on agricultural products, Polish grain exports through the port of Danzig (now Gdańsk), fell by almost half. Many debt-ridden nobles went bankrupt. At the same time, the nobles had to find ways of getting rid of their grain: this was found in the tried and tested production of alcohol, with the peasants as the principal customers. The waste, from the production process, the *Schlempe*, served to overcome the bottleneck in winter cattle fodder. As a result, the cattle trade also received a boost, and the more intensive fertilization which it made possible led to improvements in agriculture. Sheep rearing in particular—and so also the textile industry—experienced a considerable upswing.

All of this affected the Jews directly. With the ruin of many manorial lords, many of the Jews lost their positions as lessees as the impoverished nobility crowded them out. The declining grain business badly affected those Jews involved in this sector. Above all, however, the struggle for market share in the sale of spirits went against the Jews. The Polish nobility were first able to eliminate the non-Jewish, bourgeois competition in the towns, since they were exempt from the tax on the retail of alcohol (until 1844), and in 1823 the distilleries in those towns which were not in the private ownership of the nobility were closed by order of the state. The state then divided the revenues from alcohol production with the nobility after a corresponding state monopoly had been established in 1822. In order to find a substitute for their by and large declining revenues from agriculture, more and more nobles sought to drive the Jews out of the production and sale of spirits. The state—at this time still the Duchy of Warsaw—took up this idea, and on 30 October 1812 passed a decree which exluded the Jews, from 1 July 1814 on, from the production and sale of alcoholic drinks. The state forced the nobility, which was neither familiar with production techniques nor in possession of entrepreneurial skills, to adapt to a new lifestyle, while at the same time prohibiting the Jews from engaging in particular trades under any circumstances. Distillery owners were allowed to retain Jewish master brewers until 1 July 1815 strictly for the purpose of learning the requisite technical skills.

Implementing decree led to such difficulties, because of the economic shortcomings of the nobility, that its wholesale implementation had to be put off. Nevertheless, the Jews experienced severe restrictions on their economic activity which went further than under the 'Statute on the Jews,' inflicted on them in 1804 in the eastern voivodates, annexed by Russia.

After 1815 the goal remained to drive the Jews out of the alcohol business and the manorial economy, even if its realization was only attempted step by step. An opportunity to do this was provided by the introduction of a special trading license for Jews from 8 June 1814, which moreover provided the state with an additional source of income. The fees were constantly raised. From May 1816, furthermore, Jewish inn-keepers were no longer permitted to provide peasants with drinks on credit or using agricultural produce as collateral. As a result they were deprived of significant income because many peasants who did not have sufficient cash were tempted to drink heavily in the taverns in anticipation of the coming harvest. All in all, between 1819 and 1822 the number of Jews employed in this sector fell drastically. The discovery of new distilling technology which did not need Jews to operate it may also have contributed to this. When compared to 1813, only about 12 percent of Jews remained in the production and sale of alcohol in 1830, and of those only around 7 percent lived in the countryside. In this way a traditional bond which had tied the Jews to society, both noble and peasant, was broken.

The more the Polish nobility came to regard the Jews as unwanted competition which hindered their restructuring of the manorial economy and complete domination of the village, the more anti-Semitic *ressentiment* manifested itself. Nourished by demographic developments—the substantially more rapid growth of the Jewish population in comparison with the Christian—an ever more threatening picture of the Jews was painted. Jews were supposed to be cunning, persistent, undemanding, unenlightened, determined, influential in every branch of the economy, and involved in every financial transaction—in short: dangerous and harmful. It was therefore only logical for the nobility to do everything it could to prevent the Jews from obtaining equal rights. How else would it have been able to eliminate them as competitors?

The opportunity to drive the Jews from the land on the basis of the tsarist laws was another weapon in the competitive struggle. Even when these attempts did not succeed; decisively more and more Jews flowed into the towns. The remaining town privileges which prohibited Jewish residence could not halt this migration. One solution was the construction of specific Jewish quarters or ghettos. A decree of May 1822 modeled on the Warsaw ghetto statute of 1809—allowed corresponding measures for all towns.

	1816		1827	
Jews in towns	144.200	67.7%	303.800	80.4%
Jews in villages	68.800	32.3%	74.000	19.6%
Proportion of Jews in the urban population		27.3%		35.3%

The proportion of Jews in the urban population was very high, particularly in the larger towns and in the northeastern voivodates.[1] Impoverished petit bourgeois poured into the new

'Jewish districts' and competed for the few work opportunities. The mass of Jews became visibly impoverished, and often lived under unimaginable conditions with regard to accommodation, work, and income. Overmanning, particularly in skilled trades which had no future, created a large number of so-called *Luftmenshn*, literally 'air-people,' in the sense of people who 'have nothing but air to live on,' without a regular income, and dependent upon a daily scramble for casual work in order to eke out some sort of subsistence (see the section *Luftmenshn* below, especially footnote 6). With the help of illicit stills and alcohol smuggling they survived illegally, but they often became embroiled in a violent struggle with the remaining village Jews.

On the other hand, a few entrepreneurs and bankers were able to become very rich indeed. Around 40 millionaire families served as models for the figure of the Jewish 'capitalist.' They were interlinked with one another by means of complex family relationships and—being mostly immigrants to Poland—lived predominantly in Warsaw. But there was also a small upper stratum in the other towns. Their special position was as a rule due to their close co-operation with the government. For example, in 1822 finance minister Drucki-Lubecki leased the state alcohol monopoly to the Lithuanian Jew Newachowicz, at the same time as the Jews in the countryside were being driven out of the production and sale of alcohol. In 1816, Berek Szmul (Samuel) Sonnenberg leased the state salt monopoly. Jewish 'entrepreneurs'—such as Fraenkel, Neumark, and Bergson—made their profits from army supplies, to the Duchy of Warsaw, Russia, and the Kingdom of Poland. Since the government was often not in a position to pay within the period stipulated the suppliers—partly with the interposition of Jewish financiers—could dictate the terms. However, non-Jewish strata were gradually starting to find their way into the ranks of the big bourgeoisie.

The activities of Jewish army suppliers also offered an excellent opportunity to make the Jews in general responsible for the afflictions of soldiers and officers; for the poor provision of the army. Jews were demonized as deceivers, parasites, bloodsuckers, and war profiteers, in order to divert attention from the mistakes of the government and the military leadership. This runs like a red thread through the nineteenth century.

Jewish entrepreneurs practiced a new form of economic intermediation after the Jews had been broadly eliminated as intermediaries between town and countryside, between nobility, peasants, and town-dwellers, and between producers and appropriators of surplus products. The policy of the Polish nobility opened up a rift between town and countryside to which the traditional economic and social role of the Jews fell victim. As a result, the Jews were plunged into a deep identity crisis which also found expression in the life of the community and in religious or ideological attitudes. The traditional role had been bound up with simple production of goods in relation to which the Jews, on the basis of their special legal position with regard to credit and exchange, provided an exceptionally important intermediary service. With the passage to the complex production of goods—that is, to the capitalist mode of production—the Jews gradually lost their function. New social strata emerged to compete with the Jews. As a result, as society posed the 'Jewish question,' the Jews themselves questioned their new place in that society, and their understanding of themselves.

'EXPULSION' AND 'RESTRUCTURING'

It was not only migration from the countryside which worsened the Jews' situation in the towns. The industrialization which gradually set in during the first half of the nineteenth century led to a decline in the importance of traditional skilled trades. Jewish society, after many of its members had been 'expelled' from the production and sale of alcohol, village leasing, and now also skilled trades, was caught up in sustained socio-economic restructuring. The famous poet Sholem Aleichem vividly described this restructuring in his story 'Passover in the Village':

> Meanwhile, Nachman Werebjowker doesn't have such a bad life in Werebjowka. Naturally, there's no comparison with earlier times. When grandfather Arie was still alive everything was different; yes, those were the days! At that time almost the whole of Werebjowka belonged to him. There were not just one but several businesses—an inn, a grocery, a mill, and a grain warehouse—and so they wanted for nothing. But that was then. It's not like that any more. No more inn, no more grocery or grain warehouse. Nothing, absolutely nothing is left. You might well ask why the Jews still live in Werebjowka. Where else should they live? Under the earth? Even if it ever occurred to Nachman to sell his little house he wouldn't be Werebjowker any more. People would look on him as an interloper, as a stranger. At least he has his own corner, his own room, his own garden, which his wife and his daughter look after. With God's help one has enough vegetables for the summer and potatoes for the winter until after Passover. But you cannot live on potatoes alone. You also need bread, and Nachman has no bread. So he takes his stick and wanders through the village. He is always on the lookout for anything which might be traded, and when Nachman wanders through the village in order to trade he never comes back empty-handed. He sells what God bestows upon him—a little sheet iron, a pot with some millet in it, an old sack, sometimes even a fur. The fur is spread out, dried, and taken to the furrier Avrohom-Eliahu in the town. But in all these transactions you can make a profit as well as lose out: that's why you trade. 'A trader is like a hunter', says Nachman, who is always spouting Russian sayings.[2]

In another passage, from his best known novel, *Tevye der milkhiker* (Tevye the milkman), Sholem Aleichem portrays how low the standing of some craftsmen could become. Zeitel, the daughter of a dairyman, is to be married to a rich butcher. Then the poor journeyman tailor Motl Kamisol decides to call on Tevye and to ask for the hand of his daughter, whom he has loved for a long time, in person, in contrast to the usual practice of sending a marriage broker first.

> When he spoke these words I jumped up as if I had been scalded. He jumped up too, and so we stood opposite one another like two cockerels ... I would much rather someone had stabbed me in the heart with a knife than hear these words ... how could he, Motl, the tailor, ever become Tevye's son-in-law?

Motl then says:

> 'I wanted ... many times to talk to you about this, but I always put it off, until I had saved a few rubles so I could buy a sewing machine and then to kit myself out in the proper way. Because a young man who takes pride in himself needs two suits and a waistcoat these days ...'—'The ground should swallow you up', I say to him, 'you think like a child! What will you do after the wedding? Die of starvation or feed your wife with your waistcoat?'—'Oh', he says, 'I am surprised at you, Reb Tevye, for saying such a thing! I mean, you didn't have your own house when you got married. And as you see, things worked out ... Either way, whatever happens to the whole of Israel will also happen to Reb Israel ... In any case, I am a craftsman.'

Tevye allows himself to be persuaded and he is able to trick his wife Golde into agreeing, although to begin with she exclaims:

> 'How can a tailor be coming into our family', Golde asks me? 'In our family', she says, 'there have been teachers, prayer leaders, school janitors, employees of the burial association and other poor people, but, God forbid, neither tailors nor shoemakers ...'

Motl and Zeitel get married and Tevye says:

> And the young couple are living together, thank God, very happily. He is a tailor, goes to Boiberik from one summer house to another and

takes orders; and she is under the yoke day and night. She cooks and bakes and washes and cleans and carries water; and despite that they have almost nothing to eat. If I didn't bring them some cheese or milk or a couple of *groschen* every now and then, they would really be up against it.[3]

LUFTMENSHN

Jewish society was visibly differentiated economically and socially—indeed, it was polarized. The majority of Jews became poorer and poorer. They struggled along as small traders, peddlers, or even as *Luftmenshn*. Let us listen to Tevye once again:

> Now, at that time I was an out-and-out beggar. To tell the truth, I am not a rich man even now ... But at any rate compared with then I am a rich man, with my own horse and my own cart, and also, touch wood, a couple of cows, which can be milked and one of which will soon calf. Truth to tell, I have fresh cheese and butter and cream every day, and everything is made by my own hand, because we all work, and no one sits idle. My wife, God bless her, milks the cows, the children carry the milk churns and make butter, and I, you can see me there, go to the market every morning, go through Boiberik from one summer house to another and sometimes come to an agreement with people, even with the most distinguished people from Yehupets. And when you go among people and talk to people you feel that you are a person in the world too, and not just a clumsy tailor ... [this was before he had his son-in-law! H. H.]. Yes, at that time, with God's help, I was a miserable beggar, died of hunger three times a day with my wife and children, worked like a horse, dragged logs of wood out of the forest to the railway, whole wagonloads of logs, and for that I got, I hope you don't mind, 30 kopecks a day; and I didn't get even this much every day. And with this money I had to, touch wood, keep a whole room-full of mouths and, of course there's a difference between people and animals, a horse too ...![4]

Mendele Moykher Sforim seems to have introduced *Luftmenshn* into Yiddish literature when he presented the inhabitants of a shtetl in his story 'Wishing Ring' published in 1865.[5] The term quickly became popular and has since gained currency as a description of those who driven to penury, who did not know in the morning how they would survive until the evening, who took every opportunity to earn some money or food, but who also tried to adapt to their new circumstances and to 'speculate.' The term also contains overtones of self-irony and even a certain panache, and also that weightlessness which Marc Chagall (1887–1985) depicted several times between 1914 and 1922, with his images of Jews floating over the rooftops of Vitebsk, stick in hand and a rucksack over their shoulder.[6] At the end of the nineteenth century in many communities "up to 40 percent of the whole Jewish population consisted of families of so-called *Luftmenshn*, that is, people without any particular education, without capital, without a particular trade,"[7] but also those who had been "pushed out" of their former trade, and who now lived on air or engaged in "air business": "As mother says, God bless her: 'From the air you catch cold'."[8] Isaac Babel writes:

> In Odessa the '*Luftmenshn*' go around the cafes in order to earn a ruble and to feed their families, but there is nothing to be had, and in any case why should anyone give anything to a useless person, to a '*Luftmensh*'?[9]

Frequently, they were only able to survive thanks to outstanding individual and collective Jewish charity.

TRANSFORMATION OF THE OCCUPATIONAL STRUCTURE AND NEW INTERMEDIARY ACTIVITIES

This differentiation and polarization can be explained a little more clearly with a glance at the occupational structure around the end of the nineteenth and the beginning of the twentieth century. According to the census of 1897, 5.2 million Jews lived in the Russian Empire, about 4 percent of the population as a whole. Of those, 4.9 million—11.5 percent of the population as a whole there—lived in the Pale of Settlement, and in this region in the Kingdom of Poland alone there were 1.3 million Jews (14 percent of the population). Only 13.5 percent of Jews lived in the countryside, while the remaining 86.5 percent lived in the towns. At this time many Jews were active in two major areas of employment—trade, banking, and credit on the one hand, and craft, industry, and transport on the other—more than 40 percent at any given time. In this way, trade gradually became the most important source of income for the Jews, while at the beginning of the century crafts had been far more significant. The growing number of independent professions was of virtually no consequence, nor the steadily diminishing opportunities to work in agriculture or in other sectors of the economy.

Does this mean that the intermediary function of the Jews was now being established on a different basis? At first glance, the answer is yes. The Jews were particularly strongly represented in some branches of trade: in grain, furs and leather, and peddling. They were even able to advance in the production and sale of alcohol, at least temporarily. At the same time, a process of capitalist concentration is clearly discernible. Trade was increasingly dominated by a number of big merchants. The mass of Jewish traders became poorer. The 'village walker,' the typical middleman, who bought something here, and sold a little something there, acting as the agent of the big traders, and shuttled between village and town, got into ever greater difficulties. Spying out gaps in the market was more and more difficult, and opportunities for financing transactions became fewer. Even the translocal trade with the products of the ready-to-wear clothing industry, or those of Jewish craftsmen, was largely going over to the big merchants.

An interesting exception in this process is the urban trade in finished products. While Jews established big department stores in Western Europe, in Poland and in Russia large concerns were substituted by the accumulation of highly specialized small traders in markets or in the street. Retailers stood tightly packed next to one another, often with only a few nails, shoes, religious artifacts or some fruit. In the doorways they offered their wares for sale on narrow tables or in display cases. Competition was fierce and incomes extremely low. Here again what had earlier given Jewish traders an advantage over non-Jewish traders came into play: the modesty of their needs—which, in contrast to the widespread cliché, was less a sign of avarice than an adaptation to circumstances—made it possible for Jews to cope with extremely low profit margins. That ultimately diminished the value of boycott movements directed against them, which took place in token of the increasing anti-Semitism in Poland, but it also hindered the regulation of internal Jewish competition. Observers at the end of the nineteenth century noticed that Jewish traders not only offered their wares for sale particularly cheaply, but also

> that trade in Jewish towns is much more decentralized, much more adapted to the needs of the consumer than is the case outside the Pale of Settlement. In the central provinces trade is chiefly concentrated in certain 'lines' or on the surrounding area of the market place, while in Jewish towns there are bigger shops in all districts. The Jewish towns are also far ahead of the towns in the central provinces in respect of specialization ... Specialist businesses here are able to offer the public a wider choice of every article.[10]

As far as the increasing polarization of Jewish society was concerned, the bankers who, in a way, were continuing the tradition of the great financial intermediaries of governments and princes were at the top of the tree. They took advantage of the need for cash, as money transactions increased with the development of industrialization, railway construction, and wholesale trade. Although they remained a numerical minority, financiers were the richest and the most powerful Jews, and were concentrated above all in Warsaw. Within this small category there existed in the large towns as well as in the small a multitude of money changers and money lenders who carried around their "'bank' in their pockets"[11] and somehow made a living.

The intermediary function of Jewish traders became more complicated in this way. The direct exchange of goods for goods, in which money played only a subordinate role, was no longer at the center of things, but rather capitalistic financial mediation and wholesaling.

A comparable process of differentiation took place in the second major area of activity: craft, industry, and transport. As the significance of craftsmen in the national economy dwindled, the competition between them became more intense. Many of them lived under the most wretched circumstances.

Tailors and dressmakers, as well as shoemakers, all extremely over-represented craft trades—suffered hardship. From the shtetl Krasnopol'e, in the Belarussian province of Mogilev, it was reported that the craftsmen could be divided into three groups:

> The first group works to order: one part of it remains in the town to serve the urban population; the other part travels around the surrounding villages and seeks customers there. Tailors, shoemakers, carpenters, smiths, pewterers, stove fitters, and glaziers usually work at the customer's home. They wander the villages and manors, work one day in one place and the next day in another, and return home 'on the

Sabbath.' Sometimes, particularly before the high Christian holidays, before Easter and Christmas, masters go out with their entire workshop in order to carry out specific seasonal work. The tailors and dressmakers in particular do this, shoemakers much less frequently. The second group of craftsmen works only partly to order, but mainly for the market, with which it is in direct contact; for example, shoemakers, plumbers, and cap makers, who offer their products for sale on a market stall or in a booth at the fair and at the weekly market in the town itself and in the nearby villages. The third group of craftsmen is entirely without a direct relationship with the customer; it has also lost its independence and instead works for a business. Cobblers who make cheap footwear, so-called 'straps', for the undemanding peasantry, mainly belong in this group. In recent times tailors, seamstresses, embroideresses, hosiery workers, and cap makers have begun to go the same way as the cobblers.[12]

One section of craftsmen managed to find employment in expanding industries, above all in the textile industry concentrated in Łódź and its surrounding. However, it appears that Jewish workers were overwhelmingly employed by Jews in un- or barely mechanized factories. German entrepreneurs in Łódź preferred to bring in specialist workers from Germany. In this case strict observance of religious law worked against the Jewish workers. In mechanized concerns the entrepreneurs were unwilling to shut down the machines on the Sabbath. Also relevant in this connection is the fact that for the most part Jews owned larger factories than non-Jews, but at the same time these were less mechanized, and therefore less modern, and as a consequence had lower productivity.

Once again there was a small group of rich Jewish entrepreneurs who figured among the most important in the country. Many of them were continuing the tradition of the great Jewish army suppliers of the first half of the nineteenth century, who had served as the basis for the rise of a number of families, and were closely linked to Jewish trade and banking capital. In this way they could meet the enormous need for capital which Jews needed in order to make progress in the industrialization process.

Jewish entrepreneurs were particularly strong where they could link up with traditional activities. Jewish involvement in the textile industry—here one of the most important entrepreneurs in Łódź, Poznański, should be mentioned—belonged to a line of continuous development with the Jewish garment trade. For the sugar industry—in which Epstein, Kronenberg, and other Jewish dynasties from Warsaw were active—the earlier activities of the Jews in the countryside, for example, on the estates of the nobility, stood them in good stead. The third area, transport—for example, the 'railway kings' Poliakov and Bloch—of course grew out of the traditional Jewish role in trade. The fact that Jewish industrialists and brokers sought to integrate affluent branches of the economy in fundamentally different ways is actually connected with their historical experience. They played a path-breaking role in the Russian Empire.

The impoverishment of the mass of Jews proceeded incredibly rapidly. Many ruined craftsmen tried to make a living from the retail trade, although their prospects there were little better. An increasing number of Jews simply lost their economic function. In many towns the proportion of Jews without fixed employment reached 50 percent or more by the end of the century. In the second half of the 1890, the number of those who required assistance rose by around one-third. The effect of Jewish charitable organizations was no more than a drop in the ocean, however, even when the richest Jews, such as Poznański or Bloch, who had converted first to Protestantism and then to Catholicism, were involved. Even emigration did not bring significant relief.

The German rabbi Emanuel Carlebach visited Warsaw during the First World War. When he wrote home on 5 February 1917 he expressed his horror at what he had seen:

> In the last few days I have visited many Talmud Toyres [Talmud–Torah schools] where the children and the teachers—without salary—all barefoot and half naked, worked in unheated rooms. On the way I met—it was [minus] 20 or 21 degrees [Celsius], I think—a poorly dressed man *echod mini elef* [one of thousands]; I approached him, wrapped in furs and fur gloves as I was, and asked him: 'Aren't you absolutely freezing?' He replied: 'Isn't your nose freezing?' I answered, 'Not at the moment'. '*No azoy*', he said wittily, '*der orme man hat nor nozenflays!*' [the poor man has nothing but nose flesh][13]

The new, multi-layered intermediary role of the Jews in Poland and Russia must also be examined against the background of economic and social polarization. In 1912 the Moscow Association of Industrialists wrote a memorandum in which they called for the restrictions on Jews to be removed; "In the economic organism of the country the Jews perform the function of a mediating link between the consumers and the producers of goods."[14] And Isaac Babel recalled in the 1920s: "The Jews tied the ribbon of profit between the Russian peasant and the Polish *Pan* [lord], the Czech colonist and the Łódź industrialist."[15] Here Babel indicates that, despite all the changes, there was still a remnant of the traditional 'economic circulation system' involving Jewish entrepreneurs, bankers, wholesalers, and Jewish retailers, 'village walkers,' and peddlers—or rather that this circulation was continuing on a new basis. In both the precapitalist and the capitalist sectors of the economy Jews mediated production and sales, including money transactions, between Jews and Jews, Jews and non-Jews, and also non-Jews and non-Jews. However, they no longer had a monopoly in this.

COMPETITION TO OUST RIVALS FROM THE MARKET AND ANTI-SEMITISM

The changed intermediary role and the loss of their monopoly exposed the Jews to a tough economic power struggle. In Russia a large part of the nobility and the court associated the Jews with the threat of capitalism, modernization, and even revolution. Anti-Semitism became both an anti-capitalist and an anti-socialist ideology designed to hold together the existing system. In Poland the 'national question' sharpened economic competition for market share. The up-and-coming Polish bourgeoisie frequently regarded the Jews as foreigners who were blocking the best opportunities. As in Łódź, Jews were identified with the Germans and suspected of collaborating with the Russian occupying power, although many of the Jewish entrepreneurs did not lack Polish patriotism.

At the beginning of his great novel *The Estate,* Isaac Bashevis Singer describes how Count Jampolski is banished to Siberia as a result of his participation in the uprising of 1863 and his estate is transferred to a Russian prince. The Jewish grain trader Kalman Jacobi, who had previously also traded with the rebels, asks the new lord for the lease of the estate, which he is finally granted. "The peasants of Jampol [were] outraged by this Jew, an unbeliever, who in the name of a foreign oppressor lorded it on Polish soil." Kalman's business activities are successful: he opens—illegally, but tolerated by the Russian authorities—a tavern and a shop. The peasants, for whose surplus products he pays a good price, become his main customers. Kalman then opens a limestone quarry and takes a share in the railway which, commissioned by the Russian government, is being organized by the "Warsaw magnate Wallenberg ... a Jew converted to Catholicism." Here Singer obviously took the 'railway king' Jan Gotlib Bloch (see above) as a model.[16]

The economic success of the Jewish upper stratum in the changed circumstances nourished the anti-Jewish mood. Moreover, Jewish bankers or wholesalers were as a rule much less concrete and tangible as people than the village Jew whom the peasants trusted or hated as the extended arm of the lord of the manor. In the capitalistic production and distribution process, which was difficult to comprehend, it was possible—both in Poland and in Russia—to make the Jews, as traditional scapegoats in crises, responsible for economic difficulties or the negative consequences of industrialization. Here is an important starting point for understanding the relationship between industrialization and anti-Semitism.

The mood of the time, in which Poles, after the failed uprising of 1863, wanted to obtain "internal sovereignty" over the economic upswing, was described by the poet Bolesław Prus (1847–1912). At that time, he himself was not free of anti-Jewish attitudes because he feared that the Jews, who did not act as he and other 'positivists' wanted, could disturb the process of economic development. In his novel *Lalka* (The doll), set in 1880s Warsaw, a character says: "The Jews, I say, the Jews! ... They keep everything on a leash and make sure that no Wokulski [an up-and-coming Polish merchant] gets in their way, who is not a Jew, not even a Mech [a baptized Jew]." This Wokulski then employs a Jew, Schlangbaum, as a salesman, who had been unable to find employment with a Jewish firm because of the labor market surplus. In an atmosphere of growing anti-Semitism, which manifests itself in many ways, Wokulski finally sells him his business for personal reasons. His friend reacts to this by saying: "It is terrible how the Jews drive us out ... One day there'll be another riot because of the Jews." An assimilated Jew, a doctor, asks Wokulski to remain at the helm, while still taking advantage of the abilities of the Jews: "A race of genius, the Jews, but what scoundrels! ... They are ill-starred rogues, but I must acknowledge their genius and cannot deny that they have my sympathy. I feel that a dirty little Jew is preferable to a full-grown Junker ..." But

> race and common situation bind us, but we are divided by our views. We [that is, educated, assimilated Jews—H. H.] possess knowledge, they have the Talmud, we have understanding, they have cunning ... Therefore it is in the interests of civilization that it remain in our hands in which direction we should go. They can only besmirch the world with kaftans and onions, not drive it along.

Later, the above-mentioned friend again reports on the general mood:

> On my departure he [a former salesman in Wokulski's business—H. H.] told me that soon there would only be Jews here and the rest would become judaized ... The mood is increasingly rising against the Jews. All it needs is rumors that the Jews were kidnapping Christian children and killing them in order to bake matzo [unleavened bread for the Passover—H. H.].[17]

HASKALA: THE JEWISH ENLIGHTENMENT

When, in the wake of the German–Jewish philosophers around Moses Mendelssohn, Enlightenment ideas penetrated Eastern Europe, they did not have much impact on the Jewish population there. The 'Berliners,' even if they were able to build a new 'Jerusalem of the Enlightenment' in Vilnius, remained alien to the traditional way of life of the East European Jews [*Ostjuden*]. Most of them had no contact with learned texts written in Hebrew because that was not their language. The demand by the men of the Enlightenment, the Maskilim—represented by Isaac Bär (or Ber) Levinsohn (1788–1860), the "Mendelssohn of the Russian Jews"[18]—that Jews should become fully integrated in existing society, participate in the secular education system, change traditional ways of life, and in this way arrive at a new Jewish identity, was not particularly persuasive in the circumstances. Hasidism and even religious orthodoxy appeared to have better answers.

Gradually, however, a change of conviction became discernible. The rabbinical school opened in Warsaw in 1826 and the rabbinical seminaries established in Vilnius and Zhitomir in 1847 had a certain influence as a kind of substitute gymnasium (or grammar school) and counterweight to the traditional *yeshivot*, the academies of Talmudic learning. The long conflict between the Haskala and the Hasidim resulted in the appearance of a different form of *Ostjuden* which now consciously, if with different shades of opinion, advocated an autonomous Eastern Jewish nationality. A new generation of Jewish intellectuals recognized around the middle of the nineteenth century that Enlightenment and emancipation could not be forcibly imposed 'from above' or 'from outside', but rather had to come out of the historical–cultural identity of the people.

One consequence was that people began to write in Yiddish. The blossoming of a Yiddish literature from the second half of the nineteenth century, reached its peak in the form of the poets Sholem Aleichem (1859–1916), Mendele Moykher Sforim (1836–1917), Isaac Leib Peretz (1852–1915), and later on Shalom Asch (1881–1957).

The Jiddish cultural revival also found expression in the collections of Yiddish songs, anecdotes, and jokes, as well as of Jewish music, customs, and practices. The study of Jiddish folk culture was expanded and systematized in the Russian Jewish Historical Ethnographic Society founded in St Petersburg in 1908, named after a banker, philanthropist, and long-standing leading figure of the St Petersburg Jewish community Baron Horace Günzberg (Naphtali Herz Ginzburg, 1833–

1909). Particularly significant were the field studies conducted in the Pale of Settlement by S. Ansky (also spelled An-ski—Shloyme Zaynvil Rappoport, 1863–1920), the author of the famous Yiddish play *Der dibek* (1919; translated as 'The Dybbuk').[19]

The aim of introducing Jews in Biblical–Hebrew culture as well as in Russian and Polish national culture, that is, of a 'double acculturation,' was not given up, but it attained a different status. The new men of the Enlightenment overwhelmingly originated in the poorer social strata and had lived through both the clashes between Hasidim and Maskilim and conflicts generated by the military service obligation for the Jews and other harsh regulations of the reign of Tsar Nicholas I. Moreover, they were also acquainted with the debates in Russian critical–realist circles at this time which violently attacked the current state of society: they themselves belonged to the so-called 'superfluous men,' a key concept of the discussions and literary endeavors of the time: men who were social outsiders and had little chance of social advancement.

During the liberal period of Alexander II this movement was at first able to develop. Odessa was its center. The first Russian-language Jewish newspapers appeared here, for a short time. In Warsaw and other cities there were similar developments. Already subjected to increasing restrictions after the Polish uprising, of 1863, the new Jewish Enlightenment in its existing form was judged after 1881—the year of Alexander's murder—to have failed completely. Despite this failure the Haskala influenced further developments. They became part of the different nationalistic, Zionistic, liberal, and socialist-revolutionary Jewish groupings, all of which were united by one thing, however, consciousness of a special Eastern Jewish nationality.

ASSIMILATION AND ACCULTURATION

Jews did not react uniformly to radical socio-economic change and the new form of anti-Semitism which was gaining ground was not. A small group saw—in common with the majority of Western Jews—an opportunity for finding a way out of their wretched life circumstances and constant persecution in assimilation or acculturation, in the renunciation of their own culture through its alignment with another, or in the encounter with the other culture in the expectation of a new synthesis. The first signs of reform of religious practice in the synagogue and in everyday life are also relevant in this connection. The Jews in question were primarily those who had experienced economic success or who been influenced by Enlightenment ideas. The ideas included an optimism that, in the long run, complete assimilation into Polish or Russian society was possible. This cultural alignment would of course have to be preceded by the removal of discrimination. This line of argument strove for integration, while insisting on the preservation of Jewish identity.

Census data on mother-tongue and nationality help to clarify something of this consciousness of assimilation. During the Warsaw census of 1882, the Jewish community, led by assimilationists in accordance with their convictions, as a consequence of riots which had taken place shortly beforehand, tried to get the Jews to declare themselves as belonging to Polish nationality. They were successful: only 2.7 percent of Warsaw's inhabitants described themselves as having Jewish nationality.

Things were very different in 1897. This time a question was asked about the respondent's mother-tongue: 28.3 percent of Warsaw residents answered Yiddish, constituting 84 percent of all Jews, while 14 percent gave Polish as their mother tongue. One could cautiously assess this on the one hand as a sign of a desire towards assimilation. Moreover, among these 14 percent were to were found those who were gradually loosening their ties with the religious community and joining 'secular' movements—socialist or Zionist. Many of them still felt themselves to be Jews, even if they turned away from their religious faith, a tendency which gathered strength after the turn of the century. The remaining 2 percent of Warsaw Jews also show that nationality and mother tongue were independent variables: they were 'Litvaks' who had come to Congress Poland through Lithuania from Russia, mostly due to their social and economic plight, fleeing before pogroms, or Jews who had been expelled from areas outside the Pale of Settlement, who regarded themselves as Jews rather than as Russians.

In the big cities of Warsaw and Łódź, where the figures are similar, efforts to cut ties with the religious community were naturally stronger than in smaller towns. In Congress Poland as a whole, only 3.5 percent of Jews acknowledged Polish as their mother tongue.

'NECKTIED' AND 'KAFTANED' JEWS

The assimilated Jews moved away from their traditional world, and to some extent even renounced the Jewish faith. Not all, but many of them—in the literature sometimes described as *goyishe yidn*, 'necktied Jews'—came to the view that the *yidishe yidn*, the so-called 'kaftaned Jews' were a hindrance on the ladder to success.[20] It was now said in Poland and Russia what was said of immigrant Jews in the West: the dirty and uncivilized, crafty and servile Jew in his threadbare, baggy kaftan, with his temple locks dangling in spirals down to his shoulders, stinking of onions and garlic, the beggar, pickpocket, and pimp, stands in the way of assimilation and is even responsible for anti-Semitism. This abhorrence went as far as hatred of one's own origins.

> All these 'European' Jews with their contracted spirit and narrow horizons ... cannot free themselves of the thought that we are *their poor relatives*, even when we are richer than them! This inner presumption, which they feel towards everything which comes from the East, has cut me to the quick ... Wherever we may come from we are '*Ostjuden*' to them![21]

The situation became even more complicated not only because the 'necktied Jews' looked down on the 'kaftaned Jews,' but because the East European Jews had their own *Ostjuden* problem.' Just as many Western European Jews, filled consternation, rejected immigrating East European Jews, a number of Polish Jews, particularly among those keen on assimilation, regarded the Jewish immigrants from Russia with mistrust, even revulsion. These immigrating Jews—whose number totaled around 250,000—spoke another dialect of Yiddish, and outside Jewish society did not use Polish but Russian. They were largely cut off from their surroundings, both their outward appearance and behavior seemed to correspond to all the prejudices held against them. Both Jews and non-Jews in Poland were quick to hold the Litvaks responsible for the failure of a Polish–Jewish symbiosis and for the increasing anti-Semitism. People also felt at liberty to take out their hatred of the Russians on them.

> My grandfather's opinion was that relations between the Christian part of Polish society and the Polish Jews had been becoming more and more harmonious for a long time. One portion of the Polish Jews had assimilated, but even the non-assimilated Jews had already got themselves into a position from which full-blown symbiosis with the Poles would be possible ... These symbioses had now—according to my grandfather—been wrecked by the Litvaks, who had not been liberated from their 'two-faced patriotism' even by their humiliation by the tsarist administration ... My grandfather was far from being alone in his opinions, which were shared by many Polish Jews.[22]

However, it should not be overlooked that the Litvaks were more deeply integrated in Polish–Jewish society than many contemporaries acknowledged. They also established effective organizations. In addition, later on there were many supporters of Zionism among them.

BY WAY OF AN EXAMPLE: JEWS IN WARSAW AND ŁÓDŹ

As early as the first half of the nineteenth century, Warsaw and then Łódź were centers of attraction for the Jews who were migrating from the countryside because of pressure from the authorities or because the economic situation left them with virtually no other choice. With the onset of industrialization the attractiveness of the big cities increased, for impoverished Jews as for peasants in search of a living.

Warsaw, the royal capital, rich in tradition, and the biggest city in Poland (not just in the Russian area of partition), combined the central authorities of the country, the most important cultural institutions, and many of the service-industry, economic, and transport services. As a result, the prospects of finding well-paid employment were quite good. The total population rose from around 223,000 in 1864 to 884,000 in 1914, and the number of Jews from 73,000 to 337,000; their proportion of the population rose from 33 percent to 38 percent. The main growth took place after 1890. This rapid increase of the Jewish proportion of the population continued to nurture fears that the Jews would 'swamp' the city with foreign influences and stirred up anti-Semitic agitation. Another contributory factor in this was the fact that the growth in the number of Jews was not attributable to immigration alone. It was claimed that the Jews had a higher birthrate than the Christians, so that over the long term the latter were doomed to decline.

This view could be supported by past trends. It was argued that Jews had on average married earlier than Christians on religious grounds and so had had more children. If one examines the facts more closely, however, this was no longer the case in the second half of the nineteenth century and the beginning of the twentieth. Although the statistical basis is not particularly reliable we can say that the number of early marriages fell, and that the Jewish and Christian marriage practices began to converge. That more children continued to be born to Jews than to Christians can be explained by the fact that there were proportionately more marriages than among Catholics. Furthermore, the age structure of the Jewish community was younger than that of Catholics, which gave rise to more births. Finally, it appears that the greater number of children can be attributed above all to the lower mortality rate of Jewish children. Apparently, the level of care, standards of hygiene, and state of health was higher among Jews than among Christians. Moreover, among the former there were fewer illegitimate children, who at that time tended to die particularly frequently.

In Łódź a partly similar process could be observed despite very different conditions. In this factory city, founded as such in 1820 by government order, the textile industry was dominant. Since there were virtually no central administrative responsibilities—Łódź was still not a regional capital—job vacancies, services, and culture on offer were significantly more homogeneous than in Warsaw. The rapid expansion of the textile industry in the second half of the nineteenth century made Łódź the largest accumulation of workers in Poland. The population structure was complicated by the fact that Germans—workers, craftsmen, and entrepreneurs—were here in considerable numbers, although this fell from three-quarters immediately after the establishment of the factories to around 10 percent after the turn of the century. Unsurprisingly, given the nature of the city, the population grew more quickly than in Warsaw: from less than 40,000 in the 1860s to almost 480,000 by the beginning of the First World War. The proportion of Jews increased during this period from 19.5 percent to 36 percent. These figures, however, refer only to origin. Only 33 percent of the population professed the Jewish religion. From this it follows that some had converted to Protestantism—which brought them closer to the Germans in Łódź—many of them, wanting to become fully integrated in Polish society, later converted to Catholicism.

While the demographic structure of both cities were similar, the higher proportion of assimilated Jews pointed to a substantial difference in the social and occupational structure. In Warsaw, towards the end of the nineteenth century, most Jews—that is, 40 percent—were employed in trade and the credit system, which they dominated, although less and less. The next most important sphere of employment was industry and craft which was around 30 percent Jewish, Jewish participation in this sector being rather on the increase. All other sectors were virtually insignificant. By and large, circumstances in Warsaw corresponded to general developments among the Jews in Russian Poland. The increasing polarization between the few rich and the many poor, who were concentrated in retailing, peddling, or in minor trades was also to be found here. It is striking that there were a few rich—often assimilated—Jewish industrial entrepreneurs, but that most Jewish industrialists owned small businesses which mostly employed Jewish workers.

This was at first also a feature of the situation in Łódź. The businesses with the highest level of mechanization as a rule belonged to non-Jews. In the cotton industry, which was developing into a modern large-scale industry, Jews were more weakly represented than in the 'older' branches of the textile industry. Jewish workers generally found work in un- or barely mechanized firms in which they could maintain their religious observances. Moreover, assimilated Jewish manufacturers—or those with a mind to assimilate—often deliberately employed only a few Jews.

Israel Joshua Singer, Isaac Singer's elder brother, described a relatively large Jewish business whose owner declined to move with the times by converting to steam power:

> The courtyard echoed with the clattering of the looms ... On Saturday evening the workforce worked longer than usual because the work-free holiday must be observed. In the light of tallow candles, which were set up on the looms, the 50-strong workforce produced headscarves ... His factory was Jewish through and through. On every doorpost there was a *mezuzah* [small folded or rolled parchment inscribed with scriptural verses—H. H.]. And between the balls of woolen yarn and the crates in his storeroom he had even had a lectern set up with a metal candlestick so that his workers could say their afternoon and evening prayers without leaving the factory premises. In winter, when they came to work before the Morning Star had risen, they also held their morning worship there.
>
> And Chaim Alter made sure that they observed all of the laws of Jewry. Even when it was sweltering hot no young Jew dared to sit at the loom bareheaded—even if he only used a paper bag to cover his head. Prayer shawls were compulsory. And Chaim Alter made sure that the younger workers did not trim their beards or wear secular coats, but rather traditional kaftans ...
>
> Chaim Alter donated money to the Baluter synagogue of the weavers, which was called 'Love of friends' and was hemmed in between the factories, timberyards, and coal stocks. And he had even taken on a teacher who instructed the workers on the afternoon of the Sabbath. In summer he took them through 'The Sayings of the Fathers,' in winter chapters from the 'Psalter.' He was a learned man, well versed in everything which one could expect in the next world. Surrounded by exhausted weavers he gave lectures on human foolishness and on the vanity of the flesh.[23]

Up to the First World War the majority of Jewish factories in both Warsaw and Łódź were old, relatively small, or organized on the basis of manual labor. Very few were big businesses with a high level of mechanization.

The internal structure of Jewish enterprise (in the broadest sense) was varied in both cities. The proportion of Jews in this social group around 1900 was probably still approximately the same. At first sight this is also the case when one differentiates between industry and trade: in the statistics figures of around 30 percent and 40 percent respectively are quoted. Since, however, in Łódź some of the Germans—23 percent of industrialists— were assimilated Jews, who were still regarded as Jews, proportionately more Jews were engaged in entrepreneurial activities in industry here than in Warsaw.

Many of these assimilated Jews were categorized as belonging to the so-called *Lodzhermensh* ['Łódźmen'], who, according to contemporary opinion, were cunning businessmen whose success met with reluctant recognition, although by and large people disapproved of their devious and often ruthless activities. This type of industrialist was brought into being by the extraordinarily rapid, feverish expansion in the second half of the nineteenth century and the fierce competition between Germans, Poles, and Jews—and also within each of these groups—in a single branch of the economy. In Warsaw, with its rich Jewish diversification and differentiation, this was not possible.

The most socially and economocally successful Jews figured among the richest in the country. On the other side stood the mass of poor Jews attached to the Orthodox faith, often to Hasidism. Some entrepreneurs, even when they had converted to Christianity, felt a bond with these people by virtue of long tradition. For example, Bloch became heavily involved in a number of investigations, memoranda, and other ventures for the improvement of the economic situation of the Jews. Poznański, as chairman of the Jewish Charitable Association in Łódź and in other organizations, did a great deal of good for the benefit of the poor.[24]

Charity was very necessary but it could only ameliorate the misery. Around 90 percent of Warsaw peddlers were Jews, and the number of *Luftmenshn* without any economic function grew constantly. Residential conditions provide another insight into the desperately low standard of living. Although at the time in question there were no longer any clear-cut ghettos the Jews lived—both in Warsaw and in Łódź—overwhelmingly in the same part of town. Naturally, this took place in accordance with tradition; only the assimilated Jews of Warsaw moved into the fashionable streets which had still been 'free' of Jews in the first half of the nineteenth century. In 1862 these restrictions were lifted, but even for 1900 there are documents in the Warsaw State Archives which go into considerable detail concerning the Jews' residence in these streets. Immigrating Jews generally sought accommodation in districts in which they discovered co-religionists. Probably, they were also directed by ties related to family and country of origin. In this way in Warsaw, as late as 1910, around half of the Jewish population—150,000—were concentrated in the northwest of the city. Here they made up almost one-quarter of the inhabitants; in the fourth district over 90 percent.

Nalewki Street was the commercial center of Warsaw. When Alfred Döblin visited the city in 1924 he observed:

> Nalewki Street runs in northwest Warsaw just like Marschall Street and the suburb of Krakow. The wide Nalewki Street is the main artery of the Jewish part of town. To the left and the right long streets run off it, from which in turn other streets and alleys run. And everywhere is positively teeming with Jews. Streetcars travel along Nalewki Street. Its buildings have fronts much like the rest of Warsaw, crumbling and dirty. Courtyards emerge in every building. I go into one; it is square and like a market place filled with noisy people, Jews, mostly in kaftans. In the buildings in the courtyard there are furniture shops and shops selling hides. And as I go through one such building I find my-

self once more in a teeming courtyard, full of crates, with teams of horses; they are being loaded and unloaded by Jewish porters. Nalewski also houses large business premises. Colorful business plaques advertise dozens of firms: hides, furs, suits, hats, bags and cases. There are businesses in shops and on the upper floors. In the direction of the city, in the southern part on the Dluga, large, modern shops are open: perfumeries, rubber stamps, manufactured goods. I read some extraordinary names here: Waiselfisch, Klopfherd, Blumenkranz, Brandwain, Farsztandig, Goldkopf, Gelbfisch, Gutbesztand. The members of this outcast people have been given derisive names.[25]

A high proportion of the Jewish population was also found in quarters in the southwest, in the center, in the south, and in Praga. When one investigates these quarters in terms of streets and blocks, it becomes clear that the spatial separation between Jews and non-Jews was extremely strict, even in relation to Polish- rather than Yiddish-speaking Jews. That does not rule out contacts—above all economic—between Jews and non-Jews; indeed, in the period with which we are concerned, such contacts even seem to have increased. There was a similar trend in Łódź. Children often formed closer relationships, but these tended to weaken as they got older, or were finally broken off altogether. Knowledge of Jewish culture acquired by non-Jews also tended to disintegrate into fragments. The picture of the Jews as 'foreigners,' with different garb and different language, different customs and practices, proved stronger. Spatial separation reflected their social isolation. Co-existence seems to have been better in small towns with a Jewish majority population.

Living conditions for the mass of Jews were extraordinarily oppressive. In 1910, an average of 116 persons lived in Warsaw residential buildings, in Łódź the figure was 40. For Jews the figures must have been significantly worse. From memoirs and literary texts we can piece together how many people were crammed together in the buildings and dwellings, in which Hasidic study rooms and prayer rooms, cellar businesses, small workshops, or storerooms were also housed. It goes without saying that such conditions—similar to those in the slums inhabited by non-Jews—encouraged crime. Everything from pickpocketing, receiving stolen goods and prostitution; and organized crime was rife.

The very tight webs of communication within the framework of these living conditions contributed significantly to the solidarity of the Jews in both cities. Around two-thirds of Warsaw Jews professed Hasidism, which, despite all its internal religious differences, was the most united group among the Jews. The *tsaddik* of Góra Kalwaria (Ger), of Mount Calvary near Warsaw, had for a long time been one of the most respected among the Hasidim, large numbers of whom were continually making the pilgrimage to his court. In 1859 rabbi Isaac Meir Rothenberg Alter (1789–1866) had founded a dynasty here which represented a form of 'people's Hasidism' and sought to ameliorate poverty among the Jewish lower classes.

At the same time, Warsaw was also an intellectual center of the assimilationist movement among the Jews. To be sure, only a minority—mostly entrepreneurs or the self-employed—chose this path. The difficulties faced by this group can easily be imagined, including the tensions connected with industrialization, Polish nationalism, and, after 1881, the increasing discrimination against the Jews by the tsarist state, which extended to the incitement of anti-Semitism riots and pogroms.

The Warsaw Christmas riots of 1881 showed how easily the problems of radical socio-economic change could vent themselves on the Jews, and how easily envy of the few rich Jews could translate itself into violence against all Jews. A panic broke out during a Christmas mass, in the course of which 20 people lost their lives; a Jew was accused of having started the whole thing. In the excitement which had been stirred up by the wave of pogroms in Russia following the murder of Alexander II, looting broke out against the Jews. The police only intervened after three days. Jewish self-defense was only partly successful. In one proletarian quarter, Poles fought off the looters side by side with the Jews.

The social background of the unrest in Łódź in 1892 was even clearer. An initially successful strike movement turned into an anti-Jewish action, possibly stirred up by the Russian authorities so that it would be easier to send in troops to crush the 'uprising.' It was not only urban proletariat which took part in the riots, but also peasants who came to Łódź after hearing rumors of what was going on in order to punish the Jews for alleged anti-Church activities. The fact, moreover, that a number of workers—not least with reference to Jewish capitalists—allowed themselves to be diverted from their own aims shows the extent to which the Jews could take on the role of catalyst in a social conflict only dimly perceived.

Those skeptical about assimilation felt vindicated. A growing number of Jews began to join Zionist or socialist organizations. Many were profoundly unsure about what their place in society was.

THE JEWISH FAMILY

The family formed the center of Jewish life. House and synagogue constituted a unity in the religious sense, through which special consecration could come even to the poorest Jewish home. This certainly contributed to the internal consolidation of the Jews.

The father was the focal point of the family, even when he was seldom at home (as an 'intermediary between town and countryside,' as a peddler, or as a *Luftmensh*). On the Sabbath and on religious holidays, however, he could remain away only in the most pressing circumstances. He was responsible for performing the rituals and set an example to the children in respect of religious customs. In his absence, he was represented by the mother.

Alongside the theory and practice of religious laws and customs, the children learned brotherly love as practiced in the family. On the Sabbath, and often on other days, people would take in wandering beggars, poor people, or travelers, feed them, and generally be hospitable to them. Sons of poor Jews alternately ate with well-to-do families who in this way made a significant material contribution to their school attendance or even studies. In the traditional Eastern European Jewish household, faith and everyday life were fully integrated.

In liberal, assimilation-oriented families the two worlds moved apart. Here Yiddish was not much valued, and there was more emphasis on mastering the national language and manners. Children were given as good a secular education as possible. Nevertheless, people retained many Jewish symbols and customs which, however, must frequently have been regarded as purely external. As a result, many Jews came to experience an internal conflict: Jewish religion and tradition no longer provided them with any support, but secular Judaism offered no substitute of equal value to help them cope with being 'different' from the surrounding culture.

Jewish houses could be recognized from outside by the mezuzah, a narrow little tube made of glass, wood, or metal, attached at an angle to the upper third of the door post, so that the tip of the *mezuzah* pointed towards the inside of the house. It is said that by setting it at an angle, one was trying to satisfy two doctrines concerning whether the holy scriptures had to be stored standing up or lying down. In the little tube there was a small folded or rolled parchment carefully inscribed with scriptural verses from the Pentateuch (Deuteronomy 6:4–9, 11:13–21). To the observer only the word *'Shaddai'* ('Almighty') can be seen on the back of the parchment. There were as a rule many pictures and objects inside the house, too—complemented among the Hasidim by kabbalistic signs—which gave expression to one's attachment to religion and history. Often there was also a handwritten Torah roll in a special cupboard which made it possible to hold religious services at home, as long as a minimum of ten males, a *minyan*, were gathered together.

The course of the day was ordered in accordance with religious law, not least the rhythm of prayer. For this purpose Jews wrapped themselves in the prayer shawl, the *tallit*, a white woolen or silk cloth with dark blue or black stripes, and fringes (*tsitsit*) affixed to the four corners, which at a certain point during morning prayer must be raised to one's mouth. On his forehead and arm, at least during morning prayer, an observant Jew wears, in a prescribed manner, the phylactery or *tefillin*, to which a small cube-shaped case is attached which contains Torah texts written on parchment. Head, hand, and arm are all in the service of God.

MEN AND WOMEN IN JEWISH SOCIETY

'Father, what will I be when I grow up?', Deborah had asked one day, half jokingly, half seriously, because as long as she could remember Reb Avram Ber had never praised her to her mother.

Reb Avram Ber was astonished. It was the common view of pious Jews that there could only be one goal in the life of a woman for which she could hope, to bring happiness to a home by serving her husband and bearing him children. Therefore he did not even answer her. But when she pressed him he simply said: 'What will you be when you grow up? Nothing, of course!'[26]

The wife was responsible for looking after the family. This began with strict observance of religious laws and their transmission to the children. These laws constituted the focal point of domestic upbringing and resistance to them on the part of the children was not tolerated. This strictness also determined relations between parents and children. There was rarely an informal atmosphere in the home, and often children even used formal forms of address with their parents.

The principal burden of providing for the family often fell on the wife, too. Most families were poor and in many cases the husband earned too little, or even pursued religious studies which brought in nothing. As a result, we find many women who worked as market traders, small shopkeepers, or peddlers. In addition to this, of course, they were expected to run the household.

From the outside it appears that the wife had an inferior position in relation to her husband. In practice, this was often the case. From a religious standpoint, however, things were different. While the husband worshipped in the synagogue and came closer to God through study of the holy scriptures in the household the wife fulfilled the tasks which God had given her, making the home the center of religious life. Since this obligation constituted an enormous burden, the wife was liberated from other religious laws and was not required to exert herself by participating actively in worship in the synagogue. In keeping with this conception the upbringing of daughters was bound up with strict religious house rules.

In Isaac Singer's novel *The Family Moskat* the Hasid Moshe Gabriel questions his emancipated daughter Lotti, who lives in the USA and is visiting him in Poland:

> 'So, how are you, daughter? In America, you speak ... what do they call it ... English?'

'But I also speak Yiddish'.
'I hear that you have become an educated girl there. Do you go to university?'
'Yes, papa. I am now in my second year.'
'And what do you study? Do you want to become a doctor?'
'No, papa. I am studying natural science.'
'What do you mean? Electricity?'
'A bit of everything.'
'Do you at least remember that you are a Jewish daughter?'
'Don't worry, papa, the anti-Semites make sure that you never forget it.'
'Yes, that's right. Even when a Jew is a sinner he is still a Jew. From the line of Jacob.'
'They say there are too many of us in the colleges.'
'On that point they are right. "What business does a priest have in the cemetery?" What business does a Jew have in their schools?'
'But I cannot study in a synagogue.'
'The duty of a Jewish daughter is to get married, not to mess about in schools.'
'And what's the point of getting married? I would like to learn something. Acquire knowledge.'
'Why?'
'So that I can earn my living.'
'It is up to the husband to earn the money and for the wife to take care of her household duties. "The king's daughter is glorious indoors ..." Jews are known as the "children of kings".'[27]

As a rule, sexual enlightenment remained a stranger to strict Eastern European Jewish households. The girls were carefully protected from all 'indecent' things. The chastity of daughters was the highest obligation; anything which might threaten it had to be kept far away. In fact, it appears that there was little pre- or extra-marital sex. The fact that for a long time early marriage was the norm, with parents materially supporting the young couple, contributed to this significantly. Girls were often only fifteen or sixteen when they got married, the young men eighteen. Only from the second half of the nineteenth century did this practice gradually begin to change as East European Jewish families began to conform to non-Jewish social practices.

The ideal was still oriented towards the picture of the Polish Jews presented by Salomon Maimon at the end of the eighteenth century:

> The holiness of their marriages and the ever renewed affection which depends on it deserves particular mention. Every month the husband is fully separated from his wife for fourteen days (the monthly purification required by rabbinical law), they cannot touch one another or eat from the same bowl, or drink from the same cup, and by this means satiety is avoided. The wife always remains in the eyes of her husband what she was in the eyes of her lover.
>
> Finally, what innocence reigns here among unmarried people! It often happens that a boy or a girl of sixteen or eighteen years of age are married without having the least idea of the purpose of marriage, which is a very rare thing among other nations.[28]

The separation during menstruation lasted five days, in addition to which there were seven days of purification. It was concluded with a ritual immersion bath in the *mikvah*, a pool of natural water.

A love marriage did not conform with convention, even if over time it became more and more frequent: "What? Love in *my* family? Like musicians? I don't even want to hear about it!"[29] Parents sought a marriage partner with the help of the *shadkhan*, the marriage broker. The most important criterion for a future husband was by no means his ability to provide for his family, but rather his religious erudition.

> It was the custom among pious Jews to marry off their children at the age of around fifteen and then to keep them in the household until they could provide for themselves. Even Reysele, his favorite daughter, was married at the age of fifteen. And the husband who was chosen for her, a youth one year older than her, was Reb Avram Ber. On account of his enthusiasm for study and his own good reputation.

Some of his ancestors had been among the greatest of the people of Israel, in every respect famous names in the Jewish world, and furthermore, he claimed to be descended from King David. Therefore, it had looked like a very promising match. However, Reb Avram Ber proved to be a failure. To be sure, there were few people who could compare with him for his enthusiasm for learning, but he was unworldly and had to be looked after like a child. Outside the kingdom of the Talmud he was simply a fool.[30]

Gradually, however, there was more and more direct contact between potential marriage partners. At the beginning, written communications, usually of an official kind, were exchanged, predominantly based on a collection of formal letters, the *brifnshteler*. This ritual form of communication gradually became more individualized until the partners took their own affairs in hand and wrote one another love letters, and even met secretly. This led to bitter conflicts in many families.

Before the wedding the heads of young women were cropped, an event which they often found repugnant; attempts at rebellion in order to retain autonomy over one's own body usually met with failure. Afterwards, they had to wear wigs (*sheytl*), which came in two different sorts: some were for everyday wear, others for the Sabbath and the holidays. Some Hasidim did not even use wigs because they were made of fake hair. Hasidic women had to cover their hair entirely when in public. The idea behind this was that female hair had an erotic effect on men. After marriage, a woman had to be reserved with other men. She should not even offer them her hand; that could lead to the destruction of the marriage, or, if non-Jewish men were involved, to the loss of her Jewishness.

Weddings naturally required significant preparations. As a rule, getting into the right state of mind for married life took place in the *mikvah* which the bride had to visit on the evening before the wedding.

> The wife of a rabbi came in order to teach her how to count the days after her period so that she knew when she was permitted to sleep with her husband. And also how she should maintain marital purity through the prescribed washing in the women's bath.[31]

The betrothal took place under the *huppa*, the canopy under which the wedding ceremony also took place. It ended with the bridegroom stamping on a glass, in order to symbolize the fact that joy should be subdued somewhat out of sorrow for the loss of Jerusalem. After the wedding as a rule—in accordance with the matrilineal structure of Jewish families—the married couple went to the parents of the bride. The latter supported them for two years in the so-called *kes* so that the young man could continue his religious studies undisturbed.

The so-called *halitsa* divorce is a noteworthy custom. According to the Bible, the brother of a deceased man is required to marry his widow if the marriage is without issue, the so-called Levirate. If the widow or the brother-in-law had no wish to do so, their refusal could only acquire legal validity in a ceremony performed in front of a college of rabbis and a *minyan,* the minimum number of males, required to constitute a representative 'community of Israel' for liturgical purposes (ten). The brother-in-law then puts a shoe, which is kept at the rabbinical college for this purpose, on his right foot. In this way he symbolically violates a requirement of piety because the closest relatives of a deceased person must go without shoes for seven days in order to mourn him. The widow then removes the shoe from him, throws it away, and spits in her brother-in-law's face. This ceremony of removing the shoe is called *halitsa* and entitles the widow to a certificate of divorce without which she cannot remarry.

Even divorce itself had to be performed in front of a college of rabbis and a *minyan*. Extremely precise and elaborate rules had to be observed, which were probably supposed to make divorce more difficult. One particular difficulty was posed by the case of an *aguna*, a wife whose husband was a missing person. The wife could neither be considered a widow nor be divorced because, according to religious law, the husband had to play a part. As a result, the wife could not remarry, unless a number of religious Jews had confirmed the death of the husband. After the First World War, when many Jews became missing persons, relief was sought from these strict rules. For example, the testimony of non-Jews finally began to be accepted.

With the advent of bourgeois ideals, changes also began to take place within the marriage. Hitherto it had been one of the wife's obligations to make sure that her husband emulated the pious. Force of circumstances compelled more and more husbands to acquire worldly ways simply to be able to survive. From memoirs, we know that they often broke rapidly and radically with their inherited religion, declared secular education to be the measure of progress, forbade their wives—who had formerly often been their superiors in this respect—from playing a role in business activities, and even began to interfere in their wives' running of the household. The traditional power relations in a marriage were reversed. In order to legitimate their own actions and to pacify their bad consciences, many men even forced their wives to give up religious practices as well. As a result, these fundamental functions in business and in the family were lost.

As a consequence of these changes some female Jews broke free of the role which had been allotted them. From their reading they had developed other ideas about love, marriage, and life in general. In the second half of the nineteenth century, more and more young women, even from strict religious families, who not only chose their own marriage partner, but also left their parents to study or to seek their emancipation elsewhere. Many joined socialist groups, as a glance at the revolutionary movement in Russia shows. For women from the lower classes, wage labor represented a way of achieving one's independence. This often went together with impoverishment, however, particularly because there were too few work opportunities.

For women from 'bourgeoisified' families, the crisis afflicting how they had always seen themselves increasingly manifested itself in minor ailments, sickness, and emotional upset. Even Sholem Aleichem's *Tevye the Milkman* portrays this:

> 'There are people', he says, 'in Yehupets who not long ago went around without boots, who only yesterday were brokers, teachers, and servants, and who today own their own homes and whose wives already have something wrong with their stomachs and go abroad to spas ...[32]

If one could afford it, going to a health spa, became fashionable because that was what non-Jewish bourgeois women did. Many went to Vienna 'to the great doctors' who could even cure mental afflictions. It should come as no surprise, therefore, that strikingly many of the female patients and students of Sigmund Freud and of other psychoanalysts were East European Jews.

Another strategy, again in imitation of non-Jewish women, was directed towards care of the poor, public charity, and the new teaching of self-help. Some also embraced Zionism as an opportunity to bring the roots of the Jews into contact with modern values. As a mother, one could in this way once more raise one's children in 'pure' Judaism, and as a wife lead one's husband back to it. All in all, women were of the utmost importance in the formation of a new East European Jewish identity, characterized by autonomy, solidarity, and self-consciousness.

JEWISH UPBRINGING

The foundations of a child's upbringing, of course, lay in the family. Its cornerstones were law-abidingness, obedience, and piety. Religious faith and one's deeds should as far as possible form a unity, which began in the family. Therefore the teachings of the Torah and traditional religious prescriptions were closely linked with respect towards parents, which was then transferred to teachers, masters, mayors, scholars, and other respectable people.

Daughters were largely shut out from traditional, religiously oriented schooling and study. As a result, in many cases Jewish women acquired secular knowledge and non-Jewish literature earlier and to a greater extent than men, and even began to participate in public life. For a son, on the other hand, education outside the home began when he was four years old. His father took him to the *heder*, the 'room', which in Eastern Europe was usually a single-story wooden building. Often this event took on a ceremonial and celebratory form. At home

> a festive table was laid with pastries and drinks. I had the place of honor and a toast was drunk to me. My mother looked after the guests herself. Someone passed me a prayer book, two pages of which were smeared with honey which I was supposed to lick off. When I bowed my head in compliance a shower of silver and copper coins fell upon me. They had been tipped onto me—according to my grandfather—by the angels. Because the angels, he said, had faith in me, they knew that I would be a good student and because of that they were willing to give me an advance ... When the celebration was at an end my father lifted me up, covered me from head to foot in the *tallit* [prayer shawl] and took me the whole way to the *heder* in his arms. My mother could not go with us; that was a matter for men. That was our custom; the father had to carry his son all the way to the *heder* in his arms. The parents had a dim perception of the somber idea that the child was a sacrifice which they were presenting to the *heder* ...[33]

The boys sat in groups from morning until evening, devoting themselves to the study of religious books. They learned to read the Bible, to write and pray in Hebrew, the four arithmetical operations and the basics of Jewish ethics. Study was not conducted in silence, instead texts were sung or recited in sing-song fashion. What to outside observers might appear to be merely 'reeling off' the text was considered to be a very special means to aid concentration. The boys were supervised by a *melamed*, 'the learned one.' He was not academically educated, in contrast to the higher-level teacher, the *more*. The *melamed*, who as a rule lived with his family in the building of the *heder*, was paid by the parents to teach their children as much and as quickly as possible. He was therefore under pressure to obtain results and so was usually very strict. Corporal punishment was by no means infrequent. Many parents were not in a position to provide the best *melamed* for their children on account of their poverty. As a result, attendance at the *heder* was often a torment for children. It was frequently even worse at the Talmud–Torah school which, in contrast to the *heder*, was maintained by special organizations or the community. It was intended for orphans or the children of destitute families. In the same building, or nearby, was located the *bet ha-midrash*, the community's 'house of study,' in which religious studies were pursued.

When a son reached thirteen years of age he was deemed to have acquired sufficient religious knowledge to be accepted into the community as a 'Son of the Commandment' or *bar mitsvah*. This ceremony, which represented the passage into adulthood, was celebrated both at home and in the synagogue. The bar mitsvah was called up during the religious service to read from the Torah and for the first time could don phylacteries.

After the *heder* or the Talmud-Torah school, sons could go on to study at the *yeshiva*, the religious academy. Such *yeshivot* were to be found in larger communities or in Hasidic centers.

Here, eminent rabbis, learned in the Talmud, gave lectures. If a son became learned in the Talmud, this represented the greatest good fortune for a poor East European Jewish family. However, to acquire a religious education and to engage in life-long religious studies often, because of its prestige, became a rigid custom which many young men followed instead of trying to improve the living standards of their family. The acquisition of craft skills or of a trade was not held in particularly high esteem. As a rule, there were no real apprenticeships, and training often left something to be desired. To be sure, successful businessmen were well-regarded, but only a few could acquire this status. Only rich parents could afford to give their sons a thorough grounding in a trade alongside their religious education. Liberal, assimilation-oriented Jews tried to ensure that their children received the same secular education as non-Jews. The restrictions imposed by various governments—for example, the quotas for Jewish students in tsarist Russia—represented a serious obstacle. Many well-to-do Jews therefore sent their sons to school in Western Europe, or emigrated there.

Where a readiness to assimilate was predominant, as in the metropolises of Austria–Hungary, the importance of a Jewish education diminished. Instead of the *yeshivot* modern Jewish theological colleges were founded, for example, in Breslau in 1854. Elsewhere, Jews regarded the graduates of these establishments with mistrust. Suspicion also surrounded graduates of the newly created teacher-training colleges for Jews, who wanted to teach at Jewish state schools which provided an all-round education. It was feared that traditional Jewish culture would be watered down, particularly in those Jewish schools which were recognized by the state. The state determined the curriculum, of these schools, so Jewish culture played only a minor role in them.

EVERYDAY RELIGIOUS CUSTOMS

Kosher housekeeping was an important part of religious observance, and also played an educational function. Foods, drink, but also the storage of certain materials, had to satisfy rabbinical law in order to be suitable for use, that is, *kosher*.

The responsibility for keeping a kosher household lay with the wife, and the husband could not interfere. Kosher meals and their preparation imparted a feeling of inner cleanliness, self-control, and religious fulfillment. Traditional customs were therefore closely observed during preparation. Religion and tradition merged into one.

The highpoint of Jewish life was and remains the Sabbath. This work-free day with its compulsory duties is minutely regulated and should be observed from personal inclination, not with a view to receiving something from God in return. Among the East European Jews, the prescriptions of the Talmud and the directions of many eminent rabbis of East European communities were closely followed. For example, games were forbidden, as were trips and longer journeys (over two kilometers). Also forbidden were activities which were not absolutely necessary for obtaining nourishment—for example, writing, cutting, tearing, making a fire, even cooking. It was permitted to rest, eat, drink, pray, and read religious works. Business activities of whatever kind ceased between Friday afternoon and Saturday evening. Often, the streets were blocked with chains in order to stop the traffic. Even children and youths were not allowed to play, do sport, or go to the theater. Orthodox Jews avoided liberal Jews on the Sabbath. In order to alleviate the strict requirements of the Sabbath—or those of the high holidays—the *eruv* or 'blending' into one of boundaries and areas was possible: with a Sabbath-cord it was possible to extend private areas at the expense of public in order to be able to carry objects there. Nevertheless, strict rules ensured that people did not go too far.

Despite all the prohibitions the Sabbath was supposed to be a joyful time. On this day people rejoiced in the redemption and even experienced it in advance. It was even said:

> On the night of Friday and Saturday spouses should pay particular attention to their conjugal duties, because this also counts as the joy of the Sabbath. (The Cabbalists, particularly the Hasidim, even have intercourse with their wives exclusively on Friday nights.)[34]

On Friday morning the woman of the house made all the necessary preparations to be ready for the Sabbath with the cleaning, the cooking, and the baking. She also had to undergo the *mikvah* or ritual bath in order to become kosher through total immersion.

Bella Chagall recalls her childhood:

> The heat hits me in the mouth, it makes my heart bleed. 'That is Hell for all those who have sinned a lot,' I say to myself, and quickly run after mama to the ritual bath, and I am now in a room which is as dark as a dungeon. On a small platform stands the old bath-woman, holding a light and a linen cloth. Mama—I am afraid for her—silently descends the slippery steps, ever deeper into the water, until it reaches her neck.
>
> When the old woman says a blessing mama starts like a condemned person. She shuts her eyes, holds her nose, and immerses herself completely under the water as if, God forbid, for ever.
>
> 'Ko-o-o-sher!' cries the old woman with the voice of a prophet.
>
> I start as if hit by a thunderbolt, and wait there, shaking. Soon a bolt of lightning will come down from the black beams of the ceiling and kill us all. Or floods will pour in from the stone walls and drown us all.
>
> 'Ko-o-o-sher!' cries the old woman once more. Where is my mother? I no longer hear a sound.
>
> Then suddenly, as if the water of the pool had divided, my mother's head emerges from the deep. She is dripping wet and shakes herself, as if she had come from the bottom of the sea. I can hardly

bear to wait until the old woman stops crying out, until mama doesn't have to go under the water any more. She is already tired. Water is running from her hair and out of her ears.

'May you have health and long life, Alta.'

Now the old woman smiles too. Her thin hands lift up the linen cloth. Mama wraps it around her as if it were white wings and smiles like an angel.[35]

The table had to be laid for the arrival of 'the Sabbath Queen.' Wife and children had to adorn themselves festively. Over her holiday clothes, the wife often wore an expensive waistcoat, the camisole or *viestl*. The bonnet was adorned by a *shterntichl* embroidered with pearls. In the afternoon the father came home and prepared himself for the celebration. For example, he put on a black kaftan, with white socks and the *shtrayml*, the fur-trimmed black 'Jewish hat' which rabbis wore with thirteen sable-tails. Even their clothing, which had over time diverged completely from that of non-Jews, had the function of expressing piety. Moreover, in its details clothing might indicate one's membership of a particular social group or among the followers of a *tsaddik*. A *sheyner Yid* ('beautiful Jew') was a pious, learned, and—ideally—well-off Jew who manifested this to the outside world with his garb.

The father went to the synagogue with the children where the service was particularly festive. As a rule, the wife remained at home and lit the Sabbath candles when the three stars had ascended the heavens, which—around half-an-hour before sunset—signaled the beginning of the holiday.

To cite Bella Chagall once again:

Mama leaves the shop until last. She looks to see that everything is properly shut. Now I hear her small steps. She shuts the iron back-door. Now I hear her dress rustling. Now she comes into the dining room in her soft shoes. She remains for a moment on the threshold as if blinded by the white tablecloth and the silver candelabra. Then she quickly washes her hands and face and puts on the freshly washed lace collar which she always wears on Friday evenings. A completely new mama now walks up to the candelabra and lights one candle after another with a match. All seven candles are shining. They light up mama's face from below and as if enchanted she lowers her eyes. Slowly, three times, one after another, her hands close around each flame, as if she were enfolding her own heart. The cares of the week melt away with the candles. Mama covers her face with her hands and blesses the candles. Her low, murmured blessings go through her fingers and give the yellow flames even more strength. Mama's hands are lit up in the candlelight like the tablets of the law in the Ark of the Covenant.[36]

In winter, snow on the Sabbath had a special explanation.

How beloved is Israel that the angels themselves pluck their wings in its honor and lay out a carpet from the entrance of the prayer house to the entrance of their houses, while they go out to sit down to the meal of King David, peace be unto him.[37]

Joy and consciousness of duty merged into one another. Many account speak of the 'poetry' of the Sabbath. It promoted family solidarity, but also that of Jewry in general. It constituted an important source of strength for the burdens of everyday life.

The appeal to which the tension between pleasure, peace, and self-examination, on the one hand, and stricter observance of traditional prescriptions on the other gave rise, apparently seized a large number of Jews. At the same time, there was an increasing number who, because of their business relations with non-Jews or their readiness to assimilate, gradually weakened their devotion to the Sabbath. For example, they ran their businesses from the backdoor or the women no longer went regularly to the mikvah. The Sabbath rituals solidified into mere formalities. Especially for children traditional rituals ceased to be credible in such circumstances. As a result, the structure of authority of the Jewish community suffered.

The most important religious holiday was Yom Kippur at the end of September or the beginning of October, the day of atonement and of reconciliation between God and individual Jews. On Yom Kippur, absolute fasting was required from sunset to sunset. One was not even permitted to drink a mouthful of water. Pious Jewish men usually spent the night at the synagogue where worship began with the Kol Nidre, a declaration annulling all vows made to God in haste during the course of the year insofar as they concern oneself (obligations toward others are excluded, in contrast to what was often slanderously asserted).

Isaac Singer describes preparations for Yom Kippur in Warsaw at the time of the First World War:

> The *rebbe* wandered around the apartment somewhat disheveled. It was on the fourth floor; the windows looked out onto the street and onto the courtyard. You could hear the rattling of street cars and trucks and the calls of traders, who offered their wares for sale on stalls. Street musicians played and sang. Children shrieked. Only now did the full meaning of that sentence from the Talmud become entirely clear: 'It is difficult to live in big cities'.
>
> It was difficult to settle in Warsaw. The courtyard was bounded by a prayer house, but the mikvah was on the other side of the street, and when one crossed the road one took one's life in one's hands. In the kitchen the cooking had to be done on a gas flame, and who could know whether the gas was being produced under the supervision of strict Jews. The water ran out of a faucet but how could one know whether the pipes were filled with all manner of unclean things?
>
> Despite all these difficulties the preparations for Yom Kippur had been made.
>
> On the day before the holiday Reb Dan went to the prayer house where he drank a glass of wine with the other believers after morning prayers and ate a little cake. At midday his wife had prepared carp,

dumplings, and yellow turnips. In the afternoon Reb Dan put on his silk kaftan, his white rabbi's robe, and his prayer mantel with the gold embroidered hem. His wife put on her best dress and covered her head with a pearl-embroidered shawl. And his daughters and daughters-in-law also appeared in their holiday garb. After the rabbi had recited the blessings he made his way to the prayer house in order to take part in the Kol Nidre. It was very noisy in the courtyard. Women whose husbands had been conscripted lamented and sobbed. Some older women, who wore wigs covered with shawls and held gold-embossed prayer books in their hands, exchanged effusive new year's greetings. The twilight had not yet fallen but the prayer house was already brightly lit. The floor was strewn with hay and sawdust. Reb Dan was led to a seat by the eastern wall by the *shammash* [salaried sexton in a synagogue]...

As the faithful made their way home Reb Dan and quite a few other old men remained at the prayer house in order to spend the night there. The rabbi immersed himself in an old folio and brooded on the former glory of Israel ...

The candles flickered and hissed. An old man with a shriveled face and bushy white beard stretched out on one of the benches and went to sleep. Through the window could be seen the pale starry heaven and the three-quarter moon. While he waited here, dressed in his white robe and prayer mantel, Reb Dan was able to forget that he had been driven out of Tiraspol. He was in a holy place, surrounded by his fellow Jews and by the familiar books of holy law. No, he was not alone. There was still a God in heaven, angels, seraphim, and a throne of mercy. He needed only to stretch out his hand in order to touch one of the holy books whose words were the voice of the living God, the characters with which he had created the world.[38]

Yom Kippur is preceded by the ten-day New Year festival, Rosh Hashana. On the evening before New Year's day, children left letters to their father in his place at the festive table in which they promised to be more obedient to their parents in the new year and asked for forgiveness for their transgressions in the old year. Bella Chagall reports that in the afternoon, after worship, people would go to the river in order to say a prayer of purification and to throw their "sins into the flowing water."[39]

Other festivals commemorated historical events which had been passed down by means of the Bible. The Feast of Passover in April commemorates the Exodus of the Jews out of Egypt. For eight days only special crockery, cutlery, and cooking utensils may be used. Foods are prepared in accordance with strict laws, particularly the unleavened bread or matzo. Customary foods, and utensils which had come into contact with them, had to be carefully removed from the home. In many places a mock sales-contract was customary with non-Jews to whom one gave the things, which were taken back later. The father looked for the remains of any bread with leaven, or *hamets*, in it with his sons by candlelight and burned them in accordance with a strict ritual. Naturally, the mother had already prepared the crumbs.

The highpoint of the festival was the seder, an elaborate festive meal. The 'order of ceremonies' follows what is laid down in the holy scriptures for the festival meal, from which Christian communion also developed. The father sat in an easy, reclining posture in a throne-like chair beautifully adorned for this purpose. As a rule, the youngest son, if he has already learned to read Hebrew, poses four prescribed questions to the father concerning the meaning of the events. These are answered with recitations from the Haggadah, which contains the biblical story of the Exodus out of Egypt, popularized and published in many versions and in beautifully adorned books.

The official part of the seder ended with the wish: 'Next year in Jerusalem.' Many Hasidim hung *matza* from the ceilings of their homes—or in the synagogue—until the next Passover in order to keep the occasion constantly in mind.

In June the *Shavuot* ('weeks') was celebrated which commemorates the revelation of the Torah at Sinai. This was the celebration of the Torah. It was also understood as a harvest festival of biblical origin, as the Day of First Fruits. Because of this the children decorated the synagogue with tree-tops, branches, and twigs.

Sukkot ('booths') commemorated the forty-year wanderings of the Jews in the wilderness and the booths the Israelites resided in after the Exodus. The father of the family therefore constructed little huts out of boards with branches and foliage for the roof. The daughters of the family decorated them. Particularly observant Jews also slept in this hut overnight during the festival days in October. The end of the festival was the celebration of *Simhat Torah* (Rejoicing of the Law). This was one of the most joyous and boisterous festivals. There was singing and dancing. The drinking of alcohol was virtually required.

In the 1920s Joseph Roth observed one such celebration in a *shtetl*:

> The Hasidim joined hands, danced in a circle, broke the ring, clapped their hands, threw their hands to the left and to the right in rhythm, seized the Torah rolls and swung them through the air as if they were girls and pressed them against their breasts, kissed them, and cried for joy. There was an erotic passion in the dancing. It touched me deeply that a whole people could dedicate their joy in the pleasures of life to their God and make the book of the strictest laws their beloved and could no longer distinguish between physical desire and spiritual enjoyment but rather united the two. It was lust and fervor, the dancing was the worship of God and prayer a sensual excess. The people drank mead out of big pots ... I also saw how Jews lost consciousness ... after five pots of strong mead and not in triumph, but out of joy that God had given them the law and knowledge.[40]

Hanukka, the Feast of Lights—which took place in the second half of December—had a historical origin with a religious meaning. It celebrated the victory of the Maccabees in 167/164 BC over Syrian rule and the resumption of worship in the Temple. According to tradition, when the Jews had entered the

Temple desecrated by the Syrians they had found a jar of consecrated oil, enough for one day. However, miraculously, it lasted for eight days until new supplies could be obtained. As a consequence, boys—but often also women and girls—over a period of eight days lit a new candle every day on the Hanukka candelabrum and sang Hanukka songs. For this purpose in addition to the candelabra originally used in the Temple, the menorah with seven branches, there was now for the synagogue and at home on Hanukka—and the Sabbath—the eight-branched menorah which held one more *shammash* or 'servant,' a light to be used for the lighting of the candles.

One of the most interesting festivals is Purim, which takes place at the beginning of March. This commemorates the rescue of the Persian Jews from their destruction and at the same time the fact that God can help in hopeless situations if one does not lose faith. The alleged historical circumstances are set down in the Book of Esther.

The most important duty on this day was to listen to a reading from the Megillah, the Book of Esther written on a beautifully decorated roll. While the men went to the synagogue for this purpose the women and children were visited at home by a special reader. Whenever the name of Haman is mentioned in the reading the children make an dreadful racket with rattles. Three-cornered pastries called *hamantashn* ('Haman's pockets') were also eaten. The purim story was also told in folk dramas. The celebrations took place in a lively atmosphere with music and dancing, song and games. Often the young people—and also religious men—put on masks. Differences of rank and age were forgotten, and even the swapping of men's and women's clothing and drunkenness were permitted.

As a result, people often talk of a 'Jewish carnival.' This may be only a superficial analogy, however, and requires further research. It is true that there is a trace of a topsy-turvy world, but the most important thing is joy over the fact that, despite the sufferings of oppression, one will always be victorious with God's help. It is possible that aspects of the Purim festival have found their way into the Christian carnival.

Burial was also strictly regulated. Isaac Singer describes the interment of the rich Meshulam Moskat:

> In order to keep the crowds in check policemen were in attendance. They shouted at the top of their voices and laid about them with the flats of their sabers. Delegations of schoolchildren from the Talmud-Torah schools which had been maintained by donations from Meshulam were to lead the funeral procession. Women sobbed as if they were mourning a close relative. Most shopkeepers in Grzybow Street had closed their shops. Since there would probably be considerable demand for cabs at such a big funeral coachmen came from all parts of the city into the Grzybow district. A few old dodderers muttered to one another that the deceased did not deserve such honors.
>
> At around ten o'clock the hearse set off. The horses—draped with black cloth in which eyeslits had been cut—drew it slowly after them. The procession of mourning carriages stretched through Grzybow, Twarda, Krochmalna, and Gnojna streets. The carriage horses shied and whinnied. Small boys looking for a ride on the running boards of the carriages got a clout on the head with the whip. The Jews of Warsaw enjoyed nothing more than a big funeral. Long before the hearse had entered the cemetery an enormous crowd had gathered there. Youths had climbed up on gravestones for a better view. Every balcony in Genscha Street was full of people. Cemetery attendants, who wore caps with shining peaks and capes with brightly polished buttons, brought along boards and shovels. Beggars and cripples besieged the cemetery gates and the path to the grave. The spectators on the balconies and at the windows were afraid that the thronging crowds in the cemetery would overturn the hearse or shove the rabbi into the open grave. But the Warsaw Jews were used to keeping their composure in such crowds. Despite the confusion everything took place in accordance with the laws and customs. The corpse was wrapped in shrouds and then in a prayer mantel for burial. Pieces of clay had been laid on his eyes. And a stick had been put between his fingers so that

on the coming of the Messiah the deceased would be able to dig his way out to the Holy Land. The mourners sighed. The women broke into lamentations. The gravediggers recited the traditional epitaph: 'He is stone. His work is done; because everything He does is just: a God of truth and without blemish, just and truthful is He.'

When the earth had once again been shoveled into the grave Meshulam's sons spoke the Kaddish. Those gathered around the grave plucked up withered grass stalks and threw them over their shoulder...

In the house of the deceased his three sons sat '*shiva*. All four, Joel, Pinnje, Nathan, and Njunje squatted on low stools for the prescribed seven days [*shiva* mean seven in Hebrew] without shoes. The wall mirror was covered up and on the window sill there was a small basin of water and a linen towel so that the soul of the deceased could receive the ritual ablutions. In a glass candle holder a commemorative candle was burning. Early in the morning and in the late afternoon a quorum of men gathered to pray.[41]

Often some soil from the holy ground of Israel was thrown into the grave with the body. According to folk belief it was supposed to prevent the corpse from decaying so that the deceased would be able to rise again unhindered on the coming of the Messiah.

SYNAGOGUE AND COMMUNITY ORGANIZATIONS

The Synagogue was a house of assembly, prayer, and study, and therefore often known as *shul* (school). The two main functions determined the ground plan of the building. The prayer axis had to be aligned to the east, towards the lost Temple in Jerusalem which would, someday, be regained. At one end of this axis was the ark where the scrolls of the law are kept. In the middle of the room, aligned with this axis, was the symbol of wisdom, the Torah table. The law had to form the center of life.

Often the synagogue was not at ground level, but sunk into the earth to a certain extent. This can still be seen in the case of the Altneuschul in Prague. This was an attempt to follow the words of Psalm 130: "I call to you out of the depths!" Often, however, this practice was also occasioned by the prohibition of Christian authorities against synagogues being taller than Christian buildings.

Particularly worthy of mention are the many wooden synagogues in Poland. With their bold external construction and their internal layout—colorful ornaments and symbolic representations, Hebrew inscriptions, sumptuous wooden carvings—they radiated a special power. Unfortunately, today they can only be admired in pictures.

Women had to remain separated from the men in the synagogue. They either sat at ground level behind partitions around the inner room, into which they could look through slits, or in a gallery in which they were screened from the men by a lattice.

In the big cities—in addition to the structurally distinctive synagogues—there were, especially among the Hasidim, a variety of prayer rooms in back-rooms of apartment buildings, in cellars, or in adjacent buildings: the *shtibl* (prayer room) reflected the poverty of the community, yet the atmosphere in them could be just as festive and moving as in the most magnificent places of assembly. Moreover, let it be repeated that religious worship could take place wherever there was a gathering of at least ten men, a *minyan*.

The Jewish community was led by a committee, alongside which there was often a council. There was often fierce competition for the leading community offices, especially between Orthodox Jews, Hasidim, and Reform Jews, which not infrequently degenerated into violence. Social tensions in the community served only to exacerbate these conflicts. The ruling upper stratum could retain its position of power for a long time. Next to the leader of the community, the Parnas, an important role was played by the administrator of poor relief. He collected and distributed the money for the poor and organized the Sabbath meals for needy members of the community.

The rabbi was the teacher and religious authority of the community. He had no priestly functions. The priesthood had been dissolved after the destruction of the Temple in Jerusalem, even if the descendants of the caste—the Levites and the priests of Aaron—still had particular rights and duties. The rabbi had to disseminate knowledge of the Talmud in the community by giving lectures in the synagogue and holding discussions with other learned people. Furthermore, he advised the faithful on questions of religious duty and on juristic issues; he also chaired the rabbinical court. He was paid by the community. This was not a problem so long as his authority was not called into question. But the more the community was driven by dissension, and different trends in Judaism came into conflict with one another, the more the office of rabbi was caught between contending parties.

The rabbi was assisted by the *shammash*, a kind of 'sexton', in his many tasks. Often the latter took over the tasks of the *hazan* or cantor, who directed the public service, an extraordinarily demanding activity because services lasted quite a long time, and on high holidays several followed one after the other. If the *hazan* was a gifted singer, his art sometimes led him to try to give more weight to the performance than to its religious significance.

In addition to teachers, secretaries, scribes, and similar employees of the community the various associations were also important. The *hevra kaddisha* or 'holy society' was a brotherhood which was responsible for burials. It took care of the terminally ill, helped them to confess their sins, carried out all of the observances connected with death, and co-operated with the burials organization. No prohibition issued by the authorities could ever prevent this autonomous organization from fulfilling its duties.

Alongside this respected body, which often formed the core of a community, the charitable associations were probably the most important. They had a long tradition and were subordinate to the qahal which guided charitable work. Even after the breakdown of religious unity, as reflected in the various synagogues and *shtibln*, social responsibilities were the common task of the Jewish community in a particular place. Many things were done privately: on the Sabbath, Jews would play host to guests; when going to bake bread for the Sabbath, they would throw coins for the poor into collection boxes left out for the purpose. Needy *yeshiva* students were supported by well-to-do families or could at least eat their meals every day with another family. The charitable associations supported widows and orphans, the old, the sick, and the disabled, organized soup kitchens, and took care of the rehabilitation of former prison-inmates. Poorer Jews received help so that they could observe the religious festivals. Poor girls were supplied with clothes and a dowry. Furthermore, the associations helped out in the case of severe winters, illnesses, or sudden emergencies.

The rapid population growth in the nineteenth century soon pushed community charity to its limits. When the Warsaw *kahal* published its last report in 1869—it did not want to give the critics of traditional charity the chance to raise these arguments themselves—it turned out that on average only two or three rubles were available for each needy person. This situation was made distinctly worse by accelerating industrialization. Between 1894 and 1898 the number of those in need of assistance in the Pale of Settlement, including Russian Poland, increased by almost one-third. In around 1900 the average proportion of needy families was just under 20 percent; in the big cities it was significantly higher.

In the Jewish press more and more voices could be heard loudly condemning the inadequacy of the charity system. Even the increased efforts of individual rich Jews—such as Poznański in Łódź—could not change anything. The demand was that one should start with the underlying causes, particularly high unemployment. An improvement in education and new sources of employment were necessary. The reaction of the associations, the *hevrot*—co-operatives or societies, often also described as brotherhoods—was to try to organize mutual assistance or aid towards self-help instead of merely providing individual assistance. The *hevrot* of proletarian Hasidim often constituted protoforms of the workers' movement.

The most important of these efforts were the credit banks for co-operatives of craftsmen and small traders. They promoted measures for the structural improvement of trade in particular. The most significant organization was the Society for the Promotion of Craft and Agriculture among the Jews in Russia (ORT). However, it is probable that all these efforts were no more than drops in the ocean because the framework conditions for the Jews—and especially for the Jewish lower classes in Poland—did not significantly improve. However, it is clear that people did not stick only to the old ways.

The relief efforts during the First World War constituted something of a highpoint, with a number of different organizations, including the Jewish Committee for the Assistance of Victims of War (EKOPO). Donations came from all levels of Jewish society, particularly, of course, from the rich. However, there were increasing conflicts concerning the politicization of many of the participating groups. In addition, the support organizations received money from Jewish institutions abroad, and even from the Russian government.

Jews and Poles in the Łódź ghetto

Jewish women on the way to the synagogue

Prayers in the home of a deceased person in Lida

The temple of the wonder-rabbi of Sadagora

Crockery washers in Łódź, who made crockery kosher before Passover

Rabbis on the way to the synagogue in Łódź

The Jewish cemetery in Vilnius

Jewish clothing traders in Vilnius

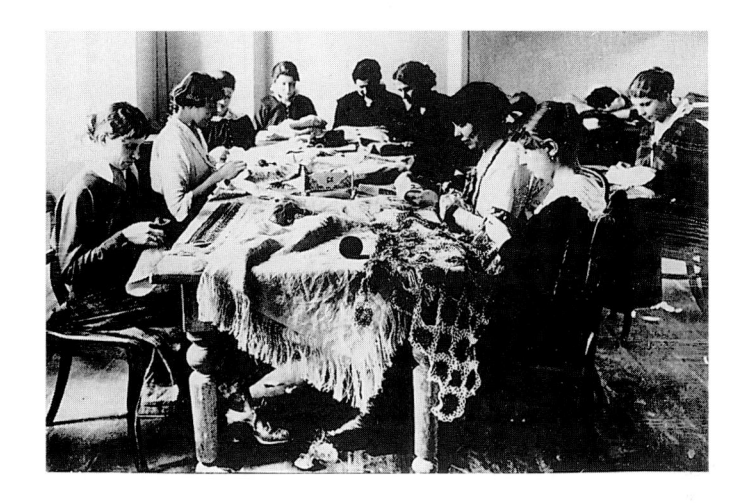

Jewish girls in the embroidery workshop of the Jewish
'Help through Work' society

Cracow Street in Lublin

Jewish paper goods salesmen in Vilnius

Jewish clothing traders in the ghetto in Vilnius

Jewish porters in front of the city theater in Vilnius

Jewish families return to their homeland

INCREASING CONFLICTS WITH THE NON-JEWISH WORLD

The altered social relations—the radical socio-economic changes, the intellectual and religious transformations, the hardening of the political situation—had their effect on Jewish identity. In his novel *The Estate,* Isaac Singer has a Jewish student who has turned his back on religion say

> The Polish Jew ... formerly had a real place in society. Before the liberation of the serfs [1864 in Poland—H. H.] his role was that of intermediary between the manorial lords and the peasants. That role was now a thing of the past and now he was little more than a parasite. He was not productive, did not speak the language of the country in which he lived, and sent his children to the *heder*. How long would the Jew still take ritual baths and go around in *tzitzits*?[42]

Assimilation to Polishness or Russianness, for which many large entrepreneurs and a part of the intelligentsia now strove, was out of the question for someone like Singer's student, even if they had become estranged from traditional Jewish ways. Society offered them few opportunities, but assimilation, above all because of the growing anti-Semitism, seemed increasingly inappropriate and implausible. Pogroms in Russia, occasional riots in Polish cities (such as those in Warsaw in 1881 and in Łódź in 1892), the many 'minor' incidents which took place ever more frequently, the boycott campaigns against Jews (and Germans)—'Each to his own!'—discriminatory newspaper articles, contemptuous remarks in the street and in drawing rooms: all had their effect.

Although economic contacts between Jews and non-Jews were deepening as a consequence of industrialization, at the same time the dividing lines were becoming sharper. Warsaw at this time is often spoken of as a 'city of two peoples.' By analogy Łódź must have been regarded as a 'city of three peoples.' In political life, too, differences became more and more conspicuous. At the council elections in 1861, this was still barely noticeable. It seemed that Poles and Jews would work together against the tsarist regime. At the elections for the Russian parliament—the Duma—in Warsaw in 1912, however, the Polish National Democrats (the strongest nationalistically inclined party so far) and the Jews clashed fiercely. The 'Jewish threat' was painted in stark colors. When a socialist was voted in with the help of Jews in the complex election procedure—and at the same time a Jew gained a majority in Łódź —the agitation got totally out of control. The National Democrats organized an economic boycott against the Jews. The conflicts were now out in the open.

SOCIALISM, ZIONISM, NEW JEWISH IDENTITY

For many Jews, doubts concerning their place in society led to self-hatred and even suicide. Others favored the revolutionary opposition and joined socialist groups. In Russia, as early as 1876, the so-called *Narodniki* ('populists') had tried, after the failure and 'going to the people' movement two years previously, to widen their support base and had founded an 'Association of the Jews in Russia.' Jews were also active in the revolutionary groups of subsequent years. However, it turned out that these groups often had a contemptuous attitude to Jewish culture when the pogroms after 1881 were, to some extent, greeted as a spontaneous uprising of the masses against Jewish exploiters, pressure began to build for greater Jewish independence. Those who had hitherto drawn closer to Polish culture tried to introduce this into national organizations, such as the Polish Socialist Party founded in 1892. But here too differences soon began to arise because of the lack of consideration for the 'Jewish question' and anti-Semitic tendencies in some sections of the party.

As a result, internationalist groups were more attractive. They promised, on the basis of Marxist theory, that world revolution would dissolve not only class conflicts, but also national conflicts. After a number of important forerunners, the most significant movements were social democracy in the Kingdom of Poland and Lithuania (1893, SDKP; from 1900, SDKPiL, Social Democracy of the Kingdom of Poland and Lithuania) and then Russian social democracy (1898, Russian Social-Democratic Workers' Party). Names such as Rosa Luxemburg (1871–1919), Jan Tyszka (Leo Jogiches, 1867–1919), Yuly O. Tsederbaum (Martov, 1873–1923), Paul Axelrod (1850–1928), and Lev Bronshteyn (Leon Trotsky, 1879–1940) give some idea of the influence which Jews exercised.

Their influence was strengthened through independent Jewish workers' co-operatives and associations which had emerged since the 1880s in Congress Poland, especially in Warsaw, and in Galicia. In 1897, finally, the General Union of Jewish Workers in Lithuania, Poland, and Russia, or 'Bund', was formed in Vilnius. Vilnius had become a center of Jewish socialism: the tradition of the rabbinical seminary, which was permitted from 1847 to 1873, had disseminated the Haskalah and included later socialists such as Aron Samuel Liberman (1845–1880) and Aron Zundelevič among its students. There was also a Jewish proletariat in the city. In a number of circles there were discussions concerning co-operation with non-Jewish organizations and the demand for a mass movement. While at first, in the spirit of the Enlightenment and assimilation, workers' movements were conducted in Hebrew or Russian, Arkady Kremer's (1865–1935) 1893 article 'On Agitation' was the turning point: one should be familiar with everyday life and concern oneself with people's everyday experiences—"*In di gasn, tsu di masn*' (Into the streets, to the masses), as Vladimir Medem (1879–1923), another theorist of the future 'Bund', expressed it. Therefore, it was necessary to communicate in Yiddish. In this way, not least via a Yiddish press, the Bund developed into a unique mass organization whose manifold influence on the Polish and Russian workers' movements cannot be overestimated. The anchoring in the Jewish proletariat made it possible to retain the character of a mass party, despite the fact that the activities of the leadership were generally illegal. Furthermore, the work of the Bund contributed significantly to the formation of a new Jewish self-image in Eastern Europe.

The decision in favor of Yiddish was not taken on tactical grounds alone. Among the Bundists—for example, Michel Goldman (Mark Liber, 1880–1937), Wiktor Alter (1890–1943), and Henryk Erlich (Wolf Hersch, 1882–1942)—socialist-international thinking was linked to the conviction that the cultural uniqueness of the Jewish people must be given due consideration and therefore that cultural 'non-territorial autonomy' was unavoidable for the Jews. The Fourth Congress of the Bund in Białystok in 1901 therefore demanded that the Russian Empire be transformed into a federation of autonomous nationalities not bound to any particular territory. In this individual membership in a national collective, the Bundists saw—similar to Austro-Marxism—an opportunity, to preserve cultural differences while overcoming nationalism, which aimed at the creation of one's own territory by the exclusion of other nationalities. These ideas found many adherents, both among the Jewish proletariat, which had often experienced anti-Semitic attitudes among non-Jewish workers, and the intelligentsia. The opportunity arose to co-operate with other workers while preserving Jewish culture, and to overstep boundary lines in order to put aside national borders in the society of the future. The significance of Jews in the workers' movement can be measured by the fact that more Jews fell at the barricades in Łódź during the 1905 Revolution than members of any other group.

Co-operation with overlapping organizations proved to be difficult, however. The Bund had at first associated itself with Russian social democracy. Its demand for organizational autonomy in a federally constructed party had in many cases met with misunderstanding, however. When its delegates lost a vote on this question at the Second Congress of the Russian Social-Democratic Workers' Party in London in 1903 they walked out. As a result, the faction sympathetic to their aims was left in a minority, which the group around Lenin immediately seized upon: the former became known as *mensheviki* ['those of the minority'], while the latter appropriated for themselves the term *bolsheviki* ['those of the majority']. After the 1905 Revolution, the Bund joined the Russian Social-Democratic Workers' Party again and worked above all with the Mensheviks, until the commencement of an entirely new phase in 1917.

An alternative to socialism was Zionism. It was more than a nationalist response to the nationalist challenge of the non-Jewish environment. For hundreds of years, since the destruction of the Temple in Jerusalem in the year 70 and the dispersal of the Jews throughout the world which followed, the longing for Zion, for a return to the land of Israel, had remained alive. God would give a sign when exile was drawing to a close and the Jews could once more gather in Israel. Then the Messiah would appear and bring redemption to all mankind. For religious Jews—and from the eighteenth century also for the Hasidim—it was the fulfillment of a life's dream to travel once to the Holy Land and to bring home a little earth to go with you into your grave when the time came. They gave no thought to the creation of their own Jewish state, however—God's will should not be anticipated.

This began to change with the 'activistic turn' among the Jews towards the end of the eighteenth century. More and more Jews wanted to contribute towards bringing forward the redemption with their own resources. In Hungary, ultra-orthodox rabbis such as Moses Schreiber, known as Hatam Sofer—'the scribe has sealed'—(1763–1839) and Akiva Josef Schlesinger (1837–1922), who, with reference to the Torah, generally rejected anything new, demanded that the Jews be regarded not only as a confession but also as a people, and that preparations should be made for the return to *Eretz Israel* ('the land of Israel'). Only in this way could the assimilation of the Jews—and so ultimately the dissolution of Jewry—be prevented. Rabbi Josef Natonek (1813–1892) developed a concrete program from the middle of the nineteenth century for the national liberation of the Jews through the creation of a state in Palestine. The influence of the Hungarian–Magyar national movement is unmistakable. Judah ben Solomon Hai Alkalai (1798–1878), rabbi in Semlin in Croatia, and Zwi Hirsch Kalischer (1795–1874), rabbi in Torun, did not go quite so far. They called for the colonization of Palestine through increased immigration; they still had no thought of an independent state.

Here were the roots of religious Zionism which wanted to maintain the unity of the Jewish people against loss of faith, emancipation, and assimilation and hoped for God's help if the Jews themselves initiated the return to Israel. A corresponding organization—'Misrahi'—was formed in Vilnius in 1902. At the same time, the foundations of religious anti-Zionism were laid: premature state-building by a secular movement such as Zionism would be blasphemy. Later representatives of Orthodoxy and of Hasidic trends would argue in this way. They joined together in Katowice in 1912 to form the *Agudas Yisrael* ('union of Israel'). In Palestine during the 1920s the ultra-orthodox group around Chaim Josef Sonnenfeld (1849–1932), who came from Hungary and considered himself to be the successor to Hatam Sofer, became increasingly influential. While *Agudas Yisrael* made its peace with Zionist efforts after the Shoah (Holocaust), the ultra-orthodox, who left these organizations, still reject the State of Israel, and consider Zionism to be a fatal threat to the Jews.

Another source of Zionism was the Haskalah which, similar to the turn to socialism, emerged from the so-called 'activistic turn.' The failed hopes that enlightenment would go hand in hand with emancipation and the integration of the Jews in society led many Maskilim to a spiritual return to Judaism, and to the conviction that a solution to the problem could only come from outside the Diaspora. In 1852, Abraham Mapu (1807–1867), originally a teacher from Kovno (Kaunas), Lithuania, published his novel *Ahavat Tsiyon* (1852, 'Love of Zion'; published in English as 'Annou: Prince and Peasant') in Hebrew. Building upon biblical motives and with a treatment schooled in contemporary novelistic technique, Mapu created an idealized picture of Israel, which at the same time gave expression to a utopian desire for the kingdom of peace—with very concrete features of a rural society with social justice and self-determination for women. The novel was a huge success and paved the way for the revival of the Zionist idea. Many writers now propagated the creation of a state in Palestine.

The increasingly violent anti-Semitism and finally the pogroms in the Russian Empire gave the impetus to match ideas and plans with actions. From 1881 small groups of *Hovevei Tsiyon* ('lovers of Zion') were formed which attached themselves loosely to the *Hibbat Tsiyon* ('love of Zion') movement. A first student organization, the Biluim—so called after the initial Hebrew letters of the quotation from Isaiah: 'O house of Jacob, come ye, and let us walk …' (Isaiah 2:5)—tried to set in motion emigration to Eretz Israel. The initial successes of the first 'Aliyah', or 'ascending', to Zion were small. Nevertheless, the desire for 'auto-emancipation', as Leo (Judah Leib) Pinsker (1821–1891) of Odessa formulated it in his book of the same name, published in 1882, became stronger among the East European Jews. They were forced to the conclusion that emancipation 'from outside' could not be expected within the foreseeable future, and it seemed increasingly humiliating and unworthy to wait in hope of being granted what they wanted, particularly when non-Jewish society was not emancipated itself.

Pinsker played a leading role in the *Hibbat Tsiyon* movement, which organized several conferences—beginning in Katowice in 1884—but soon found itself in difficulties. Religious and secular participants quarreled, emigration to Palestine was progressing very slowly, and the settlements there soon experienced a grave crisis. *Ahad Ha'am* ('One of the people'; actually Asher Ginzberg [1856–1927], born in Skvira, near Kiev, Russian Empire [now in Ukraine]) traveled to Palestine and afterwards criticized colonization as the wrong approach. State-building was not achievable for the time being. Instead, he took the view that it would be better to concentrate on a few settlements and first to try to turn Palestine into a Jewish spiritual center from which a renaissance of the Jewish people in the Diaspora would go forth. Like many other East European Jews he particularly stressed cultural autonomy, which had to be renewed. Ahad Ha'am became one of the founders of 'cultural Zionism', which was to become a distinct alternative to 'political Zionism'. Further developed by Martin Buber (1878–1965) and other important personalities cultural Zionism stressed, above all with reference to East European Jewish roots, 'Jewishness' and linked reflection upon one's own culture with a recognition of others. To this extent cultural Zionists called for a compromise with the Arabs in Palestine.

Nathan Birnbaum (1864–1937), from Vienna, linked the cultural with the political aspect. He called, under the influence of his encounter with East European Jewish culture, for Jews to find their own Jewish self-awareness; from 1885 he published the periodical '*Selbst-Emancipation*' (Self-Emancipation), and coined the term 'Zionism' in order to distinguish the new movement from general Jewish national and purely philanthropic efforts, and to establish the goal of a new unity for the Jewish people. His attempt to bring together the different tendencies got no further than a pre-conference in 1894, however.

Although they had prepared the ground for new ideas, the attempts to form a national movement originating in Eastern Europe were beginning to flag when Theodor Herzl (1860–1904), who came from an assimilated family from Budapest and lived in Vienna, made the breakthrough with his pamphlet *Der Judenstaat* (The Jewish State, 1896). In ignorance of earlier Zionistic writings and without putting forward any really new ideas, Herzl found exactly the right note with which to convince many Jews that the solution to the 'Jewish question' had been found. At the first Zionist Congress at Basel the Zionist organization was founded and the 'Basel program' was adopted. This stated that "Zionism strives to create for the Jewish people a home in Palestine secured by public law." Now Zionist associations sprang up all over the world, even if Zionism was only supported by a minority of Jews.

It was not by chance that the Zionist organization and the Bund were founded in the same year. Both orientations originated in the crisis facing the Jewish self-understanding in the nineteenth century, and both drew radical conclusions from the need to find new answers to the challenges of the time, and from the conviction that this could take place only through active participation in efforts to either improve conditions or achieve a solution. The answer of both socialism and Zionism was that the

Messiah had still not come, but the crisis of the Jews required urgent remedies; both were responses to secularization and tolerance, emancipation and liberalism, nationalism and anti-Semitism, industrialization and impoverishment, and the transformation of everyday life. Both were based on Jewish tradition and included elements of messianism, but also introduced something entirely new in Jewish history.

This common point of departure made possible, despite all the differences in respect of aims and methods, the co-operation of both these extreme alternatives on certain issues. This was also made possible by the fact that a rift soon opened up in Zionism between West European and East European Jews (*Westjuden* and *Ostjuden*). At the first Congress unity seemed a given. Even the leader of the religious wing of *Hovevei Tsiyon* and rabbi of Białystok, Samuel Mohilewer (1824–1899) sent an approving greeting address. But while many of the west-European influenced Zionists, with Herzl at the head, regarded political work as the priority, including diplomatic negotiations and the acquisition of a territory, best of all a state—which did not have to be Palestine—in accordance with international law, most East European Jews in the new movement had other priorities: rapid help for the impoverished and those under threat by practical measures, above all settlement in Palestine, which would prepare the ground for a just social order in the future. The origins of the kibbutz can be found here. This was understood as a component part of the cultural renewal of the Jews. The center of this renaissance and of the settlements could, for them, only be Eretz Israel. But at the same time they considered the 'work of the present' in the lands in which they dwelt to be necessary: the improvement of the situation of the Jews to the extent of their recognition as an autonomous national minority. This often led to tensions in the Zionist organization, particularly because many West European Jews looked down on the 'backward' *Ostjuden*. Since the material need of the Jews was greatest in the East, however, people wished to help them and, in any case, they needed them—after all, the majority of Jews lived there. In the conflict concerning the 'Uganda plan' between 1903 and 1905 the East European Zionists ultimately prevailed: they insisted on Palestine as the only field of activity for Zionism. The spokesman of the Russian Zionists, Menachem Ussishkin (1863–1941), suggested that the two tendencies—the 'political' and the 'practical'—should combine in a 'synthetic' Zionism. This—represented above all by Chaim Weizmann (1874–1952), from the Pinsk region—became the dominant strand in Zionism.

The stance of the East European Zionists was such as to make possible many forms of co-operation with other groups, particularly in relation to socialist Zionism. From 1901 the *Poale Tsiyon* ('workers of Zion') began to form in Eastern Europe, followed in 1906 by the foundation of a party. Its most important theoretician was the Marxist Ber Borohov (1881–1917). He argued to non-Zionist Jewish socialists, who regarded Zionism as a variety of bourgeois nationalism, that the Jews, even when they fought for social improvements in the Diaspora, needed Zion as a territory in which the class struggle could develop unhindered. The Arab proletariat would be an ally of the Jewish workers in this. In Palestine, David Grün, known as Ben Gurion (from Płońsk, 1886–1973), was particularly influential. He fought against Marxist and class-struggle-oriented tendencies. Even more active in this respect were the moderate Zionists–Socialists, under the leadership of Nachman Syrkin (1868–1924), who were not committed to Palestine as the ultimate goal. Influenced less by Marxism and Social Democracy, but more by the Russian Socialists–Revolutionaries, was the Jewish Socialist Workers' Party, founded in 1906. It demanded a solution to the 'national question' in the Diaspora through territorial autonomy and wanted to renew the organizations of self-administration—from the kahal to the Jewish parliament or 'Sejm'—for this reason they were also known as 'Sejmists.' The socialist Zionists certainly represented significant competition for the Bund; regional power relations were very diverse. But there was often collaboration on concrete issues which had as their object the improvement of the position of the Jewish proletariat.

Against the resistance of Orthodox Jews, who did not hold with involvement in politics, Zionist and socialist groups participated in the 1905 Revolution. As it progressed, a sort of umbrella organization of different, mostly liberal tendencies—boycotted by the Jewish Bund—came into being in the form of the Society for the Achievement of Equal Rights for the Jewish People in Russia. At first it strove for voting rights for Jews, but gradually more and more demands for national autonomy and an all-Jewish national assembly came to the fore. This was reminiscent of the Va'ad in the early modern period. Although the Society supported the national aims of the Poles, the Polish National Democrats had the slogan: 'The Poles are in danger! The Jews are coming!' After the elections to the first Imperial Duma in 1906, the new Russian parliament, the organization split.

Many members collaborated with political parties, including parties that were not specifically Jewish. All the same, the awareness grew that all Jews had common political interests. The Zionists were strongly influenced by the programmatic ideas of the Society. One of its most active politicians, the historian Simon Dubnov (1860–1941), founded the Jewish People's Party in 1906. It expressed most clearly the demand for national autonomy and for the recognition of the Jews as a national minority in the land in which they wanted to live. Starting in the 1890s, Dubnov represented the position that the Jews were a cultural–historical nation even in exile, and could therefore claim the rights of a people.

All in all, the political mobilization of many Jews was achieved—even if many Hasidim did not participate in the election because they did not regard it as compatible with their traditional religious way of life. A proactive movement was a more appropriate response to the current social conditions than the traditional pilgrimages of people from the *shtetl* or a deputation. A Political Office created in 1912 maintained contact with Jewish Duma representatives and proved extremely effective, while the Information Office subordinate to it gathered documentation on the situation of the Jews in the Russian Empire. This became extremely important in the First World War, when there were many riots against the Jews and a widespread anti-Semitic mood. It was reports of this kind which enabled Duma representatives to make representations to the authorities or to put questions to the Ministerial Council in order to obtain at least partial help.

Though socialism, Jewish nationalism and Zionism seemed offensive to faith at first sight, there was also a return to inwardness.

> Because no matter how great the need may be the future brings the most marvelous salvation. The apparent cowardice of the Jew, who does not react to a stone thrown by a playing boy and does not hear the abusive word, is in truth the pride of someone who knows that one day he will be victorious and that nothing can happen to him if God does not wish it, and that no defense can be as wonderful as God's will.[43]

Reflection upon inwardness could take the form of a rigorous, ascetic piety or of a mystical flight into Hasidism. At the same time, however, forces grew which were conscious of the distinctive Jewish folk culture and of the liberational elements of Hasidism. Pride in 'Jewishness,' in traditions and values, intensified appreciably.

From these different strands a movement emerged—still not investigated in all its manifold aspects—for an East European Jewish nationality, which claimed autonomy to the displeasure of the Polish nationalists and Russian conservatives. Yiddish experienced a renaissance. In 1908 the Czernowitz Language Conference took place, organized by Nathan Birnbaum, who in the meantime had turned his back on Zionism. A wide range of writers, dramatists, historians, sociologists, and journalists, not to mention workers and small traders, consciously considered themselves—if from different political standpoints—to be *Ostjuden* (East European Jews) and found their identity amidst industrialization, urbanization, and new ways of life. What in the West was denied by most Jews—namely, that they were a nation—was felt in Poland and Russia by an increasing number of Jews and also consciously articulated.

Despite the partial deterioration of relations between Jews and non-Jews, and despite increasing anti-Semitic trends and nationalistic polarization, the 'Jewish question' was not insoluble. The growing consciousness of a distinct nationality and culture among Jews—who were definitely not united politically, even at election time—offered the prospect of social co-existence, and not only in the sense that emancipation had to involve the renunciation of autonomy and complete integration in the dominant nation. For the first time East European Jews could envisage a means through which they could live together with other nations as a nation and "cultural personality" in their own right and on an equal footing. To be sure, this was more arduous, but possibly more desirable in the end. Perhaps in this way a new form of intermediary function could have come into being. Contemporaries raised the possibility of cultural intermediation, not least because of the multilingualism of most Jews. Unfortunately, this solution did not prove viable.

IMMIGRATION AS AN ATTEMPT TO FIND A NEW HOMELAND

The pogroms and persecutions from the 1880s were the last straw for many Jews, who now decided to emigrate. Their growing poverty, but also their dissatisfaction with community structures and existing responses to the problems of the time, gave them the impression of hopelessness. They wanted to throw off the 'fetters of the ghetto' and build a new life somewhere else. Emigration therefore also gave expression to the general crisis afflicting how the Jews saw themselves. Between the 1890s and the First World War, well over one million Jews left the Russian Empire. These were principally impoverished craftsmen and skilled workers; traders and peddlers, on the other hand, felt that they would be able to ride out the storm. The hopes of the emigrants were not always fulfilled. A considerable number—after the turn of the century, according to disputed estimates, somewhere between 15 and 20 percent—therefore had to make their way back to their old homeland. "Many come back. Others are still on the way. The East European Jews [*Ostjuden*] do not have a homeland anywhere, but graves in every cemetery."[44]

The emigrants traveled to destinations all over the world. Some chose Palestine in order to fulfill the religiously inspired dream of returning at least once to the Land of the Fathers. Many pursued Zionist ideas. Furthermore, many states in Europe and overseas—for example, in Latin America—regarded themselves as only way-stations when confronted by the influx of East European Jews. The reception was by no means always friendly. The strangeness of the East European Jewish way of life was—not least in Germany, Switzerland, and Great Britain—used to illustrate the clichés about dirty and avaricious Jews, who were 'sex fiends' and criminals. In Great Britain this line of argument was linked primarily with the social and economic functions of the immigrants, while in Germany the traditional deep-seated anti-Jewish culture resurfaced. Even the long-established Jews did not, at first, react enthusiastically because they feared, with some justification, that the negative image of the East European Jews would be transferred to all Jews and so threaten their position in society. Gradually—and this process went on until the period after the First World War—the majority of Jews came to support the *Ostjuden*. *Ostjuden* were increasingly recognized as part of a common Jewish community, the carriers of specifically Jewish values and culture.

By far the greatest number of emigrants went to the USA. Between 1881 and 1914 over two million Jews emigrated there. This stream has still not come to a halt. The genocide visited upon the European Jews shifted the center of Jewish life to the USA almost completely. In 1986, 44 percent of world Jewry—2.4 percent of the US population—lived there, as against only 27.5 percent in Israel. The immigrant East European Jews encountered long-established Jews, mostly of German origin, as well as a small number of Sephardic Jews, who had come to North America with the first 'whites.' Both groups looked on the newcomers, who as a rule were far below them in terms of social standing and had different religious and cultural traditions, with some contempt. They were 'foreign.' But it was this very culture which gave the East European Jews self-confidence. They regarded the American Jews as having deserted true 'Jewishness.' Conflicts were unavoidable. However, differences soon began to be overcome out of solidarity with the needy and in the common effort to show a positive image of Jews to society.

After the animosity with which they had been confronted in Europe, in the USA the East European Jews could breathe a sigh of relief. There was virtually no legal discrimination, most immigrants could quickly acquire American citizenship. There was not even much anti-Semitism, at least not at first sight, though it did manifest itself when, for example, one was looking for a job or wanted to join a prestigious club. Perhaps it was moderated by religious diversity and the predilection of many Protestant groups for the Jews of the Old Testament, which even went as far as 'Christian Zionism'—the belief that the Messiah would return and bring salvation when a certain number of Jews converted to Christianity or at least returned to Israel. After the First World War and the October 'Revolution' in Russia, anti-Semitism became more open as envy and hatred of Jewish capitalists combined with fear of Jewish revolutionaries. Not only the Ku-Klux-Klan, but even the automobile king Henry Ford disseminated the 'Protocols of the Elders of Zion,' a forged report of series of meetings of Jewish representatives from all over the world, allegedly held at Basel, Switzerland, which discussed a plan for Jewish world domination. This anti-Semitism was partially responsible for the immigration restrictions which were introduced between 1921 and 1924, and only relaxed after the Second World War. Immigration was now limited to a fixed proportion of the numbers of each nationality already resident in the USA. Jews were not regarded as a nationality in their own right and so were counted as being nationals of their country of origin. During the Nazi period these regulations hindered the rescue of many Jews from death.

Despite all these hindrances and disadvantages, conditions in the USA made it possible for most East European Jews to climb the social ladder. The first generation found work above all in the textile industry and in retailing, badly paid and with terrible working conditions. Second-generation Jews were often able to open their own, larger businesses or get better work as salaried employees. In the 1930s only a minority were employed as workers or salaried employees. The enormous change that has taken place since that time is indicated by the fact that today in New York a disproportionate number of lawyers, judges, dentists, and doctors have (East European) Jewish origins.

In parallel with this, the inward-looking immigrant society began to open up: many of the upwardly mobile, for example, left the Lower East Side in Manhattan and moved to upmarket neighborhoods in the suburbs. However, the cohesion of the East European Jewish community is astonishing. Despite all their hopes, the New World remained an alien environment for a long time. Sholem Aleichem, for example, who went to the USA in 1906 and then again during the First World War, has memorably described the difficulties in adapting; Shalom Asch has also written about it. As a result, it is not surprising that the immigrants joined *landsmanshaftn* (welfare and cultural associations for people from the same place), in which the *grine* ('greenhorns') were instructed by the *gelen* who came from the same region, and through which they could maintain contacts with their homeland. The regional associations in this way contributed to preserving East European Jewish culture.

To be sure, many of the immigrants wanted to flee the confinement of the ghetto, rebel against the religious laws which they no longer found compelling, and throw off the rule of the well-to-do community oligarchy who discriminated against the poor. The fear that faith and the pursuit of religious learning would be lost in the USA caused many rabbis to warn against emigration. In the inter-war period, the rabbi of Munkács (Mukačevo), Chaim Elazar Spira (Shapira, 1872–1937)—at that time the most resolute opponent of Zionism among Hasidic rabbis—described the three gates of Hell: "The lack of faith of many elements of European Jewry, the absolute subjugation to money in America, and Zionism which was gaining ground in Jerusalem!"[45] America was the greatest of these dangers. In fact, many even chose the path of complete assimilation.

The majority, however, remained attached to 'Jewishness'. Even if a large number of immigrant East European Jews sympathized with socialism and later with Zionism, they retained at least part of their traditional customs, overwhelmingly spoke Yiddish, attended Yiddish theaters and cabarets, read Yiddish newspapers, and hired *klezmer* bands for weddings, Purim, and other celebrations, including the functions of regional associations. The East European Jewish *shtetl* was reborn in many cities in the USA.

Of course, contradictions in the new self-image could not fail to materialize. Problems of adaptation found expression in the disintegration of many families—not by chance was the role of the *yiddishe mame* ('Yiddish mother') particularly important for family cohesion—but also in the relatively high rate of criminality, namely in prostitution, games of chance, fraud, and criminal gangs, and even participation in the famous gangster organizations of the 1920s; in general, however, violent crime was less prevalent among the Jews.

Politically, the majority of East European Jewish immigrants were on the side of the Bund and other socialist groupings. In 1925, 15 percent of the members of the Communist Party of America were Jewish. This was the continuation of what had begun in Eastern Europe. However, more and more Jews were attracted to Zionism, which as a result became an organization to be taken seriously. The decisive factor in this was less the desire to return to the Holy Land than solidarity with Jews in Palestine and with those who wanted to emigrate there from Eastern Europe. This trend was represented by Louis D. Brandeis (1956–1941), whose family came from Bohemia and had been connected with Frankism; on the eve of the First World War he rose to the leadership of the American Zionists. Besides supporting the colonization of Palestine he made efforts, together with the majority of Zionists in America, to help establish

Jewish centers with their own culture also there. Brandeis emphatically rejected the reproach of the 'divided loyalty' of the Zionists—to the homeland and to Israel: it was fully in accord with American ideals to fight for a better life, even for people in other countries. To that extent, it was positively a duty for American Jews to become Zionists. In 1912 the Zionist Henrietta Szold (1860–1945), from a family of Hungarian origin, founded the Hadassah, which was to become the largest Jewish women's organization in the world. She is also to be thanked for the creation of an exemplary health care system in Palestine, and for the rescue of many children and young people in Europe during the Nazi period.

The customs and practices of East European Jews, and even of the supporters of Zionism, were no obstacle to integration in American society. In this they were in accordance with the theory of the 'melting pot', as the English Zionist of East European ancestry Israel Zangwill (1864–1926) had presented it in his 1914 play of the same name: Through immigration the nationalities mix together, bringing ever new traits to the mixture, so creating a new American race without entirely losing their cultural peculiarities. Perhaps even more appropriate was the idea, also approved by Brandeis, of 'cultural pluralism,' which allowed a more thoroughgoing retention of traditions and their further development.

The wave of immigration triggered by the attempted annihilation of the Jews by the Nazis led to a renewal of East European Jewish culture in the USA. Now many ultra-orthodox and Hasidic communities arrived in the New World. They hoped at least to be able to live a religious life in accordance with their own principles. While the synagogue and the prayer room were already important meeting places in American 'shtetls', now other institutions were added, including the *heder* and the *yeshivot*. These communities are still very active today, above all the Lubavitchers, who go back to Rabbi Shneur Zalman's Habad Hasidism, and are distinguished by their ecstatic religiosity. The possibilities of self-reflection are once more part and parcel of ultra-orthodoxy and mystical Hasidism.

This is all the more the case because the crisis facing East European Jewish society in the USA is unmistakable. The clearest sign of this is the dramatic rise in the proportion of mixed marriages. The majority of Jews no longer define themselves in terms of religion. This has clearly done nothing to halt the renewal of Jewish traditions and culture, the promotion of Jewish education, the cultivation of Yiddish—the impact of Isaac Singer is relevant here—research into historical roots in Eastern Europe, and self-characterization as a 'non-religious Jew.' This situation at present exists everywhere among the Diaspora, and even in Israel.

A CENTER OF EAST EUROPEAN JEWRY: GALICIA AND BUKOVINA

In Galicia, part of the Habsburg Monarchy since the Partitions of Poland, conditions resembled those in Poland or Ukraine as much as those in Bukovina, which in 1849 was a separate crown land of the Habsburg Monarchy. Almost one million Jews lived in Galicia, and 100,000 Jews lived in Bukovina before the First World War: over ten percent of the population. The legal situation was a little more favorable than in the Russian Empire, but the East European Jews still had to endure a number of restrictions in respect of their way of life, which were intended—in the manner of the Josephine reforms—to 'civilize' them. Legal equality followed in 1867. Economic conditions were rather worse than those in, for example, Congress Poland. The impoverishment of the Galician Jews reached unimagined extremes. It was so oppressive that so-called 'white slavers' had an easy job here. Around the turn of the century infamous cases shocked the world and were exploited by anti-Semitic propaganda. Bertha Pappenheim (1859–1936) traveled around Galicia a great deal on behalf of Jewish organizations in order to counter this propaganda and to identify the roots of the misery. She saw them not only in social conditions but also in the inferior status of women in the Jewish world, which now, because of the loosening cohesive power of religion and traditional culture, seemed particularly detrimental.

A Jewish proletariat was formed in connection with mineral oil extraction in Drohobycz. A significant part of the Jews—15 percent in 1900—worked in agriculture. As a result of the relaxations in the second half of the nineteenth century there were more and more Jewish inn-keepers, as well as leaseholders and estate administrators. Alongside this development, however, the traditional pattern of conflict was renewed, with a number of additional elements. As intermediaries between town and countryside, estate owners and peasants, the Jews not only became increasingly involved in social and economic conflicts, but also came under threat from the growing national and religious conflicts of Poles, Ruthenians, and German Austrians, Catholics, Russian Orthodox, and Uniates.

When unrest broke out in the countryside in 1898, some Galician–Polish politicians tried to fan the flames with anti-Semitic propaganda. Ritual murder trials in the 1880s and a Catholic Congress in 1893 had prepared the right sort of atmosphere for this. Prominent among the many long-standing prejudices was the belief that Jewish inn-keepers lured the peasants into alcoholism and Jewish usurers drove them to ruin; responsible for all this was the government in Vienna, which favored the Jews. In this way the idea was to turn the unrest against the Habsburg administration, which had hitherto been less of a target for the anger of the peasants than the Polish landowners. The unpopular Jews were to be sacrificed and used as instruments of political manipulation.

The greater part of the Jews in Galicia and in Bukovina were Hasidim. Many *tsaddikim* dynasties gathered their followers around them. Alongside that, rabbinism also maintained its power. From the 1830s a reform-group tried to bring these strands together and thereby laid the foundation for the common struggle against the Maskilim. Life in the shtetls was shaped in all its aspects by religion and tradition. Not least because of a rich literary inheritance, the world of Galician shtetl Jews has remained alive.

To give only a few examples, Leopold von Sacher-Masoch (1836–1895), born as the son of the Galician Chief of Police in Lemberg, was an early discoverer of the Galician landscape for literature and depicted the life of Galician Jewry in many exciting tales. Karl Emil Franzos (1848–1904), son of a Jewish district medical officer in Czortków was influenced by him and wrote travel stories about Galicia and above all strove, in the spirit of the Enlightenment, to portray East European Jewish tradition, and especially Hasidism, as 'backward': indeed, one of his works was entitled *Aus Halb-Asien* or 'From Semi-Asia'. His famous novel *The Pojaz* thematized the attempt of a Jew to break out of the world of the *shtetl* and his turn towards German culture in the manner of the German *Bildungsroman*, as Franzos advocated. Alexander Granach (1890–1945), the famous actor, constructed his autobiography *Da geht ein Mensch* [There Goes a Man], on the pattern of this novel and contributed to the myth of the 'East Galicians.' Hinde Bergner (1870–1942?), born a daughter of the Jewish land-owning family the Rosenblatts in Radimno (Redim) and missing since 1942, wrote her memoirs *In den Langen Winternächten...* [In the Long Winter-nights ...] as a kind of family chronicle, although it displays qualities of high literature. Shmuel Yosef Agnon (1888–1970), grew up as the son of a rabbi in Buczacz [now Buchach, Ukraine] and wrote first in Yiddish, then in Hebrew. One of his most beautiful novels, *Eine einfache Geschichte* [A Simple Story], is set in an East European Jewish *shtetl*. Later he was active on behalf of the Zionists and eventually emigrated to Palestine/Israel. In 1966 he received the Nobel Prize for Literature, not least for his novel *Ore'ah Nata' Lalun* (A Guest for the Night, 1938) which depicts a visit to his hometown of Buczacz. He was one of the most important Hebrew writers of the twentieth century. Bruno Schulz (1892–1942) was the son of a Jewish textile merchant in Drohobycz (now Drohobych, Ukraine). He worked as an art teacher, painted, and wrote fantastical-absurd, linguistically striking stories, for example, *Sklepy cynamonowe* (Cinnamon Shops, 1934). He was murdered in the ghetto by the Nazis in 1942. Schulz belongs among the great storytellers of world literature, and is often compared to Franz Kafka. Joseph Roth (1894–1939), born in Brody, brought to life the world of the Habsburg monarchy and particularly life in Galicia in many novels, stories, and travel writings (a number of passages from his works are cited in the present volume). His friend Soma Morgenstern (1896–1976), born near Tarnopol as the son of a Hasidic steward, vividly presents Jewish life in the country, as well as various religious, spiritual, and political currents in his autobiography *In einer anderen Zeit* [In Another Time] and in the trilogy *Funken im Abgrund* [Sparks in the Abyss]. Manès Sperber (1905–1984), born in Zabłotów, was a psychologist, was active as a Zionist and then as a communist, but broke away from communism under the influence of Stalinism. He set down his life in his memoirs *All das Vergangene...* [All That Has Passed ...]—the first volume *Die Wasserträger Gottes* [The Water-carriers of God] tells us much about childhood in the *shtetl*—while much is also to be found in his novel trilogy *Wie eine Träne im Ozean* [Like a

Teardrop in the Ocean]. Rose Ausländer (1907–1988), born in Czernowitz as a daughter of a Jewish merchant family named the Scherzers, survived the Nazi period under remarkable circumstances and became famous as a lyric poet. Her vivid poetry frequently makes reference to the Galician landscape and the people living there.

In this way descriptions of the co-existence of different peoples often found their way into print.

> The East Galician soil is luxuriant and rich. It has thick oil, yellow tobacco, wheat as heavy as lead, old dreamy forests and rivers and lakes, and above all beautiful, healthy people: Ukrainians, Poles, Jews. All three see one another in a similar way, although they have different customs and practices. The East Galician is clumsy, good-natured, a little lazy and fertile like his soil ... My home village is called Wierzbowce in Polish, Werbowitz in Yiddish, and Werbiwizi in Ukrainian ... In our village of Werbiwizi lived around 150 Ukrainians, among them four Jewish families. All of them made a living from farming. The Jews also had some tatty little shops and one of them had leased the village inn from the lord of the manor. The difference between the village of Werbiwizi and the little town of Horodenka was greater than that between the little town of Horodenka and any European capital city. For Horodenka had all the features of an unsafe, bustling, and cutthroat city, while Werbiwizi was a peaceful and stable village ... The Jewish part of the town was divided into two by the main road: the upper streets and the lower streets ... The upper streets of the town were swept and sprinkled and cared for by the community servants, but no one bothered about the lower streets ... The lower streets were dirty and stank, and if no rain or frost washed away the filth or cleaned the air the people there simply suffocated. The little wooden houses stood strung together, one next to the other, because it was cheaper to build up against the neighbor's wall. One house pressed, supported itself, and leaned against the next like infirm, sickly creatures who are weak and freezing and are afraid to be alone. In these little houses lived the poor: cobblers, tailors, carpenters, plumbers, coopers, bricklayers, furriers, bakers, and all kinds of drivers and porters—all hardworking people who ran around the

whole day trying to earn some bread or five kreuzers so that the rooms full of children would have something to eat. People waited for Tuesday in particular when peasants and Jews from the 48 villages in the district came to the fair. People made their livings from Tuesdays, from this fair. Then there was a crush and running around, puffing and sweating, as if the world was coming to an end.[46]

In many literary treatments and memoirs, it is asserted that Jews and non-Jews—in common with other East European Jewish settlement areas—as a rule lived peacefully and neighborly together. In many cases the Jews served as the link between town and countryside, dealt with business matters for the peasants, and brought news and new cultural developments. Even if they remained 'strange' in many respects, had their own ways of doing things, and because of their autonomous organization made up a separate community, they were nevertheless part of the village or the town, at least among a large part of the population. To this extent they were also trusted. People knew that in general they could rely on them. For example, an Austrian officer noticed in Galicia that the Ruthenian peasants were hostile to everything from outside the village which did not "wear the kaftan of the Jew ... He trusts him [the Jew] more than imperial officials, even more than the uniform of an officer."[47]

Again and again this world, with its difficult material conditions and circumstances which were often felt as narrow and restrictive, provoked an eruption. Both hopes of Messianic salvation and the Haskalah had centers here, reform-Jewish communities developed considerable power, and after 1867 the Enlightenment movement was strengthened, particularly because the relatively good education system provided a favorable foundation. Some of these Jews identified themselves, without totally giving up their Jewish identity, with German culture, others with Polish culture, while a third group saw the future not in acculturation, but in a reflection on 'Jewish nationalism.'

One example of changing orientations is the writer and sculptor Alfred Nossig (1864–1943) from Lviv (Lemberg, Lwów/Ukraine), alongside Cracow, Brody, and Tarnopol the center of Jewish Enlightenment and a point of departure for the movement for a Jewish art renaissance. He originally strove for acculturation to Polish society and as late as the beginning of the 1880s extolled Poland as a reborn Israel continuing the Polish-Jewish symbiosis represented particularly by Adam Mickiewicz under the sign of messianism. Disappointed by growing anti-Semitic tendencies he then turned to Jewish nationalism. He now set as his goal the establishment of a Jewish state in Palestine and became one of the most important theorists of Jewish nationalism in Galicia. As early as 1886, he clearly formulated the argument that the conflicts between Jews and non-Jews could be eliminated only if the Diaspora was ended and the majority of Jews were able to fashion a full-fledged state in their original homeland. Nossig's radical views were controversial even among Zionists, however. In 1883 the first national Jewish organization had been founded in Lviv, soon to be followed by other groups. The prevalent view aimed at the settlement in Palestine of poorer and 'at-risk' Jews as colonizing farmers and safeguarding Jewish national existence in Galicia itself. The national concept was therefore supposed to be developed in the country in which one was living. This characterized the peculiar nature of Zionism in Eastern Europe and was related to the development of a new self-consciousness and common ground among East European Jews.

At the first Zionist Congress in Basel in 1897 Abraham Salz (1864–1941) from Tarnów, who was also elected as second vice-president, reported on the situation of the Jews in Galicia, and Mayer Ebner (1872–1955) from Czernowitz did the same for Bukovina. Under the surface a conflict was brewing between

Western–Jewish Zionists, who were reproached with neglecting work in the Diaspora. This erupted later when Herzl tried to hinder the colonization activities of Galicians in Palestine because he first wanted a political guarantee of certain 'settlement rights.' There were also conflicts with Orthodox Jews, however, and with assimilation-oriented Jews in Galicia, among whom the Poland-friendly line gradually became prevalent. They feared that their position would be threatened by the political activities of the Zionists—also in religious communities—and that the Jews would be drawn even more deeply into the struggle between the nationalities in Galicia.

At the beginning of the 1890s the 'Jewish National Party' was founded to make it possible to act independently in Galicia. The Jewish nationalists, concentrated overwhelmingly in Lviv, considered the Zionist movement in Galicia to be the strongest and believed that the Viennese Zionists did not represent them adequately. The latter did not want an organizational split, however, and in 1893 joined with the 'General Jewish–National Party of Austria' formed in Cracow. As long as they recognized the aspirations of the Galicians, the common organization worked. In 1895 they established a board in the form of a 'political society' in order to better coordinate regional policy. Their efforts were directed towards achieving national autonomy and equal legal status, as both people and nation, with the other peoples in Galicia and throughout the Habsburg Empire.

Concrete proposals for the alleviation of poverty, the promotion of economic activity, and the improvement of education and culture had a considerable following in the Jewish population. This support also existed in the working class; the Poale Zion was the most active group organizationally. At the Austrian parliamentary elections of 1900–1901 the Zionists were even able to return a representative for the first time, from the Galician electoral district of Brody. In 1907, at the first general and direct elections to the house of representatives of the *Reichsrat*, 13 Jewish representatives were elected. Four of them were Zionist politicians from Galicia and Bukovina. They formed the 'Jewish Club,' a unique phenomenon in Europe at that time. Recognition of Jewish nationality and of national autonomy—with Yiddish as the national language—could no longer be excluded from political discussions in the Habsburg Empire. Ultimately, recognition could not be achieved: the Austrian government feared that 'Germanness' would be weakened if the Jewish population was able to form a separate nationality. Nevertheless, the right to proclaim a Jewish nationality was granted to in Bukovina in 1910.

At the elections of 1911, however, the Zionists and the Jewish nationalists suffered a defeat. The responsibility for this lies with the assimilated Jews and the Orthodox who had tried by every means possible to hinder them. With this in view they formed alliances not only with one another but also with Polish parties. An analysis of the election results, however, shows that the support for Zionism among the Jews was still extremely broad. In the *shtetls*, the assimilated Jews and the Orthodox met with vigorous disapproval from the population influenced by the rabbis or *tsaddikim*. Even if there was support for the colonization of Palestine, only the religious Zionists of the Misrahi made inroads. At the same time, those who were beginning to liberate themselves from traditional ties frequently voted for Zionist candidates. An indication of the strength of the Zionists is given by the report from Galicia for the Tenth Zionist Congress in Basel in 1911, which talks of 103 associations and 13 youth organizations with around 10,000 members.

The workers' movement organized itself as a Jewish Section within Polish social democracy, then in 1905 in the independent Jewish Social Democratic Party of Galicia, which worked closely together with the Bund. There were also alliances with *Poale Tsiyon*, despite the general inter-Jewish rivalry. The common political demands aimed at the non-territorial autonomy of the Jews. A particular role within Galician Jewry was played by the Cracow group of 'independent Jews' who rejected both assimilation and party ideologies, and supported democracy and equal rights. At the *Reichsrat* elections of 1900 their candidate won against the president of the Jewish community of Cracow, an adherent of assimilation who had been supported by Polish conservatives.

A POSITIVE MODEL WITH CONTRADICTIONS: HUNGARY

Events in Hungary in many respects fall outside the framework of the present volume. Surprisingly, as early as the second half of the nineteenth century the magnates demanded equal legal status for the Jews, which, however, was long rejected by the Habsburg central government. Nevertheless, some improvements could be achieved. A step backwards was taken in the 1840s when surging nationalism, culminating in the Revolution of 1848, came into conflict with the interests of the Jews. On 14 March 1848 a people's assembly in Budapest held out the prospect of equal rights to the Jews, who had participated in the Freedom Fight in significant numbers. Only a few days later, however, this resolution had to be withdrawn under pressure from mass demonstrations, principally involving petit bourgeoisie and craftsmen, who saw the Jews as the cause of their parlous situation. In many places Jews were robbed and abused, and synagogues were destroyed. Even Budapest did not go unscathed. In spite of this, many Jews stepped forward to defend Hungary against the advancing Austrians, as a consequence of which they were compelled to pay enormous financial penalties. Nevertheless, the Hungarian Parliament granted them equal rights on 28 July 1849, before it was itself scattered.

In 1867 the constitution for the double monarchy of Austria–Hungary finally established equal rights; confessional equality for the Jews followed in 1895. However, there was still discrimination, if to a lesser extent in Hungary than elsewhere. People expected assimilation, however, in this case Magyarization. This led to a kind of *Kulturkampf*: Orthodox Jews—as a rule East European Jews and conservative rabbis—were unwilling to take this step. The teachings of Hatam Sofer and his successors, who rejected any kind of novelty and from an ultra-orthodox standpoint established the Jews as a nation, exercised great influence. This led to violent conflicts with the liberal reform wing. After the congress of representatives of the Jewish communities at the end of 1868–beginning of 1869, at which the reformers had the majority, the Jews split into separate organizations: the reform-oriented 'Neologi,' the largest group; the Orthodox; and the 'Status-quo-ante- faction, which wanted to maintain the state of things as it had been before the Congress. In Hungary, anti-Jewish tendencies certainly existed. On the surface they found expression in the formation of anti-Semitic groups from the 1840s and in the 'ritual murder' scandal of Tiszaeszlár in 1882–1883. All in all, however, up until the First World War the country government policies were relatively friendly to the Jews. How did this extraordinary situation come about?

The Jewish population in Hungary had grown extremely quickly. Its share of the population as a whole had been around one percent (80,000 persons) at the time of Joseph II, but by the First World War it was five percent (900,000 persons). In the early eighteenth century most Jewish immigrants—two-thirds of the Jews living in Hungary at that time—were from Moravia and, to a lesser extent, Poland. From the end of the eighteenth century, immigrants from Galicia predominated, who also bolstered the Jewish communities in the Carpathians. The upper nobility promoted their settlement. Many prospered, particularly if they already had sufficient financial means, which was often the case with Jews from Moravia. It was said, a little exaggeratedly:

> The Jew migrates to Mármaros. There he still works as a beggar, wage laborer, and inn-keeper. His son goes two counties further to the West and becomes a factory owner, merchant, or large-scale leaseholder. If he goes one or two counties further in the country he is already a large landowner and acquires a castle. In Budapest his aim is ennoblement, a seat in parliament, and a baronetcy. And when he has a couple of million he moves to Vienna.[48]

This passage in many ways provides an exemplary summary of developments. The migrating Jews–and not least the East European Jews from Galicia—took on functions which they had already occupied in Poland, and partly in Bohemia and Moravia. In this way they entered into a close symbiosis with the high nobility, which in Hungary remained in existence when it was destroyed in Poland. The Hungarian nobility, liberally disposed because of its opposition to Habsburg absolutism, wanted to play an active part in the financial economy and build up a modern agriculture. The experienced Jews could help them a great deal in this. They became once again leaseholders, administrators, and inn-keepers. They often formed part, together with the nobility, of an economic system to which Jewish wholesalers and bankers also belonged, in Pest or even in Vienna or Frankfurt. Jews who had become rich then went to the cities—as already mentioned—above all to Budapest. In 1910 Jews made up 25 percent of the population (in the downtown business quarters over 35 percent). Here a big bourgeois financial elite emerged, independent of the high nobility, but still closely linked to it economically.

In contrast to Poland, this alliance was more or less maintained in Hungary until the First World War. One may speak of a tacit 'contract of assimilation' (Viktor Karády): the majority of Hungarian Jews were ready to Magyarize and put their abilities at the disposal of the development of society as a whole. In return, their equal rights and their integration in Hungarian society was recognized and not questioned by the powers-that-be. By invoking the Khazars, even a common Hungarian–Jewish history could be constructed. The Zionists basically accepted this 'contract,' but demanded loyalty and support for endangered Jews in other countries. As a result they gave rise to violent reactions from many assimilated Jews who saw their position in Hungarian society threatened.[49]

The 'assimilation contract' was not entirely uncontentious, however. For example, debt-ridden nobles in particular were against it. The main opponents of the Jews were German burghers in the cities, however—which had no particular significance in relation to society as a whole—and above all the peasants, as in Poland and Russia. On the basis of social conflicts anti-Jewish resentments emerged, followed later by anti-Semitism. A clear sign of this was the peasant uprising in the eastern region in 1831, primarily directed against manorial lords and village Jews.

The aversion of the long-settled Jews against immigrants was a significant factor in the growth of anti-Semitic tendencies, and one which ultimately found expression in the above-mentioned religious division. The assimilated reform Jews rejected the Orthodox or Hasidic East European Jews (*Ostjuden*) because they intensified the conflicts concerning their place in society. As more and more Jews, particularly *Ostjuden*, came to Budapest the—false—impression was reinforced that hordes of Jewish 'foreigners' were immigrating. From this the concept of 'good assimilated' and 'bad Galician' Jews which after the First World

War formed the basis for open anti-Semitism. This could no longer be corrected by the Jewish upper stratum because they had themselves once promulgated this distinction.

DIFFERENT ATTITUDES TO THE EMANCIPATION OF THE JEWS IN ROMANIA, SERBIA, AND BULGARIA

Around 300,000 Jews lived in Romania at the beginning of the twentieth century, around four percent of the population. In the course of the nineteenth century the proportion of East European Jews had increased considerably because many refugees from the Russian Empire and Galicia had immigrated who wanted to escape military service and the mounting oppression. Most settled in Moldavia. In Bucharest the Jews made up around 15 percent of the population around the turn of the century, and in Iasi over 40 percent. The ruling circles regarded the immigrants as 'foreigners' and transferred this notion to all the Jews living in Romania.

Turkey, under whose formal overlordship Romania initially still stood in the nineteenth century, had had to accept the political influence of the Tsarist Empire for a further five years in the Peace of Adrianople in 1829. In this way Romania had a kind of constitution imposed upon it in 1832. It denied the Jews political rights, prohibited them from leasing settlement land, and permitted naturalization only to Christians. These legal restrictions remained in force when the constitution was abolished in 1848.

In the 1860s the discussions concerning the 'Jewish question' came to a head. In 1862 Moldavia and Walachia were united as a princedom of Romania. In 1866 Karl von Hohenzollern-Sigmaringen became the successor of the abdicating first prince, Alexandru Cuza. During the ensuing constitutional debates some politicians stirred up the masses in Bucharest to such an extent that Parliament was put under siege. The frightened deputies promised that the Jews would not be given equal rights. Nevertheless, the crowd completely destroyed the synagogue in Bucharest and abused Jewish passers-by. A number of foreign states—to start with, Austria–Hungary—intervened for the sake of their 'protected Jews' residing in Romania. But things only got worse. The liberal government took measures to drive the Jews out of the village—again primarily out of the licensed trade—and whoever did not satisfy a minimum property qualification also had to leave the towns (and so Romania) as a 'vagabond.' There were tragic scenes at the borders, some with a fatal outcome.

The Berlin Congress of 1878 turned into a highpoint of the debate concerning the equal rights of Jews. In the Russian–Turkish War of 1877 Romania had obtained its full independence from the Ottoman Empire. Not least because of the impression made by the representations of the Alliance Israélite—an organization in Paris which supported its oppressed co-religionists—the European Great Powers declared that they would only be able to recognize Romanian independence if the Jews were given equal rights. Even Russia, after some hesitation, endorsed this action. In the background was the hope that general religious equality could eliminate a trouble spot in the Balkan. This demand was laid down in Article 44 of the Treaty of Berlin.

The fact that the Romanian government had to give in to pressure did not make the already unpopular Jews any more popular. As regards the implementation of the terms of the Treaty the Romanian authorities were able to obtain concessions and delays from the Great Powers until the naturalization of the Jews only needed to be accomplished on an individual basis. Each naturalization application had to be dealt with by a special parliamentary committee. As a result, relatively few cases had a positive outcome. The Great Powers were no longer concerned or were themselves—for example, Germany and Austria–Hungary—seized by anti-Semitic tendencies. The railway line through Romania was more important to the German government than the rights of the Jews.

So Romania remained, alongside Russia, the only European state without equal legal status for the Jews. Special laws prescribed that Jews could conduct no trade in tobacco—a state monopoly—that they could not run an inn, and that they could not work on the nationalized railways or in any itinerant trade. High school attendance was permitted only when there were not enough non-Jewish applicants. Jews could not own land. In 1902 it was additionally ordered that only Romanian citizens could be accepted by the craftsmens' guilds. In this way many Jews were put out of work. A large number were forced to emigrate.

From 1876 the Jews had to undertake military service, although they could not become officers. This did little to promote their patriotism, which certainly existed. At the end of 1895 an Anti-Semitic Alliance was founded in Bucharest. Many high-ranking persons in public life belonged to it, including members of the government. The goal of this group, which tried to maintain the strictest secrecy, was to force the Jews out of economic life and to hurry along their emigration. The agitators made copious use of religious prejudices. The Alliance was responsible for a number of pogroms.

That assimilation was out of the question in such circumstances is self evident. The majority of Jews lived in the same districts and spoke Yiddish. Insofar as they were active politically, most leaned towards the left. In order to win votes some social-democratic party leaders had at first tried to build up 'Jew-free' organizations. They were defeated, however, and after their departure the party was open to Jews once more.

In 1907 a major peasant uprising broke out, which, in accordance with the relevant agitation, was in places directed against the Jews as the alleged cause of poverty. Many Jews were robbed and abused. As the unrest proceeded, however, the peasants turned directly against the big landowners. A contributory factor in this may have been the fact that the socialists, among whom there were many Jews, tried to denounce the poverty of the peasants and at the same time to reduce their hostility to the Jews. As a result, after the bloody defeat of the uprising, Jewish socialists were held responsible for the unrest and partly deported. Anti-Semitism once again proved itself as an extremely handy instrument for manipulation in any direction.

Things developed differently in Serbia and Bulgaria. Serbia, where around 5,000 Jews lived in the middle of the nineteenth century, fulfilled the terms of the Treaty of Berlin and granted the Jews equal rights. There had been an interesting disagreement at the Congress of Berlin on this subject. The tsarist foreign minister Gorchakov expressed the opinion that "the Jews of Berlin, Paris, London, and Vienna, from whom civil and political rights could not reasonably be withheld, should not be compared with the Jews of Serbia, Romania, and some Russian provinces, who constitute a veritable scourge for the native population." Bismarck retorted that "this sad situation of the Jews could probably be traced back to the restriction of their civil and political rights." In reply, Gorchakov declared that "the Russian government, to protect the interests of the population, could not avoid placing the Jews of some provinces under special regulations." Finally, the view represented by the French foreign minister, Waddington, was adopted, to the effect that "Serbia, which was striving to join the European family of states, must resolve to accept principles which in all European states form the basis of social organization."[50]

The situation in Bulgaria was similar. Here too, around 10,000 Jews received equal rights guaranteed by international law in 1879. Their number rose until the turn of the century, not least because of an expansion of territory in 1885, climbing to around 30,000, one percent of the population. Approximately one-third of them lived in the capital, Sofia. It is perhaps worth mentioning that at that time predominantly Sephardim settled there, speaking Ladino or Judeo-Spanish. The trend towards assimilation was relatively small, while the Zionists were quickly able to extend their influence after the turn of the century. Despite some anti-Jewish riots, anti-Semitism was not as open as elsewhere. One of the causes of this may have been the fact that the figure of 'the enemy' was so unambiguously represented by the Turks.

A 'RITUAL MURDER': THE CASE OF BOHEMIA AND MORAVIA

Assimilation took place most rapidly in Bohemia and Moravia. Around the turn of the century around 150,000 Jews lived in Bohemia and Moravia, 1.5 percent of the population. In Prague—together with the inner suburbs—they made up 8 percent of the population (27,000 persons). In the eighteenth century the Jews here were intermediaries between town and countryside, in symbiosis with the nobility. The apparently tolerant Josephine legislation and its consequences had worked out to the detriment of rural Jews. Already restricted by the 'familiant' policy, the Jews could by no means settle wherever they chose. In Prague, the center of the country, and in other cities they had to live in particular districts. Only a few, as a rule the extremely rich, were allowed to move to 'Christian' streets.

In 1849 the Habsburg state finally granted freedom of movement and abolished the marriage law; in 1852 the barriers of the ghetto in Prague came down; and in 1867 full legal equality was established by law. At this time a small number of Jews, particularly in Bohemia—but also in some Moravian towns, especially Brünn—belonged to the upper class. This was the consequence of rapid industrialization from the 1830s, which took place more quickly in Bohemia than anywhere else in Eastern Europe. Bohemia rose to become the industrial center of the Habsburg Empire. Jewish entrepreneurs, who were concentrated in Prague, played an exceptional role in this development. This made assimilation to the German–Austrian bourgeoisie easier for them.

In this way they entered an area of conflict which we have already encountered in another guise. It was formed and played out chiefly in the towns, while in the countryside, on account of the favorable socio-economic conditions there, more open anti-Semitism barely developed. Many Czechs identified the Jews with the Germans, the ruling class, standing in the way of national emancipation, and also with the capitalists, exploiters of the Czech proletariat. Social conflict due to industrialization was now added to the traditional anti-Jewish prejudices, together with the national conflict. Above all, urban districts became fertile soil for nationalism and anti-Semitism, since insecure and poorly educated workers from the countryside lived alongside craftsmen and traders who felt that their livelihoods were threatened.

Anti-Jewish unrest continually broke out in Prague, other parts of Bohemia, and of Moravia. Nationalist parties increasingly took advantage of this mood in order to attract followers and votes. This was as much true of the Young Czechs as of the National Socialist Party which (despite its anti-Semitic elements, should not to be confused with the later German party of the same name) and also of German-nationalist clubs and associations. As in Poland economic boycotts were organized under the motto: 'Each to his own!'

The tensions reached their climax shortly before the turn of the century. In 1897 Earl Kazimierz Badeni had to resign after the government's plan to elevate Czech to the status of an administrative language in Bohemia and Moravia failed because of German-nationalist resistance. The disappointment of the Czechs found expression at the end of the same year in an assault, sparked off by something trivial, on German institutions and businesses in Prague. This in turn became a widespread anti-Jewish riot, even against poor Jews in their traditional district of Josefov. The government was forced to impose a state of emergency in order to restore peace and order. Even after the unrest had come to an end, rabble-rousing anti-Jewish propaganda continued.

At this turbulent time a nineteen-year-old girl was found murdered on 1 April 1899 in the vicinity of an east Bohemian village, as it turned out with a large cut on her throat. Nationalist circles quickly cast suspicion on the Jews and indeed a suspect was soon discovered, a Jewish journeyman-shoemaker, Leopold Hilsner. In an unprecedented campaign, it was asserted that Hilsner had carried out a ritual murder against the Christian girl in order to obtain her blood for ritual purposes during Passover. The general anti-Jewish hysteria increased, and ritual murders were supposed to have been carried out in a number of places. Even the court could not remain aloof from the inflamed atmosphere. Hilsner was condemned to death.

The defense was able to refute the accusation of ritual murder by means of expert witnesses, however, and the trial had to be put before the appellate court. Hilsner was now assumed to have acted from sexual motives, which had already formed part of the previous charges. He was also supposed to have carried out a second, hitherto unsolved murder of a girl. Despite a lack of evidence in 1900 the court condemned Hilsner to death once again. The judgment was then commuted to life imprisonment, and in 1916 a pardon was finally granted. In 1961 the brother of the murdered girl made a deathbed confession: he had murdered the girl so he would not have to pay her dowry.

Few people turned their face against the prevailing view of the period. Among them were social democrats, the most significant political force to fight consistently against anti-Semitism. Another was the sociology professor and later President of Czechoslovakia Tomáš G. Masaryk (1850–1937), who was dubbed 'knight of the Jews' for his trouble. Masaryk had to suspend his teaching temporarily because of the demonstrations directed against him by Czech students. In 1871 August Rohling, a theology professor teaching in Vienna but originally from Westphalia, had provided in his book *Der Talmudjude* ['The Jew of the Talmud'] a pseudo-scientific proof of accusations of ritual murder. In the Austro-Hungarian Empire there were twelve such trials between 1867 and 1914. Only one ended with a guilty verdict, however.

The Jews were deeply affected by these events. Their great hopes of assimilation—not only those of the small upper class, but also those of many poor immigrant Jews—crumbled. In Prague difficulties were made worse by the 'redevelopment' of the Josefov district between 1893 and 1905, when the former ghetto was mostly torn down, and replaced by modern buildings. The Jews who lived there were now scattered throughout the city; what had been an important point of reference for them had been lost. At the same time, poverty made further inroads into the Jewish population. Economic development caused many to sink into the lowest stratum of 'scroungers,' which after the turn of the century was swelled further by the renewed influx of Jews fleeing the pogroms in Russia. Most West European Jews looked on the latter with mistrust and abhorrence. Others, however, who in the course of these conflicts increasingly reflected on their Jewishness, saw in them the roots of their identity.

The spectrum of reactions to the new situation was just as wide as in other East European countries. Assimilation tendencies are visible, for example, in census statistics on everyday speech, which was tantamount to a profession of national belonging. In Prague in 1890 74 percent of Jews stated that they used German as their everyday language, but in 1900 it was only around 45 percent. This indicates how strong the initial endeavors were to become part of the German community. The profound attachment to German culture is also reflected in the data. Franz Kafka once wrote:

> Most wanted to [leave their Jewishness behind them] and started to write in German; that's what they wanted, but with their hind legs they clung on to the Judaism of their fathers and with their forelegs they were unable to find a new footing.[51]

While the upper class barely changed its attitude, the middle stratum, because of its social and economic interests, began to reorient itself after the riots before the turn of the century. They declared themselves Czechs in the hope that this would gradually overcome Czech hostility. These 'Czecho-Jews' soon foundered, however, because of the unwelcoming stance of many Czechs who still saw Jews as significant competition as regards social advancement. The majority of the Jewish lower class tried, in their traditional contexts, to struggle through without assimilation. Some Jews join the Social Democrats, others the Zionists. Of particular significance in the search for a new Jewish consciousness was the Prague school of Zionism, influenced by Martin Buber. This put cultural and spiritual renewal at the center of things and assumed a conciliatory stance. This included the effort to find "a peaceful and friendly agreement with the Arabs" in Palestine. The historian and political scientist Hans Kohn (1891–1971) declared: "Would not all our feelings concerning our oppressors be laughable if we—no longer oppressed, but having come to power—were to deprive the Arabs of their rights or strive to deprive them of their nation?"[52]

Many found no way out of their identity crisis. The attitude of many assimilation-oriented Jews, which often went to the point of self-humiliation, led in many cases to a loss of self-esteem, in a hatred of all things 'Jewish.' Franz Kafka wrote in a letter:

> Sometimes I would like to stuff them into the drawer of the linen cupboard just because they are Jews (myself included), then wait for a while, then open the drawer a little to see if they have all suffocated, and if not, shove the drawer back in again and carry on until the job's done.[53]

Others even developed a specifically Jewish anti-Semitism, above all against the East European Jews, who people abused as 'vermin.' Openly anti-Semitic groups were financed to a not insignificant extent by donations from Jews. This was a particularly sad episode. Such tendencies also appeared elsewhere, for example, in Germany, especially against the East European Jews, who were blamed for anti-Semitism and the failure of assimilation. They were, of course, only of marginal importance, but they helped to confirm the prejudices of non-Jewish circles, because they were taken to be particularly plausible.

A large proportion of these reactions gave expression to the helplessness of many Jews, which stemmed from the poorly understood processes of radical socio-economic change. Traditional functions were lost, traditional values lost their credibility. In principle these problems resembled those of the East European Jews in Poland, Russia, and elsewhere (and we also find them, in other guises, outside Jewry).

Part IV
ATTEMPTED ANNIHILATION AND NEW HOPE

THE JEWS IN THE RUSSIAN REVOLUTION AND IN THE SOVIET UNION

During the First World War, many Jews played an important role in the growing democratic and revolutionary movement. Many left-wingers were Jews. They were active in organizations which sought to provide relief for the victims of war or were occupied with the problems—for example, economic questions—of the post-war period. They were also involved in political groups, from the Jewish Workers' Bund and *Poale Tsiyon*, through various socialist parties, to the Bolsheviks, the radical wing of Russian social democracy. Few leading well-to-do Jews supported this stance. To be sure, they were involved in humanitarian work, but they traditionally wanted nothing to do with politics. Moreover, they naturally feared a revolution, and certainly a loss of influence in Jewish communities, over which they had served as community leaders [*Gemeindevorsteher*] or in similar important posts.

The February Revolution of 1917 finally ended the special legal position of the Jews. When the Bolsheviks, who were now calling themselves communists, won power as a result of the so-called 'October Revolution' shortly afterwards, they confirmed the equal rights of the Jews. Nevertheless, the time of suffering was not yet over. The first flashpoint was Ukraine. This region had become independent as a result of the Peace of Brest-Litovsk between Imperial Germany and Soviet Russia. There was a violent struggle for power between various factions and the Bolsheviks, who also claimed legitimacy and called on the Red Army for help. Some of the anti-communist forces exploited the traditional conflict which had existed since 1648 and stirred up peasants and soldiers against the Jews, equating them with the communists. Horrific pogroms ensued. The soldiers of the 'White Army' led by Anton I. Denikin (1872–1947) and of the Ataman Symon Petlyura (1879–1926) were heavily involved in this. For the Jews, Red Army oldiers were liberators, although in the course of these cruel struggles they could never be safe from any side.

In 1920, after several armed conflicts and Soviet peace offers, when the Bolsheviks appeared to have the upper hand in Ukraine—war broke out between Poland and Soviet Russia. In Poland it was widely hoped to restore the borders of 1772. The Polish troops at first advanced far to the east. Once again many Jews were slaughtered in full-blown massacres. The Red Army counterattacked, and advanced all the way to Warsaw, hoping to carry world evolution to the West. An armistice was only reached after a Polish counteroffensive. In 1921 peace was finally agreed, which brought some degree of calm to the population in the disputed regions and so also to the Jews for the next few years.

From a legal standpoint, the situation for Jews in Russia was now better than it had ever been. Despite this new problems soon arose. The first to suffer were Jewish entrepreneurs who fell victim to the nationalization of industry from June 1918. Then the middlemen suffered, the traditional intermediaries: during the Civil War exchange between town and countryside was considerably reduced or organized by the state. The Jews lost their function and the *shtetls* became deserted. Many Jewish traders were convicted of being speculators or even shot.

There was something of a recovery when from 1921, under the so-called New Economic Policy, private capitalism was partly restored. In 1926–1927 the 2.7 million Jews in the Soviet Union constituted 2 percent of the total population, but 8 percent of urban residents, 20 percent of businessmen, and 40 percent of craftsmen. With the transition to accelerated industrialization and collectivization, not to mention Stalinism from the end of the 1920s, the situation changed once more. Private enterprise was completely forbidden. Many Jews were declared class enemies, and lost their right to vote, obtain higher education and receive medical care and food ration cards.

On the other hand, many hitherto jobless and functionless Jews now had the opportunity to find work in the new, hastily established industrial firms or to participate in colonization projects. At first, Jewish land settlements were proposed in Southern Russia or in the Crimea in order to link up with traditional centers. Former Bundists and left-wing Zionists were as active in this respect as the 'Jewish Section' within the Communist Party. After protests in the areas concerned, the Party leadership decided in 1928 to give preference to Birobidzhan in far eastern Russia, almost at the Pacific. The strategic interest of securing the borders was also behind this decision, as well as the fact that in this way the Jews could be more easily assimilated in Asia than in their accustomed environment. However, because of the harsh climate a range of inducements had to be offered in order to attract colonizers: they were supposed to be able, in accordance with the prevailing nationalities theory which stated that each nation required its own territory, to create their own 'Jewish region' as a substitute for the absent Jewish state in Israel. Naturally, propaganda benefits were also expected from this. Although the plan was not very successful—the area was too unattractive—in 1934 Birobidzhan was proclaimed a 'Jewish Autonomous Region,' and it has remained so until this day. The Jews only make up a minority of the population here, but there is still a Yiddish newspaper and Yiddish instruction in schools. Yiddish culture is supposed to be able to develop. With this the question of the relationship between Soviet power and the Jews arises.

In the first years after the October Revolution there were many Jews among the leading communists: Trotsky, Zinoviev, Kamenev, Sverdlov, Ioffe, Radek, Riazanov, and many others. Jews were appointed to important positions in public offices, the education system, company managements, and elsewhere. This gave rise to hatred in their opponents and fostered the saying that Jews are communists (and vice versa).

These Jews were assimilated: socialist ideas, world revolution, and the class struggle were more important to them than the national and religious questions facing Jewry. Other Jews integrated for the sake of social advancement. The majority of Soviet Jews, however, remained unwilling to assimilate. In 1926 three-quarters of Jews gave Yiddish as their mother-tongue, although this figure should be treated with care. They by no means had things easy: as a result of the theoretically and practically established atheism, a positive assault on religion took place in the first years after 1917: religious instruction or even the teaching of the Hebrew language were forbidden. Rabbis were prevented from fulfilling their duties. Furthermore, the development of the one-party state and the communists' monopoly of political power forced Jewish political parties, and also such groups as the Zionists, to abandon their activities. The Bund—unlike in Poland—was subsumed by the Communist Party as early as 1920, during the period of 'War Communism,' and many of its members emigrated. The last Jewish party—and at the same time the last party apart from the Communist Party in the Soviet Union in general—*Poale Tsiyon,* was dissolved in 1928. Until this time *halutsim* or 'pioneers' in socialist organized settlements had been able to prepare for life in a future state of Zion. The 'Jewish Section' endeavored to gradually expunge any form of political competition, just as it wished to repress religious Jewry, often even more harshly than the Party leadership itself.

Nevertheless, the Jews at first enjoyed cultural autonomy. Yiddish schools were permitted, as were theaters and publications. Cultural autonomy and legal equality moved many Jews who had emigrated to return to Russia. In Jewish literature, science, and journalism there was a new blossoming which could be linked to beginnings before the Revolution of 1917.

In the 1920s the Soviet government was very impressed by this. The Jewish communities had been dissolved as religious entities, after their initial recognition in 1919, and their property had been nationalized. Now soviets (councils) were being established in villages, towns, and regions which were permitted to use Yiddish as a language of administration and were given a range of rights of self-administration. Assertive action was taken against anti-Semitic tendencies.[1]

Despite many reservations—because, for example, the faith and traditions of the Jews, for whom culture, everyday life, and religion formed a unity, had outwardly been 'turned upside down'—in 1927 Joseph Roth declared:

> But everyone must respectfully observe how one people is liberated from having to suffer humiliation and another from wielding humiliation as an instrument of abuse; how the beaten are delivered from pain and those who beat them from the curse which is worse than pain. That is the great deed of the Russian Revolution.[2]

All this changed under Stalinism. The Jewish sections within the Communist Party were abolished in 1930. In the power struggle at the top of the party, Stalin and his followers used specifically anti-Jewish slogans. Since some of their opponents were Jewish, it was said, they must be petit bourgeois Jewish intellectuals who had nothing in common with the working class. Use was made of the underlying popular mistrust of the many Jews in high positions or even among the speculators and profiteers during the NEP. Countless Jews also fell victim to the Stalinist Terror, the purges, in the 1930s, not least artists and scientists. Birobidzhan was not spared either. Cultural autonomy was abolished as 'bourgeois nationalism' in favor of increased centralization and Russification—although officially it was still permitted to use Yiddish in Birobidzhan. After the Hitler–Stalin Pact of 1939, German–Jewish communists who had fled to the Soviet Union were handed over to the Gestapo. But even after the beginning of the war with Germany in 1941 there was no pause. For example, the Bundists Wiktor Alter and Henryk Erlich, who had fled from Poland, did not survive their persecution.

The action taken against them led to a new nationalist response on the part of the Jews, however. They were strengthened by the annexation of parts of Poland, Romania, and the Baltic regions by the Soviet Union in 1939–1940, since a further two million Jews were added to the existing almost three million. Life inside the Jewish community became more active. Their nationalist inclinations were strengthened by the knowledge that among the accomplices of the Nazis in the conquered territories there were many Ukrainians, Lithuanians, and Romanians who had by no means left behind their traditional anti-Semitism. Hope in the Soviet government was revived by the formation in 1942 of an 'Anti-Fascist Jewish Committee' (primarily for the purpose of obtaining support for the Soviet Union in the Anglo-Saxon countries), which initially called for the establishment of a State of Israel after the war.

These hopes were soon dashed, however. In Russia the development of Jewish life was no longer possible. On the contrary: from autumn 1948, the anti-Jewish line was resumed. The beginning of this had been marked in January 1948 by the murder, disguised as a car accident, of the famous actor and chairman of the Anti-Fascist Committee Solomon M. Michoels (1890–1948). In what followed, the Committee was abolished as 'anti-Soviet'; it was only officially rehabilitated at the beginning of 1989 by a commission of the Politburo. Many Jewish functionaries were then murdered and accused of anti-Soviet activities and contact with the West. They were supposed to be part of an 'imperialist' plot, in which 'Zionist' organizations in Israel were also involved. These 'rootless cosmopolitans' were conspirators and spies. Once again there were countless executions and deportations to concentration camps. This anti-Jewish wave also spread to other countries in the Communist block and there too was followed by persecution. The most sensational occurrences were the show trials and death sentences against leading communists in Czechoslovakia and Hungary.

At the beginning of 1953 the Soviet secret service announced that it had 'discovered' a plot involving several prominent doctors to kill the leaders of the Soviet Union with Stalin at the head. 'By chance' the members of this alleged conspiracy were mainly Jewish. It was supposed to have been financed by the US secret service and international Jewish organizations. The arrested doctors were threatened with execution. Moreover, rumors were circulating that Stalin wanted to expel all Jews from the European part of the Soviet Union. Fortunately, he died in March 1953. The doctors were rehabilitated and released. After that, state anti-Semitism disappeared, although it survived under the surface. Around 1.8 million Jews lived in the Soviet Union, though other estimates give a higher figure or very uncertain grounds. Discrimination against them remained both as regards religious practice and the entry of Jewish nationality in passports, which often led to disadvantages without the recompense of a positive expression of nationality. The link with Israel created mistrust and it was difficult to leave the country. Later, after the dissolution of the Soviet Union, the number of emigrants increased by leaps and bounds, particularly because many felt threatened by the now openly expressed anti-Semitism. On the other hand, normal religious and intellectual life was now possible again in the Jewish community. Reflection on Jewish identity commenced in earnest and more and more people began to take an interest in Jewish history and culture.

EAST EUROPEAN JEWISH NATIONALITY AND NEW WAVES OF ANTI-SEMITISM: THE JEWS IN POLAND BETWEEN THE TWO WORLD WARS

During the First World War the Jews in Poland suffered considerably under the Russian administration, which suspected them of collaborating with the Germans. The government annulled the Pale of Settlement as a consequence of the German advance, and many Jews were deported to central Russia.

The Polish National Democrats continued their familiar anti-Jewish agitation, with the difference that they now lambasted not the alleged Russophilia of the 'Litvaks,' but the Germanophilia of all Jews. Once more, Jews found themselves under attack from all sides. In the feverish atmosphere—the Poles hoped for an independent state as the outcome of the war—even accusations characteristically medieval, that Jews were poisoning streams or milk, made themselves heard. Anti-Jewish incidents multiplied. Within Polish political groups there were violent conflicts concerning the position of Jews in a future Polish state in which traditional patterns of argument resurfaced. For example, a distinction was made between assimilated Jews, with whom it was possible to co-operate, and Orthodox or Hasidic Jews, with whom it was not. The Warsaw municipal authorities, at the end of December 1916, went as far as banning from particularly attractive parks those persons who were not dressed in "clean, orderly, or European clothing", by which was meant those who dressed in traditional Jewish garb. One's attitude to assimilation was taken to be expressed by one's choice of clothes, and the authorities took it upon themselves to take action in this matter. Only after energetic protests were such measures moderated. There were similar conflicts in other areas. Time and again unrest which had arisen as a result of something quite unconnected with the Jews degenerated into the looting of Jewish businesses.

Relations between Poles and Jews deteriorated appreciably. In the turmoil caused by the creation of a national state from November 1918 the accumulated tensions erupted. Polish traders and student groups denounced the Jews as friends of the Germans, social democrats, or Bolsheviks. In 1920 the forged 'Protocols of the Elders of Zion,' which were supposed to prove the existence of a plan for Jewish world domination, were also published in Poland. The attacks escalated very rapidly to encompass violent riots, murders, executions, and pogroms. Even the Polish military became involved, particularly the units of General Jozef Haller (1873–1960), who had achieved great popularity during the struggle for Polish independence. Many Poles condemned these excesses, even in public statements. At this time, however, when the Poles were struggling for their independence, and still had to fight to establish their borders, it was difficult for many people to understand and to accept that the Jews had in the meantime become conscious of their own nationality and only within that framework wished to lay to a place in society—with demands similar to those made by the Poles before 1914 against Russia, Austria–Hungary, and Germany. Now a Jewish national council demanded recognition of the Jews as a national minority and national-cultural autonomy;

though they were not supported in this by all Jewish organizations. There seemed to be no exit from the vicious circle which had now come into being: the Jews at first reacted cautiously to the new state because of the numerous anti-Semitic incidents and the widespread traditional lack of interest in politics; many Poles took this as confirmation of their accusation that the Jews lacked patriotism. The consequence was a further deterioration in the climate.

In the unrest of this period, discontent over poverty and rising prices was directed against the Jews in accordance with the old clichés: they were usurers, hoarders, and corrupters of the nation. Alternatively, they were seen as political opponents who challenged the new order. In Galicia in 1918–19 the peasants turned against the traditional constellation of the Jews and the Polish manorial lords, a stance now underlain by the 'contemporary' argument of a 'Bolshevik conspiracy.'

But even below the level of outright violence, discrimination against the Jews increased. This affected, for example, appointments to public positions and in the education system, and even included an attempt to introduce a percentage-based restriction in respect of high-school attendance. With the law concerning the observance of Sunday opening Jewish competition was diminished because they were thus compelled to cease trading for two days a week. This also gave expression to the continuing anti-Semitism of the Church.

In connection with the Versailles peace negotiations, Great Britain, France, and the USA took up the cause of Jewish rights in Poland. The appearance on the scene of the National Democrat Roman Dmowski (1864–1939), who wanted to curtail such rights, and widespread knowledge of anti-Jewish riots made a lasting impression. On 28 June 1919 Poland had to sign an agreement which included protection of the Jews as a minority. In Poland itself this did not exactly increase public sympathy for the Jews, but on the contrary led to a new wave of anti-Jewish sentiment.

On the political right, the ever latent anti-Semitism was strengthened. The National Democrats in particular—that is, Dmowski and General Haller—came to the fore. Hatred of the Jews was by no means only racially motivated, but in many respects the result of 'pragmatic' considerations—for example, as a means to attract more votes in the prevailing turmoil. Converted 'good Jews' were by all means permitted to join the party. Time and again they were responsible for the bitterest attacks on the Jews—another expression of Jewish 'self-hatred.' The Christian Democrats represented an aggressive, religiously motivated anti-Jewishness. Anti-Semitism was also widespread in the peasants' parties and in some smaller groups. On the other hand, peasant representatives tried to tone this down in that they condemned riots and took action against unjustified accusations. The socialists defended equal rights for Jews; to them, anti-Semitism was an instrument of the right in the class struggle. However, the world of the Jews mostly remained foreign to them because it did not fit into their theoretical scheme. Politically they fought against Jewish nationalism which was ideologically detrimental since it created a distraction from social conflicts and even acted as a cause of anti-Semitism. To this extent there were also tensions between the Polish socialists and the Jewish Workers' Bund.

In the new republic, the Jews also organized political parties of every shade and color. For the Bund the class struggle remained in the foreground, but it also demanded recognition of Yiddish and the right to self-administration. In a sense it also accepted the East European Jewish (*Ostjüdische*) nationality. However, it was unable—not least because of peculiarities of the electoral law which were unfavorable to it—to win a seat in the Sejm. The alliance of all leftwing organizations for which it strove met with only qualified success. The principle, supported by all Jewish parties, of *doyikeit* or 'being-here', was most clearly represented by the Jewish People's Party (the 'Folkists'), which in 1916 had been founded separately for Poland alongside the Russian organization. Simon Dubnov was acknowledged as the intellectual authority here too. In addition to Yiddish as a language of administration they demanded a guarantee of proportionate representation in offices of state and autonomous Jewish representation. However, their extremely aggressive stance gave rise to an anti-Jewish reaction and their Jewish supporters remained few. The Zionists at first constituted the strongest party-political force. At the first elections they received the most Jewish votes. However, they were still internally divided, from the different groups of the socialist *Poale Tsiyon* to the religious Misrahi. And even the most politically influential group, the General Zionists, were split, above all between the 'Galician' and the 'Russian' wings. The causes lay in both personal conflicts and the different historical traditions and regional relations of Galicia and Congress Poland, including the history of the Zionist organizations there. They were united, apart from their support for a 'homeland' in Palestine, in the 'work of the present': to achieve national autonomy in Poland itself and improve the situation of the Jews living there. But opinions were divided over the right way to go about this. The group around Yitzhak Grünbaum (1879–1970), who for a time was the spokesman for the whole of Polish Jewry, pursued an uncompromising policy. It wanted to build up a strong position in the state particularly through active co-operation in the national minorities' block. On the other hand, the 'Galicians' around Leon Reich (1879–1929) and Abraham Ozias Thon (1870–1936) were in favor of more flexibility and accommodation with the government and the Polish political parties in order to realize their aims. They took the view that, because of their historical inheritance—namely the long period of tolerance in the former kingdom—the Poles were less anti-Semitic than the Ukrainians or Belarussians. As a consequence it would not be wise to provoke an anti-Jewish reaction from the Polish groups by becoming involved in the national minorities' block.

In this respect, the *Agudas Yisrael* ('union of Israel'), in which the parties of religious orthodoxy had combined and which knew that it could count on considerable support, took a similar political stance. Since, in their view, the situation of the Jews could only be fundamentally improved through messianic redemption they hoped for the best results from political neutrality and supported the Polish government. In this way, however, they were unable to constitute a political counterweight against the right-wing.

Polish–Jewish conflicts and anti-Semitism as a political instrument became particularly clear during the elections of 1922 and their aftermath. After the previous provisional bodies, when the borders were still undetermined, the Poles were now for the first time electing their highest constitutional bodies: the Parliament, or *Sejm*, the Senate, and the state president. In the election campaign opposing political positions played a central role, as had been the case in 1918–1919. The National Democrats represented the 'Piastic idea of the state': instead of expanding to the east they wanted to expand to the west. Political rights should only be extended to those of Polish nationality. Ranged against them were a number of groups: the Socialists (PPS), some moderate organizations, and also the block of national minorities, with its large number of Jewish politicians. They stood for an active, but not particularly aggressive policy towards the East—the 'Jagiellonian idea of the state'—for a confederation of all East European states and for political rights for minorities. For this they were dismissed as being 'unnational.' Although they were on bad terms with one another, to the right they counted as a unit. As a result the election campaign polarized between

Dmowski and Józef Piłsudski (1867–1935). Anti-Semitic vilification played a significant role in the conflicts.

The right received fewer votes in the elections than they had hoped for. Furious attacks and an extremely malicious campaign were the consequences. It was said that the Jews should have their political influence, and if possible their right to vote, taken away again. When the election of the state president was set by the Sejm and the Senate the nationalists accused the opposing candidate of being a 'Jews' president' because the votes of Jews had been decisive. Piłsudski stepped down for reasons which were not clear and Gabriel Narutowicz (1865–1922) ran instead, and on the right the big landowner Maurycy Zamoyski (1871–1939), whom the peasants' parties could not accept. As a result, Narutowicz was elected on 9 December 1922. The right reacted to this defeat with the most violent anti-Jewish attacks, although the voting stance of the peasants' parties had been decisive. People remembered the Duma election of 1912. Inflammatory rabble-rousing speeches—for example, by General Haller—eventually led to unrest in Warsaw. When the socialists were violently attacked, an exchange of fire led to bloodshed. In the Sejm there were tumultuous scenes. The hatred came to a climax on 16 December in the assassination of Narutowicz by the artist Niewiadomski, who declared that he would have killed anyone who had come to power by means of the Jews. The murder presents a typical case of a naïve and idealistic person incited to violence. After the first shock, the right performed the remarkable feat of turning the real events upside down: according to them the Jews and the socialists—especially the 'Bolshevist Jews'—were responsible for the murder because they had provoked it by their behavior. Later, the condemned murderer was hailed as a hero and savior of the fatherland.

Nevertheless, in the following years open anti-Semitism retreated. Particularly after the coup d'etat ensuring Piłsudski overwhelming influence in 1926, nationalist conflicts died down. Despite the authoritarian system, democratic elements at first became stronger. During this period a range of concessions were made to the Jews. For example, the *heder*—Jewish elementary school—was recognized by the state. The government promoted the influence of the Orthodox in the Jewish communities, the Orthodox in turn supported the government. An agreement reached with the Grabski regime in 1925 could not be realized, however, because the different Jewish groups were completely split.

The mood gradually spread that, despite some successes, Jewish political parties could achieve little through parliamentary work. As a result, more and more Jews heeded the Zionist call to build a Jewish community in Palestine. If supporters of socialist–Zionist ideas had predominated in the Second Aliyah of 1904 to 1914 and the Third Aliyah of 1919 to 1923, in the Fourth Aliyah of 1924 to 1931 for the first time mostly Jews of the Polish middle-class emigrated. The disappointment over parliamentary activity found expression in the elections of 1928, which represented a clear defeat for the Jewish parties. The Jewish faction finally split one year later over conflicts concerning the direction which should now be taken. In the subsequent elections of 1930 and 1935 the Jewish parties lost votes again. In the Sejm they no longer played a significant role, although they continued to be represented until the German invasion of 1939.

This development reflects a certain helplessness concerning how best to improve the situation of the Jews by parliamentary means in the current political circumstances. But this should not be interpreted simply as a sign of the weakness and hopelessness of the Jewish desire for equal rights and autonomy. In many towns and communities, the political representation of the Jews was extremely strong, and, in addition, the cultural variety of the Jews in Poland found expression in the different trends.

The Jews, numbering approximately 3 million, made up around 10 percent of the total population of the Republic of Poland. In the cities they constituted on average around one-third of the population, while in the east they formed the majority in many towns. As far as employment is concerned—the data refer to 1931—they were over-represented in both industry and crafts, with 42 percent, and in trade, with 37 percent; 5 percent worked in transport and communications, 6 percent in independent professions and in the administration, 6 percent as servants, and 4 percent in agriculture (a clear under-representation). The main focus of their employment can be seen in the fact that 62 percent of those in trade were Jews, 26 percent of those in industry and crafts, 27 percent in medicine, and 20 percent in education. The overwhelming majority still worked in small businesses. Mass impoverishment had increased.

Nevertheless, Jewish culture experienced another blossoming. Particularly Yiddish saw an upturn which found expression in many literary works, theater productions, and newspapers. Among the writers we might mention the expressionistic poet Uri-Tsvi Grinberg (1896–1981), who lived for a time in Lwów (Lemberg) and later went to Palestine/Israel, Perets Markish (1895–1952), who was a victim of Stalinist terrorism in 1952, Melekh Ravitsh (pseudonym for Zacharias Bergner, born 1893), Israel Joshua Singer (1893–1944), his brother Isaac Bashevis Singer (1904–1991), who was the Nobel Prize in 1978. They have both lived in the USA since the 1930s, some quotations from their works can be found also in this book. Abraham Sutzkewer (born 1913) wrote prose poems, with the 'Young Vilnius' circle. He fought as a partisan against the Nazis during World War Two, and later left for Israel. There were elements of Jewish folk music in the poetry of Mordechai Gebirtig (1877–1942). The YIVO Institute for Jewish Research, founded in Berlin in 1925, also played an important role. Many significant scholars worked at YIVO, such as Majer Bałaban (1877–1942)—in 1936 also appointed professor at Warsaw University—, Yitzhak Schiper (1884–1943), Moises Schorr (1874–1941), and Arye Tartakower (1897–1982). Their work remains unsurpassed. Emanuel Ringelblum (1900–1944), the later chronicler of the Warsaw Ghetto, and Artur Eisenbach, whose studies after the Second World War were to be foundational for further research into Jewish history in Poland, also did work there.

In painting and the visual arts, artists took up the tradition of Maurycy Gottlieb (1856–1879), the creator of modern Jewish art in Poland, as well as works influenced by Zionist ideas, for example, Leopold Pilichowski (1869–1933), Henryk Glicenstein (1870–1942), or Wilhelm Wachtel (1875–1942). At the same time, the question of the nature of Jewish art became a matter of reflection. The 'Young Yiddish' group around Jankiel Adler (1895–1949), and later also Henryk Berlewi (1894–1967), linked this to modern trends between 1918 and 1921.

There were also signs of secularization and a turning away from Judaism. While in Russian-Poland in 1900 around 85 percent of Jewish children had attended a *heder*, by 1930 the figure had fallen as low as 23 percent. In terms of language, dress, customs and behavior, more and more Jews, especially in the larger towns, conformed with Polish norms. Jews were increasingly demanding that they concentrate on obtaining rights guarantied in law instead of continuing to dream about autonomy. On the other hand, in the meantime many Poles had come to thoroughly accept the East European Jewish nationality, even the 'Yiddishness' of the Jewish people. In many memoirs there are examples of good neighborliness. Such outbursts of anti-Semitism as there were should by no means be played down, but they were not the whole story. The multiplicity of political groupings in Poland indicates the development possibilities available to Jews despite all the obstacles. It is difficult to say how these things would have progressed had it not been for the Nazis.

The deep economic crisis which began at the end of the 1920s, and the fact that anti-Jewish parties and movements were gaining strength all over Europe, led even in Poland to a new flaring up of anti-Semitism which ultimately encroached upon official policy. The National Democrats, known as the 'Endek' after their initial letters, had been marginalized under *sanacja* ('national recovery'). They then became more radical and, to a certain extent, propagated openly fascist slogans. The Camp of Great Poland (OWP), which was close to the National Democrats, called openly for anti-Jewish riots. As a result, it was banned once more.

Anti-Semitism found support among the middle class and among academics, who felt most threatened by the economic crisis. Social advance was hindered and they were threatened by 'proletarianization.' Competition with the Jews sharpened. Increasingly, Jews were not hired even as workers or as engineers. Economic boycotts were imposed on Jewish merchants and businessmen. In this the 'League of the Green Ribbon,' which was close to the National Democrats, was particularly active.

The regime lost its charismatic leader when Piłsudski died in 1935. In order to survive, it now sought an alliance with the National Democrats and with groups even further to the right. Anti-Semitism served as an effective means of binding the different groups together. The Camp of National Unity (OZN), founded in 1937 as the mass base of the regime, did not accept Jewish members. In the same year, as a result of violent anti-Semitic disorder involving students, so-called 'ghetto-benches' were set up in university lecture halls, on which Jewish students had to sit. This intensified use of the *Numerus clausus*, which had already been used unofficially in the 1920s, had the following results: in 1921–1922 Jews had made up around 25 percent of students, but in 1938–1939 the figure had fallen to only 8 percent. Many professional organizations introduced open or concealed rules which in effect precluded Jews from membership. In 1937, the government also approved the 'Polification' of the economy through boycotts on the part of the authorities and the Catholic church. Already in 1936, meat slaughtered in accordance with ritual for Jews, Muslims, and Karaites had been limited to certain regions; the proposal of a general prohibition could not be carried through. In succeeding years rabble-rousing led even to pogroms with many dead and injured. All these measures and the renewed anti-Jewish climate impoverished the Jewish population even more. The number of those in need became ever greater. Since they no longer had a monopoly on the role of economic intermediary, the Jews could increasingly be relegated to the margins.

Reactions to the new situation included resignation and a rising number of suicides, but also increased political activity. At the beginning of the 1930s, the radical Zionists–Revisionists, who uncompromisingly demanded the establishment of a state in Palestine—even by force of arms—gained popularity. Many Polish Jews took part in the Fifth Aliyah between 1932 and 1939. In 1936, however, the British mandatory authorities closed the border and it was only possible to enter illegally. The policy of the Bund was increasingly seen as the only way of countering anti-Semitism. Important in this respect was the fact that the Bund had organized self-defense units and had allies in the leftwing Polish parties. It now became the strongest individual Jewish party and was able to attain a leading position in the big cities at the municipal elections in 1938 and 1939. A common complaint during these years was the tendency towards demoralization among Polish Jewry. On the other hand, there is much evidence to the effect that the consciousness of a common (East European) Jewish tradition and culture was strengthened once more, even in many people who had turned away from the Jewish faith.

The Catholic Church actively encouraged the anti-Jewish mood and, like the National Democrats and the government, spoke of the Jews as 'alien', economically troublesome, and morally inferior elements. In this it was simply repeating the traditional stereotypes. The behavior of the government, on the other hand, was not without contradictions: for example, it still co-operated with the Orthodox group *Agudas Yisrael*. The latter enjoyed government support and, from fear of a left-wing revolutionary takeover, did not shrink from manipulating elections in Jewish communities. Moreover, the government also maintained contact with the Zionists. However, although it still condemned pogroms and riots, it actively considered how Jewish emigration could be promoted. Even in the Foreign Ministry plans were developed to resettle Jews not only in Palestine, but also in Madagascar—a plan which the Nazis also considered for a while. Some political groups let themselves be carried away by trains of thought similar to those behind the 1935 Nurenberg 'race laws.' But in contrast to the situation in Germany, in Poland such ideas were not followed up by concrete measures or discriminatory laws.

The Polish government also tried to prevent Polish Jews who had settled abroad—for example, in Germany—from returning home. In its view, the number of Jews in Poland must not be allowed to increase. At the same time, this served to counter the actions of the German government which had intervened in response to discrimination against German citizens in Poland. The Jews were now an international political target. This led to conflicts with the National Socialist regime which wanted to expel the East European Jews (*Ostjuden*). They had to be removed, principally on account of their status as foreigners, by means of boycotts and similar measures.

In 1938 this policy reached its first climax. In January, the German government expelled all Soviet Jews, as retaliation for the expulsion of 150 German citizens from the Soviet Union. However, the Soviet government refused to take back its Jewish citizens. As a result, they simply disappeared in Nazi concentration camps. In autumn 1938, after the *Anschluss*, the Polish government withdrew Polish citizenship from the 20,000 Polish Jews living in Austria in order to prevent them from returning home. The assets of these Jews played a not inconsiderable role in this decision. The German government now changed the law to make it easier to expel Polish citizens. Dealings between the two governments soon ran aground. In October, as it were 'in the dead of night,' the Nazis transported between 17,000 and 20,000 Polish Jews to the border in order to deport them to their native land. This was the model, and a rehearsal, for later deportations. The Polish government barred the entry of the Jews, and, after a few had managed to get in, closed the border. As a countermove, they began to expel German Jews. In a rage over the deportation of his parents, who had lived in Hannover and were being kept under inhuman conditions at the border, a Polish–Jewish student named Herschel Grynszpan shot the German diplomat Ernst vom Rath in Paris. This assassination served as pretext for the pogrom known as '*Kristallnacht*' ('night of broken glass') which began on 9 November 1938 and continued over the next few days. Negotiations between the Polish and German governments resumed, and in 1939 Poland accepted its Jewish citizens deported from Germany.

Shortly afterwards, when German troops advanced into Poland on 1 September 1939, the Jews stood shoulder to shoulder with the rest of the Polish population to defend the country. "The Warsaw Jews were gripped by an enthusiasm which vividly recalled the year 1861, the era of 'eternal friendship'," wrote the Jewish historian Emanuel Ringelblum. In addition to many donations, assisting in the setting up of civil defense, and helping with the wounded, the Jews participated in fortification work, even on the Sabbath. Bernard Mark, another Jewish historian, remembers a group of people in Warsaw: "In the first row there were five well-known rabbis in long, heavy silk kaftans and sable hats ... They were followed by youths from the rabbinical colleges with shovels on their shoulders".[3]

> The war was not really a surprise for anyone—as early as July ditches were being dug and barricades erected in the streets of Warsaw. Even rabbis took up spades and dug ditches. Now, when Hitler was on the point of advancing into Poland, the Poles forgot their grudge against the Jews and we became—God help us!—*one* nation.[4]

After the victory of the German Wehrmacht many Jews, along with many other Polish citizens, fled to the Soviet Union. There they awaited an uncertain fate. If a few were able to make it on to Palestine, many of those who remained in the USSR fell victim to the Stalinist Terror, deportations, and work details under appalling conditions.

A PRECARIOUS SITUATION IN INDIVIDUAL EAST EUROPEAN COUNTRIES

The 'Jewish question' was directly linked to industrialization, capitalism, emancipation, and nationalism. Social and national conflicts exacerbated one another, and were in turn stirred up by religious conflict. The antagonism to the rich Jewish upper stratum which the rising classes felt in the ruthless competitive struggle with leading capitalists was carried over to all Jews, together with prejudices concerning the 'strangeness' of the East European Jews (*Ostjuden*). The cliché of cunning, harmful, corrupting Jews—who, into the bargain, sided with the nation's enemies—had become general. In the turmoil after the First World War and during the construction of the successor states to the Habsburg, Russian and German Empires, this conflict came out into the open almost everywhere and erupted in violence. People held the Jews responsible for defeat and all manner of problems. Populist groups attempted to win a mass following by mean of anti-Semitic agitation.

In this context, there was anti-Jewish unrest in Hungary and Czechoslovakia. The 'Czecho-Jews' had made themselves unpopular during the war. Because of the experience of Jews in Russia, they could not bring themselves to regard the Russians as liberators, and so clashed with the public's Slavophile sympathies. Nevertheless, the first president of the new republic, Masaryk, managed to defuse the situation somewhat, applying the whole force of his personality to it. A bearable armistice was arrived at between Czechs and Jews which, typically, was only called into question by the German minority, who were concerned about their own situation. To be sure, the fact that the Czechoslovak constitution included a provision making it possible to profess Jewish nationality contributed to the hopeful situation. In the censuses of 1921 and 1930 those Jews who took advantage of this provision made up more than one percent of the population of the republic, while those who professed to be Jewish on religious grounds made up around 2.5 percent (350,000 persons). The initial economic and socio-political successes of the new state begot a favorable climate and strengthened Czecho-Jewish assimilation tendencies. The Jewish Party was rejected by both assimilated and Orthodox Jews, because it emphasized the notion of nationality and got involved in politics—moreover, with significant results. As all these currents came tohether, Prague once more became a Jewish intellectual and cultural center. However, the situation was always precarious. Slovakia became as autonomous region with the government of Catholic priest Josef Tiso (1887–1947) in 1938, and the a puppet state of the Third Reich. Not only was anti-Semitic legislation stepped up, there were deportations and the Slovak Hlinka guard collaborated in the murder of Jews.

In Hungary, from the beginning of the 1920s, a period of consolidation set in after the riots and bloody pogroms in the wake of revolution and counterrevolution. The 1920 *Numerus clausus* law restricting Jewish admission to university was one outcome of persecution, but for a long time it remained the only official discrimination. Due to Hungary's territorial losses as a result of the First World War, the number of Jews fell from almost one million in 1910 to just over 470,000 in 1920, 6 percent of the population. By 1930 this proportion had fallen to 5 percent as a result of conversions and, above all, a falling birth rate. Almost half of Hungarian Jews lived in Budapest. Reform Jews were also concentrated here, making up around 65 percent of the total in 1930. The Orthodox Jews, basically *Ostjuden*, suffered something of a decline in comparison with the pre-War period, because many of them had settled in areas which now belonged to either Czechoslovakia or Romania. They now accounted for 30 percent of the Jewish population. The remaining 5 percent were so-called 'status quo' communities which stood between the two extremes. The anti-Jewish actions in the initial period of the new Hungarian state had caused many Jews—regardless of their different religious or political views—to reflect deeply on the nature of Jewishness. This unquestionably enabled them to obtain social recognition. In the 1930s, however, anti-Semitism began to grow again, and increasingly—not least under German influence—shaped legislation. At first the government resisted handing over the Hungarian Jews to the Nazis. In 1944, however, under German pressure and with the help of the fascist 'Arrow-Cross' organization the Jews were included in the 'Final Solution.' At least some could be saved by various means, however.

In Romania many Jews were persecuted during the First World War as alleged allies or even spies of the Habsburg monarchy. With the acquisition of Bessarabia from Russia, Bukovina from Austria, and Transylvania from Hungary at the end of the First World War, Romania's Jewish population grew to around 800,000 or 4.5 percent of the population as a whole in 1920. At the end of the 1920s it was around one million and so the biggest in Eastern Europe after Poland (three million), and Russia (almost as many). The Jews demanded equal rights enshrined in law, which they had enjoyed in, for example, Bukovina. Under pressure from the Entente, the Romanian government finally agreed to full naturalization. Equal rights were included in the constitution of 1923. Only one year later, however, restrictions were introduced regarding the newly obtained rights. Only the socialists protested, but they were much too weak. Rabble-rousing anti-Semitic speeches suggesting that the Jews had snapped up all the best jobs from Romanians found much more resonance. These ideas found particular favor in the academic world, among students and professors. At the same time, the specter of social revolution—led by 'Jewish bolshevism'—was raised.

Among students the first members of the later 'Legion of the Archangel Michael' gathered; founded in 1927, this organization gave birth in 1930 to the Iron Guard [the name commonly applied by outsiders to the organization as a whole]. The latter did not shrink from murdering judges and—in 1933 and 1938—even presidents who took action against it. Particularly from the economic crisis of the end of the 1920s, it won a mass following. At this time it was already receiving financial support from German groups. The National Socialist regime stepped up its assistance for the Iron Guard and for other anti-Semitic parties, even after the assassination in 1938, when the Iron Guard lost support. General Antonescu (1882–1946) came to power after the 1940 Hitler–Stalin pact, which was unfavorable for Romania. For a short time his government also included members of the Iron Guard. The Iron Guard staged an unsuccessful putsch against Antonescu in January 1941, hoping to concentrate all power in their own hands. This was closely followed by an anti-Jewish pogrom which led to the deaths of 600 Jews in Bucharest alone. At the end of June 1941, immediately after the outbreak of war with the Soviet Union, Romanians and Germans rioted among the Jews of Iaşi, accusing them of being accomplices of the Russians. These were at least 12,000 victims. The killing then continued in the conquered parts of Bessarabia, Bukovina, and Ukraine. However, in the following years it was possible—not least due to the courageous representations of the Chief Rabbi of Romania, Alexander Safran, to the Orthodox Metropolitan and the papal nuncio in Romania—to save many Jews, including many refugees from Poland and Hungary, from deportation.

In Bulgaria in 1943, where the number of Jews had in the meantime grown to around 50,000, the protest of many citizens—to the point of a public demonstration—prevented the transportation of 8,000 Jews to the death camps, despite the government's promise to the Nazis.

In Yugoslavia before the Second World War, anti-Semitic views had had relatively little impact on politics. In 1930 around 70,000 Jews lived here, mostly in Croatia, where they had immigrated above all from Hungary. However, the Croatian Ustaša movement denounced them as the enemies of Croatian nationalism and sponsors of the Serb dominated united Yugoslav state. Under the rule of governments dependent on the National Socialists and their allies the Jews here too fell victim to the 'Final Solution.' Albania, on the other hand, occupied first by Italy and then by Germany, refused to hand over its Jews.

After the October Revolution in 1917, the Baltic states seceded from the Russian empire. Plagued by political and economic instability the question of the national minorities played an important role in these countries. In Lithuania around eight percent of the population were Jews, in Latvia six percent, and in Estonia less than one. The constitutions envisaged extensive minority rights, with cultural autonomy and opportunities for parliamentary representation. In Lithuania, in connection with the historical rights of self-administration, there was even a Jewish national council, and a minister with specific responsibility for Jewish affairs. When the internal situation came to a head, however, nationalist agitation was stepped up, and after the transition to an authoritarian regime at the end of 1926 Jews lost their political representation. Latvia also followed this pattern. Only in Estonia could the Jews continue to work together, with the minorities' cultural council despite the existence of an authoritarian regime. After this region was conquered by the German army in the Second World War, the Jews were subjected to a systematic policy of annihilation.

THE ATTEMPTED EXTERMINATION OF THE JEWS

It was not clear from the beginning what was meant by the 'extermination' of the Jews. Hitler spoke as early as 1919 of the "removal of the Jews from our people," and in *Mein Kampf* in 1924 of "gassing," and also of the eradication of "parasites" and "vermin." The chief party ideologue Rosenberg spoke in similar terms; he saw the Jews as vampires, corrupters of the race, and political conspirators—Bolshevik, naturally—who must therefore be annihilated.[5]

After the Nazis had come to power, Jews in Germany were at first deprived of their rights step by step. Among the most important measures taken against them were the boycott of 1 April 1933, the law of 7 April 1933 which led to Jewish personnel being dismissed from local governments, law courts, and universities, the Nuremberg 'race laws' of 15 September 1935, and the law eliminating Jews from the German economy of 12 November 1938 after '*Kristallnacht.*' Drastic measures against the Jews, above all those of 1933 and again in 1938, were, as a rule, stage-managed, to provide an outlet for anti-Semitic thugs, and on the other, to prepare legislative controls, describe them as "expressing of popular sentiment," and so legitimate them. The laws and administrative acts were warmly welcomed by traditional anti-Semites in the bureaucracy, but also by those business circles which had enthusiastically taken over Jewish companies. In 1988, an astonishingly large number of firms were able to celebrate their fiftieth anniversary, a result of the 'Aryanization' of the German economy in 1938.

Joseph Roth saw things clearly in 1937:

> The Jews could only attain complete equality of rights and the worth which external freedom bestows when the host population [*Wirtsvölker*] attains inner freedom and the worth conferred by an understanding of what it means to suffer. It is—without a miracle from God—scarcely to be believed that the host population will attain this freedom and this worth. To the religious Jew only the consolation of heaven remains. To the rest, 'vae victis.'[6]

The SS, which from the beginning of 1939, on Goering's orders, had been responsible for policy on the Jews, sought to solve the problem by means of a clear 'racial' separation: that is, through the expulsion of the Jews. To begin with, few German Jews had taken up the option of emigration. Most wanted to stay in Germany; naturally, they could not even have begun to imagine what was in store, and believed that, despite their lack of rights, they would be able to live within the framework of their own culture. For the time being, Jewish culture was consciously promoted: Jewish theater, Jewish education, Jewish religion all experienced an upsurge in popularity, not least because it was the Nazis' intention to further separate the Jews from the rest of society in this way. As discrimination increased, better-off Jews in particular emigrated. Towards the end of the 1930s an average of 23,000 Jews a year were taking this route. In Poland at this time the figure was already 100,000. On the other hand, the outcome of international refugee conferences and the reluctance of Western countries to support Jewish emigration did not make the decision to emigrate any easier.

After the Jews had lost all their rights and more or less all their property—around 70 percent of gainfully employed Jews could no longer work for a living— the SS decided that the time was right to deport them. One-third of German Jews had already emigrated. Until October 1941, the SS—partly against the wishes of the Party and also of the Foreign Ministry—made arrangements for the emigration of a further one-third. Adolf Eichmann, then leader of the Jewish section of the *Reichssicherheitshauptamt* (RSHA), had been in contact with Jewish organizations since 1935 in this connection. The final one-third of the Jewish population, around 160,000 people, remained in Germany.

With the defeat of Poland in 1939, the policy of pressurizing Jews to emigrate became more and more difficult. The almost three million Jews in Poland could hardly be sent abroad, apart from anything else because they simply would not be accepted anywhere. From the beginning, the SS, and special units set up for the purpose, dealt with these Jews ruthlessly; to a certain extent this period served as a rehearsal for the extermination of the Jews. A plan emerged to settle all the Jews who could be found in a 'reservation' south of Lublin. At the beginning of 1940 the first deportations began. But sections of the Party thwarted this plan because they did not want any Jews in the German '*Lebensraum*' or 'living space.'

As a result, an older project was taken out of mothballs: the creation of a Jewish state in Madagascar, if possible under German overlordship. Himmler favored this plan because at first he regarded the mass murder of the Jews as 'un-German.' Hitler sounded out Mussolini. The Jews from Baden and the Saar-Pfalz region were intended to be the 'advance guard'; at the end of October 1940, they were deported to Gurs and other camps in France to await their transportation to Africa. The course of the war frustrated these plans: Britain did not make peace, and with the invasion of the Soviet Union on 22 June 1941 all Jews were passed on to be murdered by so-called *Einsatzgruppen* (special task forces) and SS units, though regular units of the Wehrmacht were also involved. Local forces often participated too. The idea of deporting the remaining Jews to an uninhabited part of the Soviet Union, once it had been conquered, could not be realized. As a result, the decision began to form from the summer of 1941 to implement systematic mass extermination, which Hitler in December 1941, at the same time as the declaration of war on the USA, elevated to a decision of general principle. The 'Wannsee conference' of 20 January 1942 discussed the organization of the extermination which was now pursued methodically throughout the Nazi sphere of influence. The gas chambers in Auschwitz commenced operations in spring 1942: many other extermination camps followed. About six million Jews fell victim to the 'Final Solution.'

The life of the Jews in the East under the German occupation, in the ghettos and in the camps can scarcely be described. They had to form 'Jewish councils' who organized administration—including arrangements for transports to the gas chambers. Many Jewish councils tried to save the lives of those in the ghetto by seeking to persuade the Nazis that the skills of particular persons were absolutely necessary, or they sacrificed some in the hope that the rest would survive. The Łódź Jewish elder Mordechai Chaim Rumkowski is perhaps the most outstanding example of this. Despite a number of deportations, the ghetto continued until 1944, when it too was 'liquidated.' Rumkowski went to his death along with the rest. The leader of the Warsaw Jewish council, Adam Czerniaków (1880–1942), chose suicide when he had to arrange a deportation of children. This was not a unique case; others refused to carry out the orders of the Germans, preferring to be shot instead. The records of the Jewish council in Warsaw from 1940 until 1942 may be found in the National Archive in Warsaw. Alongside multifarious data concerning housing conditions, food, and schooling, there are also documents concerning 'work battalions' and the terrible conditions in the work camps. At the beginning of 1942 there were still 400,000 Jews in the Warsaw ghetto. Of those able to work, 47 percent were employed in crafts, 24 percent in trade, 5 percent in industry, and 24 percent in other occupations. Starvation rapidly increased the mortality rate from 1941 onwards. The records end with the raising of gas charges in the Jewish residential quarters.

Some Jews tried armed resistance. There were uprisings in different ghettos, for example, in Warsaw in April–May 1943, in Lviv (Lemberg) in June 1943, in Białystok in August, and in Vilnius in September 1943. All were brutally repressed, and few Jewish participant survived. One of the leaders of the Warsaw uprising, Marek Edelman, survived and worked later as a doctor in Łódź. He was one of the founders there of the independent trade union Solidarność. Remarkably, he has always been against the glorification of the ghetto fighters. Since 1945, it has often been asked why Jews did not heed the call to arms issued in Vilnius by Abba Kovner (1918–1987) at the end of 1941, instead of going "like lambs to the slaughter."[7] This often conceals a bad conscience, since more could have been done to help those being persecuted. Even the Zionists sought, in their struggle for the State of Israel and in their view of history, to emulate those who had participated in the uprisings. Marek Edelman, on the other hand, declared that

> Death in the gas chambers should be valued no less than death in battle, and a death is unworthy only when someone tries to save his own life at the expense of others ... it is terrible when someone goes to their death in this fashion. It is perhaps more difficult than any shoot-out; shooting is a much easier death.[8]

It has long been common to describe Jews—and especially East European Jews—as obsequious and cowardly. Their history shows, however, that under particular circumstances they could certainly fight and put up resistance. But armed action was not seen as a virtue. As a rule, people responded to violence with patience. Behind this stood faith in the will of God and the coming redemption, a different set of values, which recognized higher ideals than those of the warrior—for example, learning—and not least an insight into the senselessness of violence. Violence only begets violence. These considerations also influenced how the Jews conducted themselves under the Nazis, particularly because the scale of the approaching extermination was at first so unimaginable that no resistance could be organized. To be sure, in the ghettos and in the extermination camps there were also attempts to obtain greater or smaller advantages, and even to save one's life at the expense of others. Who among those who were not there may stand in judgment? At the same time, in the bearing of the Hasid who went to his death with the prayer 'Shema Israel'—'Hear, O Israel: The Lord our God is one Lord' (Deuteronomy 6:4)'—; of the wife who would not allow her husband to meet his end alone; of the teacher and the governess who accompanied their children into the gas chamber and comforted them; and of the person who, almost out of his mind with fear and humiliated beyond measure, dug his own grave, although he knew what was awaiting him, there is every bit as much honor as in direct struggle against the murderer.

Could the Poles have done more to help the Jews? This is perhaps as much the subject of violent argument in Poland today as it is among the Jews themselves. There is agreement that the Polish relief organizations for Jews were unique in Europe and that there were many individual acts of assistance. In virtually no other land did so high a proportion of people help the Jews, to which the list of those honored for this reason at Yad va-Shem, the place of remembrance in Jerusalem, bears impressive testimony. However, many take the view that such acts were rather the exception. Anti-Semitic tendencies had always played a decisive role, and Polish-Jewish relations had remained distant. Even in the underground there was little contact between Jews and Poles. In any case, we must take into consideration the fact that many attempts at rescue remained unknown or unsuccessful and that many people who would have been ready to help simply did not turn thought into deed out of fear of the Nazis: anyone caught helping Jews in any way would pay for it with his life. Almost every Polish family was worried about one of its members in a concentration camp, in prison, or in forced labor. The continual raids, the public executions, and the burning down of whole villages had their perpetrators' desired effect.

THE JEWS IN POSTWAR POLAND: NEW SUFFERING AND NEW HOPE

With the end of the war, the suffering of the Jews in Eastern Europe was far from over. Many of them had to remain in Germany under degrading conditions as 'displaced persons' in camps. We have already said something of the fate of the Jews in the Soviet Union and in other countries in their sphere of influence. In Poland the Jews were in a curious position. Shortly after the end of the war, when the future political order was in question, there were new pogroms in Cracow, Parczew, Kielce, and other places which claimed the lives of hundreds of Jews. In Kielce alone, on 4 July 1946, 42 people were murdered. As a rule, rumors of ritual murder once more served as the precipitating cause. The atmosphere was heated up still more by conflicts between the communists and their opponents. Some of them—and here the Catholic Church must once more bear some of the responsibility—took advantage of anti-Jewish prejudices in the struggle against the communists: many members of the Polish Communist Party were Jews who had joined partly in the hope that socialism in Poland would finally create the kind of society in which Jews could feel at home. Some were also active in the political police and were involved in crimes; their behavior was then taken to be characteristic of Jews in general. In addition, there was the problem that Jewish property was now in new hands and the new owners usually did not want to give it back. There is much that we still do not know about the course of the pogroms. The first steps are now being taken in Poland to research these events, at the prompting of Solidarity. At the time, the main consequence was a new wave of Jewish emigration.

The elimination of Jewish party functionaries on the basis of Stalinist policy followed. However, this was not as brutal as it was in Czechoslovakia or Hungary. Even in later years, various party factions used anti-Semitism in order to get rid of political opponents. In 1968 this form of conflict reached its peak. Under the ossified Gomułka regime new power struggles broke out within the Party. In an explosive situation student demonstrations for greater freedom in high schools led to clashes with the police. The unrest spread and one party faction held the Jews responsible. Reference was made to the Arab–Israeli war of 1967 in which the Zionists were made out to be the aggressors.

Whoever spoke up for Israel was supporting their policies. With this 'argument' the Jews in Poland were portrayed as the supporters of a policy of aggression. In order to preserve his influence, Party chief Gomułka attached himself to this position. A sharply anti-Jewish reaction resulted, which first affected those in the Communist Party, and then those in other parts of society—above all in science and the arts. Many lost their jobs, were interrogated, and even arrested. Shocked by this unexpected wave of anti-Semitism most of the remaining Jews left the country. Only around 5,000 remained.

Motivated by the relatively open discussion of the relations between Poles and Jews in *Solidarność,* in Catholic publications, but also in the official government press and public declarations, and in 1988 even within the Communist Party, a discussion got under way concerning the events of 1968, which led to the condemnation of anti-Semitism and the behavior of the Party leadership at that time, although without fully bringing to light the background. All in all, for some time official policy on the Jews has taken a different line. Discrimination began to diminish and Jewish institutions once again received more state support. After the fall of the communist regime in 1989/90, Jewish life could develop completely freely, even when anti-Semitism found renewed expression. However, of the three million Jews who lived in Poland before the Second World War only 5,000 remain. Does that not spell the end of the *Ostjuden*?

In fact, the Jews living in Poland today mostly live under wretched conditions. Many are alone and sick. The average age is 70. Often there are too few to form a *minyan* for a religious service.

When two young Poles were researching the traces of the last Jews, an old Jewish woman said to them:

'I am angry with our God.'
'Why?', I ask, surprised.
The old woman nodded her head:
'Well, after all ... we are supposed to be the chosen people, but what has that brought us? Blood, more blood and hatred and terrible slaughter ... I've thought about this and I sometimes think that it would have been better if he hadn't chosen us. He should have left us alone to live like all the rest.'[9]

Yet there are still hopeful signs. Some Jews are making every effort to preserve the old traditions and to pass them on to posterity. In 1985, a Bar-mitsvah celebration took place in Warsaw for the first time in 30 years, as a thirteen year old boy was accepted into the community. That was the source of a tremendous impetus. Many people who had 'hidden' their Jewishness in postwar Poland now returned to it. The number of Jews continues to increase. There are reports of young people who were not brought up in the Jewish tradition consciously acknowledging their Jewishness, often under difficult circumstances.

> Behind me stands the history of my family and the long history of my people. The most important thing for us Jews is always to raise our children as Jews. If I were to turn my back on the traditions of Polish Jews today, in full knowledge, that would be a betrayal of everything which our people has done over the centuries. It would mean that the Jews in Poland should have assimilated long ago and that ultimately the Holocaust was a kind of punishment for their stupidity. Then the horror to which the thought of the millions of our dead gives rise would be the only outcome of the genocide.[10]

Szymon Datner is a noted historian. He was born in Cracow in 1902. As a teacher he dwelt with his family in Białystok where he lived through the Second World War and the German occupation. In the ghetto he joined a resistance organization which could not prevent most of the Jews from being killed. Datner's wife and two daughters were among the dead. At the Jewish

Institute of History in Warsaw, he experienced the contradictory and often anti-Jewish developments in postwar Poland. In 1953 he left the Institute and worked as a bricklayer. Later on, he was able to work as a historian once again. In 1968 he was 'pensioned off,' but soon afterwards became director of the Institute for a short time. His daughter from his second marriage worked there later as a historian.

Concerning the behavior of the Poles in the course of the extermination of the Jews in the Second World War he says:

> 'I must stress that 90 percent of these murderous deeds was the work of Germans ... There was a range of different attitudes among the Polish population. Most Poles were passive as regards the fate of the Jews. This can be explained in terms of the prevailing terror and the fact that Poles were also subject to planned mass murder by the Germans. Their passivity I regard as justified in a situation in which every act required heroism. What I condemn is the indifference which one also encountered.
>
> Finally, there were two active groups. The first was made up of those who denounced, robbed, and murdered Jews; the second was made up of those who hid Jews and helped them. The second group was larger and more representative of the Polish population and the Polish resistance. The first enjoyed greater success.'
>
> 'What do you mean by that?'
>
> We often forget that in order to save a single Jew someone needed the help of several other people and a long period of time, usually several years. To betray one Jew one person sufficed and a brief moment. Furthermore, many rescue attempts were unsuccessful, which means that both the Jew and the Pole met their death — and so did not come to be included in the positive statistics.' ...
>
> 'Is it your personal opinion that the Poles did their best?'
>
> 'I wouldn't say that, but on the question of whether a people should be judged in terms of those who risk their lives for others or in terms of its informers I have no doubt.

Concerning the future, he thinks that:

> It looks as if the Polish Jews will die out. But our people has been dying out for two thousand years and it still remains alive.
>
> The Jewish community in Poland is very small, but perhaps it will survive. Recently some new, young people came to us. It seems that they had fallen away from their Jewish lineage, but they have returned. Three months ago I had an experience of great joy: a bar mitzvah celebration. I hope that someone will remain when we are no longer here ... I look to the future with confidence. The Polish Jews were exterminated, but in its place American Jewry grew magnificently. There are six million of them, as many as those who were exterminated in Europe. There is the State of Israel, where new generations have already grown up. Even though a number of branches have been cut off and others have withered and fallen, the Jewish people lives and will continue to live.[11]

The extermination of the Jews in Eastern Europe, despite the countless victims and unspeakable suffering, did not succeed, and neither did the extermination of the *Ostjuden*. The culture of these Jews will, to be sure differently from before, persist and continue to have an effect, also in the places where it originated. Memory will help make sure of that.

AFTERWORD: THE SIGNIFICANCE OF MEMORY

Memory is an essential part of the Jewish conception of the world. The following words are ascribed to Ba'al Shem Tov: "The desire to forget prolongs exile; the secret of redemption is memory." To remember the Holy Land and the Holy Scriptures, as well as the history of the Jewish people before and after their expulsion from Israel, is to recall the prehistory of the redemption. The Messiah may come at any time. In the figurative sense this is also true for the secular realm. Whoever rejects the history and culture of the Jews loses his Jewish identity, his 'Jewishness,' and with it the solidarity and the strength to assert himself as a Jew in society. To break with convention and to find one's path in another way requires self-reflection and securing oneself in memory.

Memory, recollection, and history belong to the essence of the Jews. By this means they continually renew themselves. Not only historical knowledge is understood here, but also existential concern. The past does not lie behind us, but in front of us; we experience it in memory. The significance which is attributed to memory follows from the particular history of the Jews. Scattered over the whole world, they have often been without a homeland; they were not permitted to have one. Therefore their history, the history of them all and of each individual, is a homeland in memory.

Manès Sperber writes:

> When the Jewish shtetls still existed for me they belonged only in a distant past; since they have been destroyed ... Zablotow henceforth belongs to my present. It has its home in my memory.[1]

Jewish communities make a record of the names of their members, particularly of those who were persecuted or murdered, to safeguard them from being forgotten. No Jew can avoid this, and though it is an experience of sorrow, it is also one of strength. Today the strength which memory may give is more necessary than ever, and perhaps the ability to know what to do grows directly from the memory of the past.

To remember also means to become conscious of history and to take a critical look at it. The esteem in which tradition, nurtured in centuries-old, even millennia-old rituals, is held in Jewish historical thought is incalculable. At the same time, however, the old writings are continually discussed anew, as is the path of history. Characteristic in this regard is, for example, the Hasidic tale in which the *tsaddik* sought to emulate his teacher to such an extent that he abandoned him, just as the latter had turned away from his own teacher.[2] Memory of this kind is a painful process.

The quotation from Ba'al Shem Tov stands above the exit gate of the Place of Remembrance Yad Vashem in Jerusalem. It tends to be quoted by high ranking politicians, at commemorative events related to the German crimes against the Jews. It even adorns a stamp issued by the German Post Office on the occasion of the 50th anniversary of the organized pogroms of 9 and 10 November 1938, usually known as '*Kristallnacht.*' Memory has significance not only for Jews, but for all of us. It frequently comprises recognition of loss, for which we can only mourn. But it leads beyond that. It makes it possible for us to get to know our own history, in which we find our identity, and to uncover the roots of forms of behavior, ways of thinking, and feelings in terms of history. An elaboration of this kind of history and confrontation with it may lead to some disquiet; but only in this way can attitudes and behavior change.

Those who shy away from such a confrontation, those who would like to protect their fixed view of the world from such disquiet, will much more easily have their self-confidence shattered. Our desire to forget does not stop history from catching up with us again. The desire to forget only prolongs our own uncertainty and helplessness in dealing with problems and critical issues. Memory, on the contrary, frees us and gives us strength to consciously form our present and future.

The history of the Jews in the modern period—also in Eastern Europe—urgently brings the 'Dialectic of Enlightenment' before our eyes. The thinkers of the Enlightenment wanted to emancipate humanity, to liberate it from its—according to Kant, self-caused—intellectual immaturity. Whoever did not correspond to the image of such a liberated person had to be 'improved' or educated. Until this aim was achieved his rights were of a lesser order.

It was not only the lower social orders who were 'in need of improvement' in this sense, but also the majority of Jews, particularly the *Ostjuden*. In the dispute over their place in society which followed the catastrophe of 1648, they had begun to form a 'distinct cultural personality,' and most were not ready to give up their 'Jewishness.' Their religion was to them not merely a private affair—the progressives would have tolerated that—but part of their social and historical identity.

The transition from an agrarian to an industrial society based on capitalism was bound up with the Enlightenment. Not only thought turned against the conventions holding humanity in ignorance, but also economic and social developments increasingly dissolved traditional communities. Enlightenment and capitalism frequently liberated people from their shackles in the realm of thought—for example, in relation to Church dogma—and in the economy, for example, serfdom, guild rules, and other regulations. At the same time, this freedom also required one to surrender oneself to new dependencies—for example, wage labor in industrial enterprises—or it brought difficulties for those who had to find a new way in the world after old ties had been destroyed. The way of life of many people was 'colonized' (Habermas), eclipsed by the intervention of new statehood with extended powers, and by new economic relations.

The Jews could not avoid the appearance of being the 'colonizers of progress.' The peasant could trust 'his' Jew absolutely, the one who traded with him, who took care of everything for him, who often served as counselor in family matters, or on tax or legal issues, and who even represented him against the state should the need arise. However, his feelings towards the Jews were conflicting: traditionally, the Jew was an 'instrument' of the feudal lords, with the result that the accumulated hatred could be vented on the 'intermediary.' Apart from that, the Jews had brought a different form of economy into the village: the focus was not the—to be sure, frequently broken—'moral economy' (E. P. Thompson), making a living through careful management in accordance with certain concepts of honor, but rather thinking in terms of 'capitalist' criteria even when the profit obtained in this way was only sufficient for subsistence. As a result, the Jew was both trusted and alien at the same time.

It was all the easier to identify Jews with the threat posed by the coming apart of traditional communities under the pressure of socio-economic developments. The more the Jews lost their position as intermediaries the more they began to lose their place in old communities. They took on new social and economic functions, but were unable to win back the trust which they had formerly enjoyed, or at least not to the same extent. The traditional ties were destroyed. At the same time, however, it was possible for most Jews to maintain their own communities and to give them new life: through a new religious reflection in Hasidism and Orthodoxy, in conflict with the Haskalah and its consequences, in the common feeling of an East European Jewish nationality.

The strangeness and isolation of most Jews could easily be exploited to make them scapegoats in crises and emergencies, particularly because the real causes were usually hidden in economic and social processes which had become much more complex. Insofar as one felt able to shift the blame onto the Jews, one could assume an apparent identity while in reality it was often not possible to find one's way. The fact that the majority of Jews wanted recognition of their own nationality with equal rights was not accepted by the Poles, who were fighting for their own national consciousness and national independence. Rather they saw the Jews as national opponents, who at the same time took away from them the best jobs and social positions—a development which was in fact the outcome of the 'jockeying for position' characteristic of the new capitalist economy. The Jews became the 'other,' so that people could hold their own in the socio-economic transformation.

The recognition of East European Jewish culture, way of life, and nationality on equal terms could not be achieved in Eastern Europe. Ranged against it stood the traditional anti-Jewish attitude of the Christian churches, robust material interests, and above all the fact that society in Eastern Europe itself had only just begun to reach out for its own emancipation and had not yet found itself. The prayer of Rabbi Israel, the Maggid of Kozienice who lived around the turn of the nineteenth century, was not fulfilled:

Lord of the world, know that the children of Israel suffer too much; they deserve redemption; they need it. If, however, you do not yet want to grant this, on grounds that are unknown to me, then at least redeem the other peoples, the other nations ... but quickly![3]

Nevertheless, the assertive efforts of the Jews to obtain equal rights had begun to change the minds of more and more non-Jews. The Nazi Terror brought this development to a brutal halt. Today, when we remember the world of the Jews in Eastern Europe in its multifacetedness; when we recall the ways of life, the culture, the customs, and the rituals of the Jews; we hope for a continuation of the inner strength of the Jews. And perhaps we will ourselves obtain the freedom to make the stranger into a friend, and to consider the 'other' as part of our own.

NOTES

PART I: POLAND AS A PLACE OF REFUGE FOR JEWS

1 S. J. Agnon, 'Polen—die Legende von der Ankunft' [Poland—the legend of the arrival [of the Jews]], in *Das Buch von den polnischen Juden* [The book of the Polish Jews], ed. S. J. Agnon and Ahron Eliasberg (Berlin, 1916), p. 3.
2 *Das Buch von den polnischen Juden*, p. 11 (the Privilege of Grodno).
3 Shlomo Netzer, 'Wanderungen der Juden und Neusiedlung in Osteuropa' [The migrations of the Jews and resettlement in Eastern Europe], in *Beter und Rebellen. Aus 1000 Jahren Judentum in Polen* [Praying men and rebels. 1000 years of the Jews in Poland], ed. Michael Brocke (Frankfurt am Main, 1983), pp. 33–49, here p. 44.
4 Marian Fuks, Zygmunt Hoffmann, Maurycy Horn, and Jerzy Tomaszewski, *Polnische Juden. Geschichte und Kultur* [Polish Jews. History and culture] (Warsaw, n. d. [ca. 1983]), p. 14.
5 Reiner Bernstein, *Geschichte des jüdischen Volkes* [History of the Jewish people], Information zur politischen Bildung 140, 4th edition (Bonn, 1985), p. 23.
6 Fuks et al., *Polnische Juden*, p. 15.
7 Agnon et al., *Das Buch von den polnischen Juden*, p. 38.
8 Fuks et al., *Polnische Juden*, p. 30.
9 Jürgen Hensel, 'Polnische Adelsnation und jüdische Vermittler 1815–1830. Über den vergeblichen Versuch einer Judenemanzipation in einer nicht emanzipierten Gesellschaft' [Polish nation of nobles and Jewish intermediaries 1815–1830. On the futile attempt at the emancipation of

the Jews in an unemancipated society], *Forschungen zur osteuropäischen Geschichte* 32 (1983), pp. 7–227, here p. 93.

10 Michał Strzemski, *Das abgebrochene Gespräch. Erinnerungen* [The uncompleted conversation. Memoirs] (Leipzig, 1985), p. 85.

11 Netzer, 'Wanderungen', p. 44.

12 Ibid., p. 47.

13 Jörg K. Hoensch, *Sozialverfassung und politische Reform. Polen im vorrevolutionären Zeitalter* [Social structure and political reform. Poland in the pre-Revolutionary era] (Cologne–Vienna, 1973), p. 180. As late as 1924 Alfred Döblin heard the following version of this: "Poland, Heaven for the nobleman, Paradise for the Jews, Hell for the peasants" (*Reise in Polen* [Journey in Poland], [Munich, 1987], p. 73). To be sure, an anti-Jewish attitude is being expressed here, but it can be taken to indicate the relatively favorable situation of the Jews.

14 Agnon et al., *Das Buch von den polnischen Juden*, p. 21–31.

15 Herman Greive, *Die Juden. Grundzüge ihrer Geschichte im mittelalterlichen und neuzeitlichen Europa* [The Jews. Outlines of their history in medieval and modern Europe] (Darmstadt, 1980), p. 124.

PART II: EAST EUROPEAN JEWRY AS A 'CULTURAL PATTERN OF LIFE' IN EASTERN EUROPE

1 Jörg K. Hoensch, *Geschichte Polens* [History of Poland] (Stuttgart, 1983), pp. 148, 150 (after Henryk Sienkiewicz, who first applied the term "Flood" to the war against Sweden in 1656).

2 Herman Greive, *Die Juden. Grundzüge ihrer Geschichte im mittelalterlichen und neuzeitlichen Europa* [The Jews. Outline of their history in medieval and modern Europe] (Darmstadt, 1980), p. 127f.

3 Shmuel Yosef Agnon, *Eine einfache Geschichte* [A simple story] (Frankfurt am Main, 1987), p. 166f.

4 Gershom Sholem, *Die jüdische Mystik in ihren Hauptströmungen* [Major trends in Jewish mysticism] (Frankfurt am Main, 1980), p. 88.

5 Gershom Sholem, *Zur Kabbala und ihrer Symbolik* [On the Kabbala and its symbolism] (Frankfurt am Main, 1973), pp. 255–258; Egon Erwin Kisch, 'Den Golem wiederzuerwecken' [To reawaken the golem], in *Geschichten aus sieben Ghettos* [Stories from seven ghettos] (Frankfurt am Main, 1982), pp. 177–194.

6 Sholem, *Die jüdische Mystik*, p. 142.
7 Ibid. pp. 224f.
8 Isaac Bashevis Singer, *Old Love. Geschichten von der Liebe* (Munich–Vienna, 1985), p. 38 ('Die beiden' [Both of them]).
9 Scholem, *Die jüdische Mystik*, pp. 287, 301, 305.
10 Marian Fuks, Zygmunt Hoffmann, Maurycy Horn, and Jerzy Tomaszewski, *Polnische Juden. Geschichte und Kultur* [Polish Jews. History and culture] (Warsaw, n. d. [ca.1983]), p. 26.
11 Cited by Scholem, *Die jüdische Mystik*, pp. 347, 346.
12 Simon Dubnow, *Weltgeschichte des jüdischen Volkes. Von den Uranfängen bis zur Gegenwart* [World history of the Jewish people. From the first beginnings to the present day] (Berlin, 1928), vol. 7, p. 197.
13 Scholem, *Die jüdische Mystik*, p. 349.
14 Cited in *Kirche und Synagoge. Handbuch zur Geschichte von Christen und Juden. Darstellung mit Quellen* [Church and synagogue. Handbook on the history of Christians and Jews. Presentation with sources], ed. Karl Heinrich Rengstorf and Siegfried von Kortzfleisch (Munich, 1988), vol. 2, p. 459.
15 Cited by Karl E. Grözinger, 'Die Hasidim und der Hasidismus' [The Hasidim and Hasidism], in *Beter und Rebellen*, p. 148.
16 Elie Wiesel, *Chassidische Feier* [English translation, *Souls on Fire*] (Vienna, 1974), p. 85.
17 Gershom Scholem, 'Drei Typen jüdischer Frömmigkeit', in *Lust an der Erkenntnis. Jüdische Theologie im 20 Jahrhundert. Ein Lesebuch* [Desire for knowledge. Jewish theology in the twentieth century. A reader], ed. Schalom Ben-Chorin and Verena Lenzen (Munich–Zürich, 1988), pp. 311, 317f.
18 S. A. Horodecky, *Religiöse Strömungen im Judentum. Mit besonderer Berücksichtigung des Chassidismus* [Religious trends in Judaism. With particular reference to Hasidism] (Bern–Leipzig, 1920), p. 183.
19 Elie Wiesel, *Chassidische Feier*, p. 190.
20 Scholem, *Die jüdische Mystik*, p. 382.
21 M. A. [presumably Mathias Acher, pseudonym of Nathan Birnbaum], 'Polnische Juden', in *Der Jude* I (1916/17), p. 561. Nathan Birnbaum describes the East European Jews as a "separate cultural community": "We have come to know them as a large Jewish cultural 'block'—perhaps the largest there has ever been—pervaded with inner movement, rich in history, strongly oriented towards the present, and full of future," *Was sind Ostjuden? Zur ersten Information* [What are East European Jews?

Preliminary information] (Vienna, 1916), p. 15. He had already spoken at the first Zionist Congress in 1897 of the *Ostjuden* as having a separate culture as something entirely self-evident (Zionisten-Congress in Basel [Congress of Zionists in Basle] [29, 30, and 31 August 1897], *Officielles Protocoll* [Vienna, 1898], pp. 82–94). The history of the concept *Ostjude* must still be written. In any case, it must be emphasized that it originated in Jewish linguistic usage. The fact that the 'Ostjude' subsequently played an important role as a cliché in anti-Semitic agitation should not lead to the term being relinquished.

22 Salcia Landmann, *Jiddisch. Das Abenteuer einer Sprache* [Yiddish. The adventure of a language] (Frankfurt am Main, 1986), pp. 53, 23. At the forefront of research into Yiddish language and culture is the Yiddish Scientific Institute (YIVO), founded in Berlin in 1925, and with its first headquarters in Vilnius, Lithuania. In 1940, it was moved to New York. Since the dissolution of the Soviet Union the Institute is again operating in Vilnius. The Institute of Jewish History in Warsaw has carried on the tradition of the Institute of Jewish Studies there; at the University of Cracow there is an Institute for Jewish History and Culture. In the meantime, similar institutions have been established in other East European countries.

23 M. Samuel, *The World of Sholem Aleichem* (New York, 1943), p. 26f, cited in *Versunkene Welt* [Sunken world], ed. Joachim Riedl (Vienna, 1984), p. 16.

24 Mendele Moykher Sforim, *Fischke der Lahme. Bettlerroman* (Leipzig, 1978), p. 19f.

25 Rose Ausländer on Cernăuţi (Czernowitz) where she was born in 1907. Cited in *Dein aschenes Haar Sulamith. Ostjüdische Geschichten* ['Dein aschenes Haar Sulamith.' East European Jewish stories], ed. Ulf Diederichs in association with Otto M. Lilien and Germania Judaica (Munich, 1988), new edition, p. 33.

26 Manès Sperber, *Die Wasserträger Gottes. All das Vergangene...* [The watercarriers of God. Everything that has passed ...] (Frankfurt am Main, 1993), Vol. 1, p. 23f. Sperber was born in 1905 in Zabłotów, Galicia.

27 Heinrich Heine, *Über Polen* [On Poland], in Heinrich Heine, *Werke*, vol. 2, ed. Wolfgang Preisendanz (Frankfurt am Main, 1968), p. 66f.

28 Joseph Roth, *Das falsche Gewicht. Die Geschichte eines Eichmeisters* [The false weight. The story of an inspector of weights and measures] (Cologne, 1977), p. 26ff.

29 *Salomon Maimons Lebensgeschichte. Von ihm selbst geschrieben und hrsg. von Karl Philipp Moritz* [Salomon Maimon's life story. Written by himself and edited by Karl Philipp Moritz]. Newly edited by Zwi Batscha (Frankfurt am Main, 1984), p. 13.
30 Simon Dubnow, G*eschichte des Chassidismus* [History of Hasidism] (Königstein, 1983—reprint of the first edition, 1931), vol. 1, p. 32f, compare p. 34.
31 *Salomon Maimons Lebensgeschichte*, p. 229; on the otherwise wretched conditions on landed estates, compare, for example, pp. 14–23, 37–39, 66–72.
32 Heinrich Heine, *Über Polen*, p. 67f.
33 Dubnow, *Weltgeschichte*, vol. 8, p. 340f.
34 Concerning the discussions and suggestions here and in what follows the quotations are to be found in Jürgen Hensel, 'Polnische Adelsnation und jüdischen Vermittler 1815–1830. Über den vergeblichen Versuch einer Judenemanzipation in einer nicht emanzipierten Gesellschaft' [Polish nation of nobles and Jewish mediators 1815–1830. On the futile attempt at the emancipation of the Jews in an unemancipated society], *Forschungen zur osteuropäischen Geschichte* 32 (1983), pp. 179, 180, 201, 205, 206; Dubnow, *Weltgeschichte*, vol. 8, pp. 317, 364.
35 Singer, *Old Love* ('Jochna and Shmelke'), p. 17f.
36 Hensel, 'Polnische Adelsnation,' p. 174f (Denkschrift 1815 [Memorandum 1815]). Details vary concerning Satanower's dates.
37 Shmuel Yosef Agnon, *Der Verstoßene* [The outcast] (Frankfurt am Main, 1988), pp. 108–109.
38 John Doyle Klier, *Russia Gathers Her Jews. The Origins of the 'Jewish Question' in Russia, 1772–1825* (Dekalb, Illinois, 1986), p. 34.
39 Joseph Roth, 'Juden auf Wanderschaft' [The wandering Jews] (1927/1937), in *Werke*, ed. Hermann Kesten, vol. 3 (Cologne, 1976), pp. 293–369, here p. 345f.
40 Benjamin Nathans, 'Conflict, Community, and the Jews of Late Nineteenth-Century St Petersburg', in *Jahrbücher für Geschichte Osteuropas* 44 (1996), p. 178–216.
41 François Guesnet generously made this source available to me. It reflects the same kind of thinking as the forged 'Protocols of the Elders of Zion'.
42 Manfred Hildermeier, 'Die jüdische Frage im Zarenreich. Zum Problem der unterbliebenen Emanzipation', in *Jahrbücher für Geschichte Osteuropas* 33 (1984), pp. 321–357, here p. 350 (from Sergei Witte's memoirs).

43 Here I am indebted to Frank Michael Schuster's unpublished M.A. thesis, 'Der Krieg an der 'inneren' Front—Russlands Deutsche und Juden im westrussischen Kriegsgebiet 1914–1916' [The war on the 'home' front—Russia's Germans and Jews in the west Russian war zone 1914–1916] (Giessen, 1997).

44 Dubnow, *Weltgeschichte*, vol. 8, p. 301 (after a Russian report of 1810). Brody, near Lviv, was also Joseph Roth's birthplace. The Jewish innkeeper at the center of his novel *Tarabas* (Frankfurt am Main, 1987) was modeled on a well-to-do Jew who lived there.

PART III: THE CRISIS OF THE JEWS IN EASTERN EUROPE A NEW IDENTITY

1 Figures from Jürgen Hensel, 'Polnische Adelsnation und jüdischen Vermittler 1815–1830. Über den vergeblichen Versuch einer Judenemanzipation in einer nicht emanzipierten Gesellschaft' [Polish nation of nobles and Jewish mediators 1815–1830. On the futile attempt at the emancipation of the Jews in an unemancipated society], *Forschungen zur osteuropäischen Geschichte* 32 (1983), pp. 7–227, here pp. 107, 124f. According to newer estimates a figure of around 243,000 Jews must be accepted for 1816, which was around 8.7 percent of the population. In 1827 this proportion was 9.3 percent. In 1830 10 percent was finally achieved. As a result of the Partitions of Poland, around 500,000 Jews came into the Russian sphere of governance outside the Kingdom of Poland (cf. *Philo-Lexikon. Handbuch des jüdischen Wissens* [Königstein, 1982, p. 632. Reprint of 1936 edition]).

2 Sholem Aleichem, 'Ein Pessach im Dorf' [Passover in the village], in *Jiddische Erzählungen von Mendele Mojcher Sforim, Jizchak Lejb Perez, Scholem Alejchem* [Yiddish tales by Mendele Moykher Sforim, Isaac Leib Peretz, and Sholem Aleichem], ed. Leo Nadelmann (Zürich, 1984), pp. 310–325, here p. 313f.

3 Sholem Aleichem, *Tewje, der Milchmann* [Tevye the milkman] (Leipzig, 1984), pp. 64f, 68ff.

4 Aleichem, *Tewje, der Milchmann*, p. 9ff.

5 I am grateful to Desanka Schwara for this reference.

6 The term also played an important role for the Zionists. At the First Zionist Congress in 1897 in Basle, David Farbstein spoke of the poor who

"live on air" (Zionisten-Congress in Basel [Congress of Zionists in Basle] [29, 30, and 31 August 1897], *Officielles Protocoll* [Vienna, 1898], p. 104), and at the Fifth Congress in Basle in 1901 Max Nordau described the '*Luftmenschen*' as "a specific Jewish type." "Many 'air persons' together constitute an 'air people'." That was why the Jewish people finally needed their own land (Max Nordau, *Zionistische Schriften* [Zionist writings], ed. Zionist Action Committee [Cologne–Leipzig, 1909], pp. 117–118, cf. p. 129). On the other hand, he considered colonization in Palestine without political safeguards—in a phrase directed against the Zionist *Ostjuden*—with contempt as "Luftarbeit von Luftmenschen ['air work by air people']" (from an interview in 1907 in *Welt*, cited by Angelika Montel, 'Herzl's Maitresse. Zur Gründung der Welt' [Herzl's Maitresse. On the founding of *World*], in *Wandlungen und Brüche. Von Herzls 'Welt' zur 'Illustrierten Neuen Welt' 1897–1997*, ed. Joanna Nittenberg with Anton Pelinka and Robert S. Wistrich [Vienna, 1997], pp. 19–66, here p. 43). The Marxist Zionist Ber Borokhov labeled Jewish workers as the 'air proletariat' because they could barely find employment in modern industry (Matityahu Mintz, 'Ber Borokhov', in *Studies in Zionism* 5 [1982], pp. 33–53, here p. 36). Just to indicate the term's range of usage, let me cite Hannah Arendt, who referred to those intellectual "air people of western Jewry" who despite economic security could not find a place in either Jewish or non-Jewish society (Hannah Arendt, *Die Krise des Zionismus. Essays und Kommentare* 2 [The crisis of Zionism. Essays and commentaries], ed. Eike Geisel and Klaus Bitterman [Berlin, 1989], p. 64).

7 Salo W. Baron, *The Russian Jew under Two Tsars and Soviets* (New York, 1987), 2nd edition, p. 95.

8 Sholem Aleichem, *Menachem Mendel, der Spekulant* [Menachem Mendel the speculator] (Munich–Zürich, 1964), p. 12.

9 Isaac Babel, *Werke*, ed. Fritz Mierau, vol. 2 (Berlin, 1973), p. 93.

10 Anselm Hillmann, *Jüdisches Genossenschaftswesen in Russland* [Jewish cooperative systems in Russia] (Berlin, 1911), p. 33.

11 Bernard D. Weinryb, *Neueste Wirtschaftsgeschichte der Juden in Russland und Polen. Von der 1. polnischen Teilung bis zum Tode Alexanders II (1772–1881)* [The recent economic history of the Jews in Russia and Poland. From the first partition of Poland to the death of Alexander II *(1772–1881)*] (Hildesheim–New York, 1972), 2nd edition, p. 56.

12 Hillmann, *Jüdisches Genossenschaftswesen*, p. 101f (after L. Rochlin, 1909).
13 Alexander Carlebach, 'A German Rabbi Goes East', in *Leo Baeck Institute Year Book* 6 (1961), pp. 60–121, here p. 108. The letters show vividly the circumstances of Warsaw Jewry as well as the experience of meeting *Ostjuden*.
14 I. M. Dijur, 'Jews in the Russian Economy', in *Russian Jewry (1860–1917)*, ed. Jacob Frumkin, Gregor Aronson, and Alexis Goldenweiser (New York–London, 1966), pp. 120–143, here p. 143.
15 Babel, *Werke*, vol. 1, p. 68.
16 Isaac Bashevis Singer, *Das Landgut* [The estate] (Munich, 1981), pp. 11, 16.
17 Bolesław Prus, *Die Puppe* (Berlin, 1954), pp. 87, 658, 773, 774, 776, 834f.
18 Cf. Inge Blank, 'Haskalah und Emanzipation. Die russisch–jüdische Intelligenz und die "Jüdische Frage" am Vorabend der Epoche der "Grossen Reformen"' [Haskala and emancipation. The Russian–Jewish intelligentsia and the 'Jewish question' on the eve of the 'great reforms'], in *Juden in Ostmitteleuropa. Von der Emanzipation bis zum Ersten Weltkrieg* [Jews in Central and Eastern Europe. From emancipation until the First World War], ed. Gotthold Rohde (Marburg, 1989), pp. 197–231, here p. 213.
19 Cf. 'Leben im russischen Schtetl. Auf den Spuren von An-ski. Jüdische Sammlungen des Staatlichen Ethnographischen Museums in Sankt Petersburg' [Life in a Russian shtetl. In the footsteps of Ansky. The Jewish collections of the State Museum of Ethnography in St Petersburg]. Katalog zu einer Ausstellung (Cologne–Frankfurt am Main, 1993).
20 Cf. *Versunkene Welt* [Lost world], ed. Joachim Riedl (Vienna, 1984), pp. 77–90.
21 Panaït Istrati, *Familie Perlmutter* [The Perlmutter family], in *Werkausgabe*, vol. 8, ed. Heinrich Stiehler (Frankfurt am Main, 1988), p. 165.
22 Michal Strzemski, *Das abgebrochene Gespräch. Erinnerungen* [The uncompleted conversation. Memoirs] (Leipzig, 1985), p. 86.
23 Israel Joshua Singer, *Die Brüder Aschkenasi* [The brothers Ashkenazi] (Munich–Vienna, 1986), p. 59ff.
24 At the end of the nineteenth century, a new Jewish cemetery was established in Łódź with the help of Israel Poznański. He was buried there himself in 1902 and a massive and magnificent mausoleum was erected in

his memory. Cf. *Cmentarz Żydowski w Łodzi. Największy cmentarz żydowski w Europie (The Jewish Cemetery of Łódź-, the Oldest Jewish Cemetery in Europe)*, Ed. Muzeum Sztuki w Łodzi (Łódź, 1988).
25 Alfred Döblin, *Reise in Polen* [Journey in Poland] (Munich, 1987), p. 74.
26 Esther Kreitmann, *Deborah—Narren tanzen im Ghetto* [Deborah—Fools dance in the ghetto] (Frankfurt am Main, 1984), p. 6.
27 Isaac Bashevis Singer, *Die Familie Moschkat* [The Family Moskat] (Munich, 1987), 2nd edition, p. 573.
28 *Salomon Maimons Lebensgeschichte. Von ihm selbst geschrieben und hrsg. von Karl Philipp Moritz* [Salomon Maimon's life story. Written by himself and edited by Karl Philipp Moritz]. Newly edited by Zwi Batscha (Frankfurt am Main, 1984), p. 230. Maimon himself was married at the age of eleven and had had his first son by the age of fourteen; cf. pp. 52–66.
29 Israel Joshua Singer, *Die Brüder Aschkenasi*, p. 136.
30 Kreitmann, *Deborah*, p. 11.
31 Isaac Bashevis Singer, *Old Love. Geschichten von der Liebe* [Stories of love] (Munich–Vienna, 1985), p. 13 ('Jochna und Schmelke').
32 Aleichem, *Tewje, der Milchmann*, p. 38.
33 Shmarya Levin, 'Mottje der Melamed', in *Dein aschenes Haar Sulamith. Ostjüdische Geschichten* ['Your Ashen Hair Sulamith'. Eastern European Jewish Stories], Ed. Ulf Diederichs in association with Otto M. Lilien and Germania Judaica (Munich, 1988), new edition, pp. 135–142, here p. 14.
34 Ulrich Gerhardt, *Jüdisches Leben im jüdischen Ritual. Studien und Beobachtungen 1402–1933* [Jewish life in Jewish ritual. Studies and observations 1402–1933]. Revision with commentary by Zwi Sofer. Edited by Dietrich Gerhardt, with Malwine Maser and Peter Maser (Heidelberg, 1980), p. 145.
35 Bella Chagall, *Brennende Lichter* [Shining lights] (Reinbek, 1966), p. 30f.
36 Ibid, p. 42. As a rule, two Sabbath candles were lit.
37 Shmuel Yosef Agnon, *Der Verstossene* [The outcast] (Frankfurt am Main, 1988), p. 23.
38 Singer, *Die Familie Moschkat* [The Family Moskat], pp. 360–363.
39 Bella Chagall, *Brennende Lichter* [Shining lights], p. 66.
40 Roth, 'Juden auf Wanderschaft' [The wandering Jews], pp. 293–369, here p. 315.
41 Singer, *Die Familie Moschkat*, pp. 253ff.
42 Singer, *Das Landgut* [The estate], p. 307. For the heder and tzitzits see the previous section.

43 Roth, 'Juden auf Wanderschaft' [The wandering Jews], p. 308f.
44 Roth, 'Juden auf Wanderschaft' [The wandering Jews], p. 298.
45 Cited in Arthur Hertzberg, *Shalom, Amerika! Die Geschichte der Juden in der Neuen Welt* [Shalom, America! The History of the Jews in the New World] (Munich, 1992), pp. 88–89.
46 Alexander Granach, *Da geht ein Mensch. Roman eines Lebens* [There goes a man. Novel of a life] (Munich, 1990), pp. 1, 15, 67, 70–71.
47 Freiherr Fenner von Fenneberg, *Österreich und seine Armee* [Austria and its army] (Leipzig, 1847?), p. 82f. In my view, this attitude is also characteristic of a later period. I am grateful to Richard Widor for the reference.
48 Károly Eötvös, defense lawyer in the Tiszaeszlár trial. Cited after Walter Pietsch, 'Die jüdische Einwanderung aus Galizien und das Judentum in Ungarn' [Jewish emigration from Galicia and Hungarian Jewry], in *Juden in Ostmitteleuropa* [Jews in Central and Eastern Europe], pp. 271–293, here p. 281f. I am also grateful to Walter Pietsch for other references based on his ongoing research.
49 For details see Peter Haber, *The Anfänge des Zionismus in Ungarn (1879–1904)* [The Beginning of Zionism in Hungary (1879–1904)] (Cologne–Weimar–Vienna, 2001).
50 Simon Dubnow, *Weltgeschichte des jüdischen Volkes. Von den Uranfängen bis zur Gegenwart* [World history of the Jewish people. From the first beginnings to the present day] (Berlin, 1928), vol. 9, pp. 425, 491.
51 Franz Kafka, *Briefe 1902–1924* [Letters 1902–1924] (Frankfurt am Main, 1958), p. 337. Cf. his Diaries for examples of an encounter with East European Jews: *Tagebücher 1910–1923* [Diaries 1910–1923] (Frankfurt am Main, 1951), for example, pp. 178, 210ff, 465, 478f.
52 Hans Kohn, 'Zur Araberfrage' [On the Arab question], in *Der Jude* 4 (1919/1920): pp. 566–571. Cited in *Die Juden in Böhmen und Mähren. Ein historisches Lesebuch* [The Jews in Bohemia and Moravia. A historical reader], ed. Wilma Iggers (Munich, 1986), pp. 232–237, here pp. 234, 235.
53 Franz Kafka, *Briefe an Milena* [Letters to Milena] (Frankfurt am Main, 1952), p. 57.

Part IV. Attempted Annihilation and New Hope

1. A detailed portrayal of the example of Odessa is given by Walter Kaufmann in his unpublished Master's thesis, '"Der Kampf auf der jüdischen Strasse". Die Politik der Jüdischen Sektionen der Kommunistischen Partei am Beispiel Odessas, 1920–1925. Vorgeschichte und Verlauf' [The struggle in the Jewish street. The policy of the Jewish sections of the Communist Party taking Odessa as an example, 1920–1925. Prehistory and course] (Berlin, 1994).
2. Joseph Roth, 'Juden auf Wanderschaft' [The wandering Jews] (1927/1937), in *Werke*, ed. Hermann Kesten, vol 3. (Cologne, 1976), pp. 293–369, here p. 357.
3. Both quotations in Marian Fuks, Zygmunt Hoffmann, Maurycy Horn, and Jerzy Tomaszewski, *Polnische Juden. Geschichte und Kultur* [Polish Jews. History and culture] (Warsaw, n. d. [ca. 1983]), p. 44.
4. Isaac Bashevis Singer, *Old Love. Geschichten von der Liebe* [Stories of love] (Munich–Vienna, 1985), p. 226 ('The manuscript').
5. Cited after Bernd Martin, 'Judenverfolgung und -vernichtung unter der nationalsozialistischen Diktatur' [Persecution and extermination of the Jews under the National Socialist dictatorship], in *Die Juden als Minderheit in der Geschichte* [The Jews as a minority in history], ed. Bernd Martin and Ernst Schulin (Munich, 1981), pp. 290–315, here pp. 295–298; Wolfgang Scheffler, 'Wege zur "Endlösung"' [Paths to the 'Final Solution'], in *Antisemitismus. Von der Judenfeindschaft zum Holocaust* [Anti-Semitism. From hatred of the Jews to the Holocaust], ed. Herbert A. Strauss and Norbert Kampe (Bonn, 1985), pp. 186–214, here p. 191. These quotations should make clear what kind of ideas influenced the thought processes of leading Nazis and Nazi propaganda. I do not mean to suggest that there was a direct line of continuity from earlier manifestations to the later murder of the Jews during the Second World War.
6. Joseph Roth, 'Juden auf Wanderschaft' [The wandering Jews], Preface to the new edition, pp. 368–369.
7. Cited in *Ess firt kejn weg zurik ... Geschichte und Lieder des Ghettos von Wilna*, ed. Florian Freund et al. (Vienna, 1992), p. 53. The simile follows Isaiah 53:7.
8. Hanna Krall, *Dem Herrgott zuvorkommen* [To forestall God] (Frankfurt am Main, 1992), pp. 47–48.

9 Malgorzata Niezabitowska and Tomasz Tomaszewski, *Die letzten Juden in Polen* [The last Jews in Poland] (Schaffhausen et al, 1987), p. 55.
10 Ibid. pp. 57–75, here p. 74; Bar-mitsvah celebration, pp. 137–150; example of the conscious transmission of tradition, p. 104.
11 Ibid. pp. 153–172. Citation, pp. 163–164, 172, partly corrected after the Polish original which appeared in 1993 (with thanks to Klaus-P. Friedrich).

AFTERWORD

1 Manès Sperber, cited after *Dein aschenes Haar Sulamith. Ostjüdische Geschichten* ['Dein aschenes Haar Sulamith.' Eastern European Jewish stories], ed. Ulf Diederichs in association with Otto M. Lilien and Germania Judaica (Munich, 1988), new edition, p. 56.
2 Gershom Scholem, *Die jüdische Mystik in ihren Hauptströmungen* [Major trends in Jewish mysticism] (Frankfurt am Main, 1980), p. 382.
3 Elie Wiesel, *Chassidische Feier* [English translation, *Souls on Fire*] (Vienna, 1974), p. 124.

SELECTED BIBLIOGRAPHY

A full list, with titles in German and Polish, can be found in the German edition of the book.

BIBLIOGRAPHIES, LEXICONS, AND OTHER AIDS, PERIODICALS

Encyclopaedia Judaica. 16 vols. Jerusalem, 1971–1972.
Hundert, Gershon D., Gershon C. Bacon. *The Jews in Poland and Russia. Bibliographical Essays*. Bloomington, 1984.
Jewish Social Studies.
Jews in Eastern Europe.
Lerski, George Jews, and T. Halina. *Jewish–Polish Coexistence, 1772 to 1939. A Topical Bibliography*. New York, 1986.
Nationalities Papers.
Polin. A Journal of Polish–Jewish Studies.
Studies in Contemporary Jewry.
Yearbook. Leo Baeck Institute.
Yivo-Annual of Jewish Social Science.

GENERAL OVERVIEWS AND COMPREHENSIVE WORKS

Baron, Salo W. *The Russian Jew under the Tsars and Soviets.* 2nd edition. New York, 1987.

Biale, David. *Eros and the Jews. From Biblical Israel to Contemporary America.* New York, 1992.

Dubnov, Simon. *History of the Jews in Russia and Poland from the Earliest Times until the Present Day,* 3 vols. Philadelphia, 1916–1920.

East European Jews in Two Worlds. Studies from the Yivo Annual, ed. Deborah Dash Moore. Evanston, 1990.

Essential Papers on Hassidism. Origins to Present, ed. Gershon David Hundert. New York–London, 1991.

The First Zionist Congress in 1897. Causes, Significance, Topicality, ed. Heiko Haumann. Basel, 1997.

Gay, Ruth. *Unfinished People. Eastern European Jews Encounter America.* New York–London, 1996.

Gitelman, Zvi. *A Century of Ambivalence. The Jews of Russia and the Soviet Union, 1881 to the Present.* New York, 1988.

The Golden Tradition. Jewish Life and Thought in Eastern Europe, ed. Lucy S. Dawidowicz. New York, 1967.

Greenberg, Louis. *The Jews in Russia. The Struggle for Emancipation,* 2nd edition. New Haven–London, 1965.

Hagen, William W. *Germans, Poles, and Jews. The Nationality Conflict in the Prussian East, 1772–1914.* Chicago–London, 1980.

Hoffman, Eve. *Shtetl. The Life and Death of a Small Town and the World of Polish Jews.* Boston–New York, 1997.

Hungarian–Jewish Studies, ed. Randolph L. Braham, 3 vols. New York, 1966–1978.

Israel, Jonathan I. *European Jewry in the Age of Mercantilism, 1550 to 1750.* Oxford, 1985.

The Jewish Family. Myths and Reality, ed. Steven M. Cohen and Paula E. Hyman. New York–London, 1986.

Jewish History. Essays in Honour of Chimen Abramsky, ed. Ada Rapoport-Albert and Steven J. Zipperstein. London, 1988.

The Jews of Czechoslovakia. Historical Studies and Essays, 3 vols. Philadelphia–New York, 1968, 1971, 1984.

Jews in the Hungarian Economy 1760–1945. Studies Dedicated to Moshe Carmilly-Weinberger on his Eightieth Birthday, ed. Michael K. Silber. Jerusalem, 1992.

Jews and Jewish Life in Russia and the Soviet Union, ed. Yaakov Ro'i. Ilford, 1995.

The Jews in Poland. Vol. 1. Dedicated to Józef A. Gierowski. ed. Andrzej K. Paluch. Cracow, 1992.

———. Vol. 2, dedicated to Rafael F. Scharf. ed. Sławomir Kapralski, Cracow, 1999.

The Jews in Poland, ed. Chimen Abramsky et al. Oxford, 1986.

Kahan, Arcadius. *Essays in Jewish Social and Economic History*. Edited by Roger Weiss. Chicago–London, 1986.

Klier, John Doyle. *Russia Gathers Her Jews. The Origins of the 'Jewish Question' in Russia, 1772–1825*. Dekalb, Illinois, 1986.

Levitats, Isaac. *The Jewish Community in Russia, 1772–1844*. New York, 1970 [1943].

———. *The Jewish Community in Russia, 1844–1917*. Jerusalem, 1981.

McCagg, William O. *A History of the Habsburg Jews, 1670–1918*. Bloomington, Indianapolis, 1989.

Patai, Raphael. *The Jews of Hungary. History, Culture, Psychology*. Detroit, 1996.

Pogroms: Anti-Jewish Violence in Modern Russian History, ed. John D. Klier and Shlomo Lambroza. Cambridge, 1992.

Rabinowicz, Tzvi. *Chassidic Rebbes. From the Baal Shem Tov to Modern Times*. Southfield, Michigan, 1989.

Roskies, Diane K., and David G. Roskies. *The Shtetl Book. An Introduction to East European Jewish Life and Lore*. 2nd edition. New York, 1979.

Rothkirchen, Livia. 'Deep-Rooted Yet Alien: Some Aspects of the History of the Jews in Subcarpathian Ruthenia,' in *Yad Vashem Studies* 12 (1977), pp. 147–191.

Rubin, Ruth. *Voices of a People. Yiddish Folk Song*. New York–London, 1963.

Weinryb, Bernard D. *The Jews of Poland. A Social and Economic History of the Jewish Community in Poland from 1100 to 1800*. Philadelphia, 1973.

Żborowski, Mark, and Elizabeth Herzog. *Life is with People. The Jewish Little-Town of Eastern Europe,* 2nd ed. New York, 1953.

BIBLIOGRAPHY TO PART I:
POLAND AS A PLACE OF REFUGE FOR JEWS

Dunlop, Douglas Morton. *The History of the Jewish Khazars.* Princeton, N. J., 1954.

Golb, Norman, and Omeljan Pritsak. *Khazarian Hebrew Documents of the Tenth Century,* 2 vols. Ithaca, NY–London, 1982.

Goldberg, Jacob. *Jewish Privileges in the Polish Commonwealth. Charters of Rights Granted to Jewish Communities in Poland–Lithuania in the Sixteenth to Eighteenth Centuries.* Jerusalem, 1985.

Hundert, Gershon David. 'On the Jewish Community during the Seventeenth Century. Some Comparative Perspectives,' *Revue des études juives* 142 (1983), pp. 349–372.

———. 'The Role of the Jews in Commerce in Early Modern Poland–Lithuania', *Journal of European Economic History* 16 (1987), pp. 245–275.

BIBLIOGRAPHY TO PART II: EAST EUROPEAN JEWRY AS A 'NEW CULTURAL PATTERN' OF LIFE IN EASTERN EUROPE

Fishman, David E. *Russia's First Modern Jews: The Jews of Shklov.* New York–London, 1995.

Goldberg, Jacob. 'Poles and Jews in the Seventeenth and Eighteenth Centuries. Rejection or Acceptance,' *Jahrbücher für Geschichte Osteuropas* 22 (1974), pp. 248–282.

Hundert, Gershon David. *The Jews in a Polish Private Town. The Case of Opatów in the Eighteenth Century.* Baltimore–London, 1992.

Levine, Hillel. *Economic Origins of Anti-Semitism. Poland and Its Jews in the Early Modern Period.* New Haven–London, 1991.

Rosman, Murray J. *The Lords' Jews. Magnate–Jewish Relations in the Polish–Lithuanian Commonwealth during the Eighteenth Century.* Cambridge, Mass., 1990.

Schochet, Elijah Judah. *The Hasidic Movement and the Gaon of Vilna.* Northvale, N. J.–London, 1994.

Weiss, Joseph. *Studies in Eastern European Jewish Mysticism.* Oxford, 1985.

BIBLIOGRAPHY TO PART III. THE CRISIS OF THE JEWS IN EASTERN EUROPE AND A NEW IDENTITY

Berk, Stephen M. *Year of Crisis, Year of Hope. Russian Jewry and the Pogroms of 1881–1882.* Westport, Conn.–London, 1986.

Best, Gary Dean. *To Free a People. American Jewish Leaders and the Jewish Problem in Eastern Europe, 1890–1914.* Westport, Conn.–London, 1982.

Cohen, Gary B. 'Jews in German Society. Prague, 1860–1914', in *Jews and Germans from 1860 to 1933. The Problematic Symbiosis*, ed. David Bronsen. Heidelberg, 1979, pp. 306–337.

Corrsin, Stephen D. 'Poles and Jews in a Conquered City. Warsaw', in *The City in Late Imperial Russia*, ed. Michael F. Hamm. Bloomington, 1986, pp. 123–151.

———. *Warsaw before the First World War: Poles and Jews in the Third City of the Russian Empire, 1890–1914.* New York, 1989.

Frankel, Jonathan. *Prophecy and Politics. Socialism, Nationalism, and the Russian Jews, 1862–1917.* Cambridge, 1981.

Gassenschmidt, Christoph. *Jewish Liberal Politics in Tsarist Russia, 1900–1914. The Modernization of Russian Jewry.* London, 1995.

Haberer, Erich E. *Jews and Revolution in Nineteenth-Century Russia.* Cambridge, 1995.

Judge, Edward H. *Easter in Kishinev. Anatomy of a Pogrom.* New York–London, 1992.

Kieval, Hillel J. *The Making of Czech Jewry. National Conflict and Jewish Society in Bohemia, 1870–1918.* New York–Oxford, 1988.

Klier, John Doyle. *Imperial Russia's Jewish Question, 1855–1881.* Cambridge, 1995.

Lederhendler, Eli. *The Road to Modern Jewish Politics. Political Tradition and Political Reconstruction in the Jewish Community of Tsarist Russia.* Oxford–New York, 1989.

Levin, Nora. *While Messiah Tarried. Jewish Socialist Movement, 1871–1917.* Oxford–New York, 1977.

Mahler, Raphael. *Hasidism and the Jewish Enlightenment. Their Confrontation in Galicia and Poland in the First Half of the Nineteenth Century.* Philadelphia, 1985.

———. *A History of Modern Jewry 1780–1815.* London, 1971.

McCagg, William O. *Jewish Nobles and Geniuses in Modern Hungary.* New York, 1986 [1972].

Mendelsohn, Ezra. *Class Struggle in the Pale. The Formative Years of the Jewish Workers' Movement in Tsarist Russia.* Cambridge, Mass., 1970.

Nathans, Benjamin. *Beyond the Pale: The Jewish Encounter with Russia, 1840–1900.* Unpublished dissertation, University of California at Berkeley, 1995.

———. 'Conflict, Community, and the Jews of Late Nineteenth-Century St. Petersburg', in *Jahrbücher für Geschichte Osteuropas* 44 (1996), pp. 178–216.

Opalski, Magdalena. *The Jewish Tavern-Keeper and his Tavern in Nineteenth-Century Polish Literature.* Jerusalem, 1986.

———, and Israel Bartal. *Poles and Jews. A Failed Brotherhood.* Hanover–London, 1992.

Parush, Iris. 'Women Readers as Agents of Social Change among Eastern European Jews in the Late Nineteenth Century,' in *Gender and History* 9 (1997), pp. 60–82.

Rogger, Hans. *Jewish Policies and Right-Wing Politics in Imperial Russia.* Basingstoke, 1986.

Russian Jewry (1860–1917), ed. Jacob Frumkin, Gregor Aronson, and Alexis Goldenweiser. New York–London, 1966.

Sarna, Jonathan D. 'The Myth of No Return. Jewish Return Migration to Eastern Europe, 1881–1914,' in *Labor Migration in the Atlantic Economies. The European and North American Working Class during the Period of Industrialization*, ed. Dirk Hoerder. Westport, Conn.,–London, 1985, pp. 423–434.

Stanislawski, Michael. *Tsar Nicholas I and the Jews. The Transformation of Jewish Society in Russia, 1825–1855.* Philadelphia, 1983.

Stampfer, Shaul. 'Heder Study, Knowledge of Torah and the Maintenance of Social Stratification in Traditional East European Jewish Society', *Studies in Jewish Education* 3 (1988), pp. 271–289.

———. 'Remarriage among Jews and Christians in Nineteenth-Century Eastern Europe,' *Jewish History* 3, no. 2 (1988), pp. 85–114.

Tobias, Henry J. *The Jewish Bund in Russia. From His Origins to 1905.* Stanford. Cal., 1972.

Towards Modernity. The European Jewish Model, ed. Jacob Katz. New Brunswick, N. J.–Oxford, 1987.

Weinberg, Robert. 'Workers, Pogroms, and the 1905 Revolution in Odessa,' *The Russian Review* 46 (1987), pp. 53–75.
Wertheimer, Jack. *Unwelcome Strangers. East European Jews in Imperial Germany*. New York–Oxford, 1987.
Wróbel, Piotr. 'The Jews of Galicia under Austrian–Polish Rule, 1869–1918,' *Austrian History Yearbook* 25 (1994), pp. 97–138.
Zipperstein, Steven J. *The Jews of Odessa. A Cultural History, 1794 to 1881.* Stanford, Cal. 1985.

BIBLIOGRAPHY TO PART IV: ATTEMPTED ANNIHILATION AND NEW HOPE

Brym, Robert J. with the assistance of Rozalina Ryvkina. *The Jews of Moscow, Kiev, and Minsk. Identity, Anti-Semitism, Emigration*, ed. Howard Spier. Houndmills–London, 1994.
Cała, Alina. *The Image of the Jew in Polish Folk Culture*. Jerusalem, 1995.
Chary, Frederick B. *The Bulgarian Jews and the Final Solution 1940–1944.* Pittsburgh, 1972.
The Chronicle of the Łódź Ghetto, 1941–1944, ed. Lucjan Dobroszycki. New Haven, 1984.
Gitelman, Zvi Y. *Jewish Nationality and Soviet Politics. The Jewish Sections of the CPSU, 1917–1930.* Princeton, NJ, 1972.
Gutman, Yisrael, and Shmuel Krakowski. *Unequal Victims. Poles and Jews during World War Two*. New York, 1986.
Heller, Celia S. *On the Edge of Destruction. Jews of Poland between the Two World Wars*. New York, 1977.
Jews and Non-Jews in Eastern Europe 1918–1945, ed. Bela Vago and George L. Mosse. New York, 1974.
Kagedan, Allan Laine. *Soviet Zion. The Quest for a Russian Jewish Homeland*. Houndmills–London, 1994.
Katzburg, Nathaniel. *Hungary and the Jews. Policy and Legislation 1920–1943*. Ramat-Gan, 1981.
Krakowski, Shmuel. *The War of the Doomed. Jewish Armed Resistance in Poland 1942–1944.* New York–London, 1984.
Levin, Dav. *Fighting Back. Lithuanian Jewry's Armed Resistance to the Nazis, 1941–1945*. New York–London, 1985.
Levin, Nora. *The Jews in the Soviet Union since 1917. Paradox of Survival.* 2 vols. New York–London, 1988.

Marcus, Joseph. *Social and Political History of the Jews in Poland, 1919–1939*. Berlin, 1983.

Mendelsohn, Ezra. *The Jews of East Central Europe between the World Wars*. Bloomington, 1983.

——. *Zionism in Poland. The Formative Years, 1915–1926*. New Haven–London, 1981.

Perspectives on the Holocaust, ed. Randolph L. Braham. Boston, 1983.

Pinchuk, Ben-Cion. *Shtetl Jews under Soviet Rule. Eastern Poland on the Eve of the Holocaust*. Oxford, 1990.

Rabinowicz, Harry M. *The Legacy of Polish Jewry. A History of Polish Jewry in the Inter-War Years 1919–1939*. New York–London, 1965.

Ringelblum, Emanuel. *Polish–Jewish Relations during the Second World War*, ed. Joseph Kermish and Shmuel Krakowski. New York, 1976.

The Tragedy of Hungarian Jewry. Essays, Documents, Depositivs, ed. Randolph L. Braham. New York, 1986.

Trunk, Isaiah. *Jewish Responses to Nazi Persecution. Collective and Individual Behavior in Extremis*. New York, 1979.

——. *Judenrat. The Jewish Councils in Eastern Europe under Nazi Occupation*. New York–London, 1972.

Weinberg, Robert. 'Purge and Politics in the Periphery: Birobidzhan in 1937', *Slavic Review* 52 (1993), pp. 13–27.

INDEX

Abulafia, Abraham 44
acculturation 121, 122, 186, 187
accusations 4, 9, 11, 12, 14, 29, 38, 64, 77, 201, 214, 217
accusations of ritual murder 4, 9, 11, 12, 14, 29, 38, 64, 78, 89, 182, 191, 198, 200, 201, 240
activism (activist turn) 50, 166, 167
Agnon, Shmuel Yosef 183
Agudas Yisrael 166, 167, 219, 226
aguna 141
Ahad Ha'am (Asher Ginzberg) 168
Aleichem Sholem 107, 120, 142, 178
Alexander I of Russia 74, 78, 84, 86, 87, 91, 121, 133
Alexander II of Russia 87, 88
Alexander III of Russia 89
Aliyah 168, 221, 225
Alkalai, Judah 166
Alliance Israélite 195
Alter, Isaac Meir Rothenberg 132
Alter, Wiktor 164, 212
An-ski, (Shloyme Zaynvil Rappoport) 121

Anti-Fascist Jewish Committee 212, 213
anti-Judaism, anti-Semitism 7, 11, 14, 15, 21, 63, 70, 78–80, 82, 89, 90, 104, 112, 117, 118, 122–125, 132, 133, 137, 161, 163, 164, 167, 170, 173, 174, 176, 177, 182, 187, 191, 193, 194, 196–199, 200–203, 211–214, 216, 217, 219, 220, 223–225, 229–232, 234, 239–241, 249
Anti-Semitic Alliance 196
Antonescu, Ion 231, 232
Arab–Israeli war 240
army suppliers 106, 114
Aryanization 234
Asch, Schalom 120, 178
Ashkenazim 6, 11, 92
assimilation 51, 72, 75, 88, 91, 98, 122–124, 132–134, 145, 161, 163, 166, 178, 188, 190, 191, 193, 196, 198, 199, 202, 203, 215, 229
Association of the Jews in Russia 162

August III of Poland 49, 64
Auschwitz 236
Ausländer, Rose 185
Austro-Marxism 164
autonomy 37, 69, 80–82, 87, 139, 142, 164, 165, 168, 172, 174, 188, 189, 190, 211, 212, 215, 218, 212, 223, 233
Axelrod, Paul 163

Ba'al Shem Tov 51, 245, 246
Babel, Isaak 110, 116
Badeni, Kazimierz Felix 200
banking, banker 4, 18, 39, 89, 91, 102, 105, 111, 113, 114, 116, 118, 120, 160, 192
bar mitsvah 144, 244
Basel 10, 169, 177, 187, 189
Báthory, Stephan 20
beggar 62, 109, 123, 134, 155, 192
Beilis, Mendel 89
Béla IV of Hungary 97
Ben Gurion, David (Grün) 171
Berdichev 60
Bergner, Hinde 183
Bergson (entrepreneur family) 105
Berlin 75, 76, 92, 119, 195, 197, 222
bet ha-midrash 55, 144
Białystok 23, 164, 170, 237, 242
Biluim 167
Birnbaum, Nathan 169, 174
Birobidzhan 209, 212
Bismarck, Otto von 197
Black Death 7
Bloch, Jan Gotlib 115, 117, 129
block of national minorities 219
Bolesław the Pious 4

Borohov, Ber 171
boycott 112, 161, 162, 172, 199, 224, 225, 226, 233
Brandeis, Louis 179, 180
Breslau 145
Brest-Litovsk 5, 35, 207, 208
brifnshteler 139
Brody 97, 184, 187, 188
Buber, Martin 168, 202
Bucharest 98, 194, 196, 232
Budapest 169, 190, 192, 193, 230
Bydgoszcz (Bromberg) 13

Camp of Great Poland (OWP) 224
Camp of National Unity (OZN) 224
Capistran, John 12, 13
capitalism 89, 117, 209, 228, 247, 248
Carlebach, Emanuel 115
Caro, Joseph 24
Casimir III, the Great 4, 5
Casimir IV 12, 13
Catherine II of Russia 80–82, 84
Chagall, Bella 147, 148, 151
Chagall, Marc 110
chamber servants 4
charity institutions 110, 130, 142, 159
Charles V, Emperor 45
Charles VI, Emperor 93
Christian Democrats 217
Clement VII, Pope 45
Clement XIII, Pope 64
clothing 8, 11, 19, 21, 87
 (Eastern-) Jewish 9, 11, 19, 21, 87, 112, 135, 147, 148, 154, 155, 159, 215
collectivization 209

Communists, Communist Party 179, 184, 207–209, 213, 240, 241
concentration camps 213, 227, 239
Congress of Berlin 195, 197
Constantinople 47
conversion 14, 19, 47, 230
Cossacks 35, 36, 37
Council of Basel 10
Counter-Reformation 14, 19, 24, 25, 63, 65, 79
Cracow 12, 13, 17, 23, 24, 27, 30, 46, 68, 188, 190, 240, 242
craftsmen 15, 17–19, 22, 27, 28, 64, 69, 70, 87, 88, 92, 101, 107, 108, 111–115, 123, 126, 127, 145, 160, 175, 190, 196, 199, 209, 222, 237
Crimean Tatars 35, 36
crusade 4, 13, 78
custom (also religious) 41, 57, 58, 61, 73, 75, 120, 131, 134, 138, 140, 143, 145, 146, 152, 155, 179, 180, 185, 223, 250
Cuza, Alexandru 194
Czacki, Tadeusz 69
Czartoryski, Adam, Jerzy 72, 75
Czerniaków, Adam 237
Czernowitz 174, 185, 187
Częstochowa (Tschenstochau) 38

Danton, Georges 49
Danzig (Gdańsk) 13, 102
Datner, Szymon 242
death 7, 14, 23, 25, 43, 77, 93, 141, 158, 177, 200, 201, 213, 232, 237, 238, 243
Decembrists 85
devekut 44, 52

displaced persons 239
Dmowski, Roman 216, 217, 220
Döblin, Alfred 130
Dov Baer of Międzyrzecz 52
Drohobycz 182, 184
Drucki-Lubecki, Franciczek Ksawery 105
Dubnov, Simon 172, 218
Duma 89, 162, 172, 173, 220

Ebner, Mayer 187
Edelman, Marek 237, 238
education 21, 25, 26, 39, 47, 57, 75, 87, 88, 96, 110, 120, 134, 141, 143, 145, 146, 160, 181, 186, 188, 209, 210, 216, 222, 234
Eichmann, Adolf 235
Elbing (Elbląg) 13
Elia of Chełm 43
Elijah of Vilnius, *see* Gaon
Elisabeth of Russia 49, 80
emancipation 50, 71, 84, 87, 120, 141, 166, 167, 168, 169, 170, 174, 194, 199, 228, 249
emet 43
enlightenment 25, 48, 51, 57, 64, 75, 76, 79, 80, 81, 85, 94, 96, 119, 120–122, 137, 163, 167, 183, 186, 187, 247, 248
entrepreneurs 91, 101, 105, 106, 114–117, 126, 127, 129, 132, 161, 199, 208
Epstein (entrepreneur family) 115
Erlich, Henryk (Wolf Hersch) 164, 212
eruv 146
excommunication 77
Ezofowicz, Michel 19

farmers 15, 18, 30, 187
'Final Solution' 230, 232, 236
Florence 17
Ford, Henry 177
Fraenkel (entrepreneur family) 105
Frank, Eva 95
Frankfurt a. M. 17, 85, 92, 192
Franzos, Karl Emil 183
Frederick II Emperor 4, 9
Frederick II of Prussia 81
Freud, Sigmund 142
Frey Junius 49

Gaon (*gaon*) 76, 77
General Jewish–National Party of Austria 188
General Union of Jewish Workers in Lithuania, Poland, and Russia, or 'Bund' 163, 164, 166, 169, 179, 207, 217, 225
Gestapo 212
ghetto 9, 10, 71, 85, 104, 130, 175, 178, 184, 199, 201, 223, 224, 236, 237, 238, 242
Goering, Hermann 234
Goldman, Michel 164
Golem 42, 43
Gomułka, Wladyslaw 240, 241
Gorchakov 197
Grabski, Władysław 221
Granach, Alexander 183
Grodno 5
Grynszpan, Herschel 227
guild 15, 17, 19, 64, 81, 87, 92, 196, 248
Gurs 236

Habermas, Jürgen 81, 248

Hadassah 180
Haggadah 152
Haidamak uprisings 98
Haller, Józef 215, 217, 220
halutsim 210
Hamburg 17
hamets 152
Hannover 227
Hanower, Natan 25, 26, 30
Hanukka 153, 154
Hasidism, Hasidim 42, 51, 52–56, 71–78, 96, 98, 120, 121, 129, 131, 132, 135, 139, 144, 147, 152, 153, 157, 160, 165, 166, 173, 178, 180, 181, 183, 184, 193, 214, 246, 249
Haskala 76, 119–121, 163, 167, 186, 249
hazan 158
Hebrew 6, 12, 21, 23, 25, 42, 44, 57, 67, 77, 81, 119, 121, 144, 152, 156, 157, 163, 167, 184, 210
heder 143, 144, 161, 180, 221, 223
Heine, Heinrich 61, 67
Herzl, Theodor 169, 170, 188
hevra kaddisha 86, 158
Hibbat Tsiyon 167, 168
Hilsner, Leopold 200
Himmler, Heinrich 236
Hitler, Adolf 228, 233, 236
Hitler–Stalin Pact 212, 232
Holocaust (*see also* Shoah) 242
Horodenka 185
Horowitz, Yeshaya 46
hostility against the Jews, *see* anti-Judaism, anti-Semitism
Hovevei Tsiyon 167, 170
huppa 140

Iaşi 98, 232
identity 10, 99, 106, 120, 122, 142, 161, 162, 174, 186, 201, 203, 214, 245, 247, 249
independent Jews 190
industry 102, 111–115, 125, 127, 129, 177, 208, 222, 237
Institute for Jewish Research 222
intermediary function 27, 29, 40, 54, 58, 63, 101, 106, 111, 113, 116, 117, 133, 161, 174, 225, 248
Ioffe, Adolf A. 210
Iron Guard 231, 232
Isaac of Trokai 4
Israel ben Eliezer, *see* Ba'al Shem Tov
Isserles, Moses 24, 30
Ivan IV 78, 79

Jerusalem 55, 60, 76, 119, 140, 152, 156, 158, 165, 178, 239, 246
Jewish Club 189
Jewish Committee for the Assistance of Victims of War 160
Jewish councils 236, 237
Jewish Institute of History 242
Jewish legion 70
Jewish National Council 215, 233
Jewish National Party 188
Jewish party 210, 225, 229, 240
Jewish People's Party 172, 218
Jewish Social Democratic Party of Galicia 189
Jewish Socialist Workers' Party 171
Jewish State 21, 85, 145, 165, 169, 187, 209, 236
Jezierski, Jacek 69
Jogiches, Leo 163

John II Casimir of Poland 38
Joselewicz, Berek 70
Joseph II, Emperor 94
Judah the Hasid 42
'Judenfleck' 10

Kabbala 42–47, 56
Kaddish 86, 156, 158
Kafka, Franz 184, 202, 203
kahal 20, 26, 39, 41, 48, 59, 69, 73, 74, 75, 77, 78, 82, 86, 88, 96, 159, 172
Kalischer, Zwi Hirsch 166
Kalisz *see* Statute of Kalisz 4, 17
Kamenev, Lev B. (Rozenfel'd) 210
Kamionka Strumiłowa 19
Kamisol (Motl) 108
Kant, Immanuel 81, 247
Karamzin, Nikolai 85
Karl von Hohenzollern-Sigmaringen, Prince and King of Romania 194
Kazimierz 12, 13, 27, 46
kehilla 20
kes 140
Khazar 6–8, 78
Khmelnytsky, Bohdan 36, 37, 60
kibbutz 170
Kielce 240
Kiev 7, 35, 168
Kisch, Egon Erwin 43
Kishinev 89
klezmer 179
Kohn, Hans 202
Kol Nidre 150, 151
korobka 87
Kościuszko, Tadeusz 70

kosher 44, 87, 146, 147
Kosoy, Feodosii 79
Kovner, Abba 237
Kovno (Kaunas) 167
Kozienice, Israel of 249
Koźmian, Kajetan 72
Krasnopol'e 113
Kristallnacht ('night of broken glass') 227, 234, 246
Kremer, Arkady (Aron) 163
Kronenberg (entrepreneur family) 115
Ku-Klux-Klan 177

labourer/worker 51, 114, 126–128, 133, 160, 163–165, 171, 174, 175, 177, 189, 199, 224
Ladino 198
Lateran Council 11
League of the Green Ribbon 224
learning 21–26, 39, 42, 76, 103, 120, 139, 178, 238
lease, rent 14, 15, 18, 21, 28, 88, 96, 105, 117, 182, 185, 192
Legion of the Archangel Michael 231
Leipzig 17
Lelewel, Joachim 91
Lemberg, (Lwów, Lviv) 12, 183, 187, 222, 237
Lenin (Vladimir Ilyich Ulyanov) 165
Levi, Juda ha 6
Levinsohn, Isaak Bär 119
Lewko 4
Liber, Mark 164
Liberman, Aron Samuel 163
Litvaks 123–125, 214
living circumstances 66, 84, 113

Łódź 114–117, 123, 125–129, 130, 131, 133, 160–162, 165, 236, 237
London 165, 197
Löw, Rabbi 43
Lublin 3, 14, 20, 21, 24, 30, 31, 235
Luftmenshn 105, 109, 110, 130
Luria, Isaac 45, 46
Luria, Salomon 24
Luxemburg, Rosa 163

Maccabees 153
Maggid 52, 54, 56, 249
Maimon, Salomon 64, 66, 75, 138
Mapu, Abraham 167
Maria Theresia 94
Mark, Bernard 228
Máramaros 192
marriage 21, 44, 55, 59, 69, 93, 96, 108, 126, 137, 138, 139, 140, 141, 181, 198, 243
Martov (Yuly O. Tsederbaum) 163
Masaryk, Tomáš G. 201, 229
Maskilim 75, 119, 121, 167, 183
matzo 119, 152
Maximilian von Habsburg 30
Medem, Vladimir 164
Megillah 154
melamed 144
Mendelssohn, Moses 57, 64, 75, 119
menorah 154
Messiah 44, 46–48, 50, 52, 54, 60, 156, 165, 170, 177, 245
Messianism 6, 45, 50, 51, 170, 187
met 43
mezuzah 128, 134
Michoels, Solomon M. 213
Mickiewicz, Adam 50, 187

Międzybóż 51
Międzyrzecz 52
migration 4, 5, 12, 31, 40, 91, 98, 104, 106, 115, 125, 166–168, 175, 177, 178, 180, 196, 226, 234, 235, 240
mikvah 138, 139, 147, 149, 150
military service, conscription 22, 71, 87, 94–96, 98, 121, 194, 196
Minsk 35
Minyan 135, 140, 157, 241
Misnagdim (*Mitnaggedim*) 75, 76
Misrahi 166, 189, 218
Mohilewer, Samuel 170
Molcho, Salomo 45
money-lending 7, 12, 18, 58, 113
Mongols 78, 97
Morgenstern, Soma 184
Moscow 14, 36, 79, 82, 84, 89, 116
Moses de León 44
Mountain Jews 7
Mühlhausen 24
Munkács (Mukacevo) 178
Mussolini, Benito 236

Nachman von Bracław 107
Napoleon 70, 71, 101
Narodniki 162
Narutowicz, Gabriel 220
Nathan of Gaza 47, 48
National Socialist 226, 231, 232
National Democrats 90, 162, 172, 214, 217, 219, 224, 226
nationalism 132, 164, 170, 171, 173, 186, 187, 190, 199, 212, 217, 228, 232
Natonek, Josef 166
Neologi 191

New Economical Policy 209
New York 178
Newachowicz, Leon 105
New Jerusalem 69
Nicholas I, Tsar of Russia 121
nobility 12, 14, 17–19, 28, 29, 37, 40, 58, 61, 65, 66, 70, 74, 81, 91, 101–104, 106, 115, 117, 192, 198.
Nossig, Alfred 187
Novgorod 14, 79
Novosiltsev, Nikolai N. 73
Nuremberg 'race laws' 226, 234

Odessa 62, 110, 121, 168
Offenbach 49, 95
Oleśnicki, Zbigniew 12
Orthodoxy, Judaism 48, 56, 74, 75, 95, 96, 98, 120, 129, 146, 157, 166, 167, 172, 188, 189, 191, 193, 214, 219, 221, 226, 229, 230, 249
outsiders 59, 93, 121, 231

Pale of Settlement 83, 90, 121, 214
Pappenheim, Bertha 182
Paris 195, 197, 227
Parnas 157
Paul I of Russia 77
Peace of Adrianople 194
Peace of Brest-Litovsk 207, 208
Peace of Versailles 216
peasants 18, 28, 29–31, 35–38, 58, 59, 61–63, 72, 81, 82, 84, 88, 92, 101–103, 106, 144, 116, 118, 125, 133, 161, 169, 182, 186, 193, 197, 208, 216, 217, 220, 248

peasants' parties 217, 220
peddler, hawker 17, 18, 28, 58, 61, 74, 92, 101, 109, 111, 116, 127, 130, 133, 136, 175
Peretz, Isaac Leib 120
Pestel', Pavel 85
Peter I, the Great 38, 79
Peter III of Russia 80
Petersburg 120
pilpul 23, 24, 26, 41, 48, 76
Piłsudski, Józef 220, 224
Pinsk 171
Pinsker, Leo 168
Piotrków 14
Pius II 13
Płońsk 171
Poale Tsiyon (Zion) 171, 188, 189, 207, 210, 218
pogrom 7, 13, 25, 35, 39, 46, 88–90, 123, 132, 133, 161, 162, 167, 175, 189, 196, 201, 208, 215, 225, 226, 227, 230, 232, 240, 246
Poliakov, S. S. 115
Polish Legion 70
Polish Socialist Party 162
Poznański (entrepreneur family) 115, 160
Prague 9, 10, 23, 27, 43, 92–95, 157, 198–202, 229
Privileges de non tolerandis Christianis 13
privileges *de non tolerandis Judaeis* 13
property, Jewish 211, 235, 240
Prus, Bolesław 118
Przemyśl 17
public law 169

Purim 154, 155, 179

rabbis 19, 23, 24, 26, 30, 41, 43, 49, 50, 52, 54, 56, 73, 74, 76–78, 85, 115, 132, 140, 145, 146, 148, 166
'race laws' 226, 234,
Radek, Karl (Sobelsohn) 210
Rebecca, daughter of Rabbi Meir Tiktiner 23
Reform Jews 157, 193, 230
Regensburg 27
Reichsrat 189, 190
Reichssicherheitshauptamt 235
Reubeni, David 45
Revolution in Russia 89, 90, 175, 177, 207–214, 232
Revolution of 1848 190
Ringelblum, Emanuel 223, 227
Rohling, August 201
Rosenberg Alfred 233
Rosh Hashana 151
Roth, Joseph 62, 63, 153, 184, 211, 234
Rumkowski, Chaim 236, 237
Russian–Turkish War 195
Rzeszów 60

Sabbath 41, 43, 86, 94, 96, 97, 114, 128, 133, 134, 139, 146–149, 154, 158, 159, 228
Sabbathism 97
Sacher-Masoch, Leopold von 183
Safed 24, 45
Safran, Alexander 232
Salz, Abraham 187
Sandomierz 12
Sanhedrin, Great 71
Satanower, Mendel 75

Schlesinger, Akiva Josef 166
Schulz, Bruno 184
Seder 152
Sejm 22, 40, 68, 69, 172, 217, 219, 220, 221
Semlin (Zemun) 166
Sephardim 6, 10, 98, 198
sex 10, 47, 49, 137, 200
Sforim, Mendele Moykher 59, 110, 120
Shabtai Tsevi 47–51, 52, 56, 76
Shaddai 135
shadkhan 138
shammash 151, 154, 158
Shavuot 152
Shekhina 44
sheytl 139
shiva 156
Shoah (Holocaust) 167
shtadlan 22
shterntichl 148
shtetl 59, 60, 61, 110, 113, 153, 173, 179, 180, 183, 184, 189, 208, 246
shtibl 157, 159
shtrayml 148
Sigismund I, the Old 20
Sigismund III of Poland 30
Simhat Torah 153
Singer, Isaac Bashevis 44, 117, 128, 136, 150, 155, 158, 161, 181, 222
Singer, Israel Joshua 128, 222
Skvira 168
slaughter 41, 225, 237
Smyrna 47
Social Democrats, Social Democracy 163, 165, 171, 189, 201, 202, 207, 215

socialism, Socialists 51, 117, 121, 123, 133, 141, 162, 163, 164, 165, 167, 169, 171–173, 179, 197, 207, 210, 217, 218, 210, 221, 231, 240
Society for the Achievement of Equal Rights for the Jewish People in Russia 172
Society for the Promotion of Craft and Agriculture among the Jews in Russia 160
Sofer, Hatam (Moses Schreiber) 166, 167, 191
Sofia 198
Solidarność 237, 241
Sonnenberg, Berek Szmul 105
Sonnenfeld, Chaim Josef 166
Speransky, Michail 73
Sperber, Manès 184, 246
Spira, Chaim Elazar (Shapira) 178
Stalin 211, 213
Stalinism 184, 209, 211
Stanisław II, August Poniatowski 70, 72
Staszic, Stanisław 72
Statute of Kalisz 4
Statute on the Jews (1804) 84
sukkot 153
SS 234–236
Sverdlov, Jakov M. 210
Svyatopolk II, Prince of Kiev 7
Svyatoslav, Prince of Kiev 6
Synagogal supervision 86
synagogue 22, 27, 31, 40, 43, 63, 64, 78, 122, 128, 133, 136, 137, 144, 148, 150, 151–154, 156–159, 180, 190, 195
Synod of Prague 10

Syrkin, Nachman 171
Szold, Henrietta 180
Szybuscz 40

tallit 135, 143
Talmud 3, 23, 24–26, 41, 44, 45, 58, 60, 72, 76, 85, 116, 119, 120, 135, 144–146, 150, 155, 158, 201
Talmud–Torah School 116
Tarnopol 184, 187
Tarnów 187
tefillin 135
Thorn (Torún) 13
tikkun 46
Tiszaeszlár 191
Torah 21, 22, 30, 42, 44, 48, 55, 77, 86, 116, 135, 143, 144, 152, 153, 155, 156, 166
trade, tradesman 5, 15, 17–19, 28, 37, 41, 51, 58–60, 63, 64, 67, 69, 70, 72, 74, 78, 79, 80, 81, 84, 96, 98, 101–103, 105, 107, 109–115, 117, 127, 129, 136, 145, 150, 160, 174, 175, 195, 196, 199, 208, 215, 222, 237, 248
Trotsky Leon (Lev Bronshteyn) 163, 210
tsaddik 52–56, 76, 77, 132, 148, 183, 189, 246
Tsederbaum, Yuly O. 163
Tyszka, Jan 163

Uganda plan 171
Uprising in Poland 50, 51, 70, 85, 91, 118, 121
Ussishkin, Menachem (Usyškin) 171

Va'ad 21, 22, 40, 68, 172
Venice 17, 25
Vienna 68, 92, 142, 169, 182, 192, 197, 201
Vilna 76, 77
Virgin of Lubomir 55
Vitebsk 110
Voltaire 25

Waddington, William Henry 197
Wahl, Saul 30
Wannsee conference 236
War Communism 210
Warsaw 13, 68–71, 91, 102, 104, 105, 113, 115, 117, 118, 120–123, 125–132, 150–155, 159, 161–163, 208, 214, 220, 223, 227, 228, 237, 242, 243
Weizmann, Chaim 171
Werbermacher, Hanna Rachel 55
Wielopolski, Aleksander 91
Wierzbowce (Werbowitz, Werbiwizi) 185
Witold of Lithuania 5
Witte, Sergei 89
Władysław II, Jagiełło 5
World War, First 68, 84, 90, 115, 127, 128, 141, 150, 160, 173, 175–179, 181, 191, 193, 207, 214, 229–231
World War, Second 177, 223, 232, 233, 241–243
Worms 27

Yad Vashem 246
yeshiva 26, 144, 159
Yiddish 23, 57, 58, 67, 70, 110, 120, 121, 122, 124, 131, 134, 137,

164, 174, 179, 181, 185, 189,
196, 210, 211, 212, 217, 218,
222, 223
YIVO 222, 223
Yom Kippur 150, 151
Young Czechs 199

Zabłotow 60, 184
Zamość 30
Zamoyski, Maurycy 69, 220

Zangwill, Israel 180
Zasław 25
Zhitomir 120
Zinoviev 210
Zionism, Zionist 51, 121, 123, 125,
133, 142, 162, 165, 166–180,
184, 187–189, 193, 198, 202,
209, 210, 214, 213, 215, 218,
221, 223, 225, 226, 237, 240
Zundelevič, Aron 163

Also available from CEU Press

A Suburb of Europe

Nineteenth Century Polish Approaches to Western Civilization

By **Jerzy Jedlicki**, Institute of History, Polish Academy of Sciences; Graduate School for Social Research, Warsaw

The story of a century-long Polish dispute over the merits and demerits of the Western model of liberal progress and industrial civilization. As in all peripheral countries of Europe, Polish intellectuals – conservatives, liberal, and (later) socialists – quarrelled about whether such a model would suit and benefit their nation, or whether it would spell the ruin of its distinctive cultural features.

"... an important and profoundly insightful analysis of the intellectual debate about economic development in the partitioned lands of nineteenth-century Poland, as writers like Kamjeński came to the defense of industry, capitalism, economic progress, and something more vague that went by the name of "civilization". Obviously, those forces would not have needed to be defended if they did not face intellectual criticism from a variety of perspectives—conservative, national, sentimental, messianic, socialist—which Jedlicki explores with great erudition." – **The American Historical Review**

"... a brilliant example of intellectual history, whose importance far transcends the period on which it focuses. In important ways, in the post-communist 'transition' of the 1990s, the issues of the 19th century are profoundly relevant to the beginnings of the 21st. Moreover, Jedlicki's book raises issues and examines positions that were and are not unique to Poland, but that every society faces as it confronts social change." – **Choice**

"... an excellent volume about philosophy, political economy, the creation of nationalism, and a host of other subjects. It is an enlightening and engrossing read. Anyone with an interest in Poland and East Central Europe will find this an invaluable and enjoyable book." – **Austrian Studies Newsletter**

308 pages, 1998
963-9116-27-0 cloth $49.95 / £31.00
963-9116-26-2 paperback $21.95 / £13.95

**AVAILABLE TO ORDER AT ALL GOOD BOOKSHOPS
OR CHECK OUT OUR WEBSITE WWW.CEUPRESS.COM
FOR FULL ORDERING DETAILS**

Also available from CEU Press

Foreword to the Past

A Cultural History of the Baltic People

By **Endre Bojtár**, Institute of Literary Studies of the Hungarian Academy of Sciences

"It will supersede all that has been written in English on the roots of Lithuanian, Latvian and Old Prussian ethnicity, culture and religion" – **The English Historical Review**

Over time at least four meanings have been attributed to the term 'Baltic' – drawing on thirty years of extensive research, *Foreword to the Past* is the first modern introduction to the enigma of the Baltic origins and the self-identification of the Baltic people.

The book is divided into three distinctive parts: the first part recounts the history of the Baltic peoples relying on archaeological sources; the second part provides an objective linguistic history and a description of the Baltic languages; the third part provides an original and fresh insight into mythology in the ancient history of the Baltic peoples.

With its helpful maps and figures, *Foreword to the Past* is an un-paralleled and original cultural exploration of the Baltic people.

419 pages, 7 maps, 2000

963-9116-42-4 cloth $49.95 / £31.95
963-9116-41-6 paperback $23.95 / £14.95

**AVAILABLE TO ORDER AT ALL GOOD BOOKSHOPS
OR CHECK OUT OUR WEBSITE WWW.CEUPRESS.COM
FOR FULL ORDERING DETAILS**

Also available from CEU Press

Jewish Budapest

Monuments, Rites, History

Edited by **Géza Komoróczy**, Eötvös Loránd University, Budapest, with **Kinga Frojimovics, Viktória Pusztai** and **Andrea Strbik**

"Unlike most works concerning Jewish Budapest, which have taken a strictly historical approach, this work also introduces the Jewish elements and traces which exist still today in Budapest. The work is an immense archival undertaking by the Center of Jewish Studies at the Hungarian Academy of Sciences." – **Slavic and East European Journal**

"The rich variety of photographs, maps and drawings make lore and history come alive. Encyclopedic in scope and detail, this volume will certainly become the basic English text on the Jews of Budapest and Hungary. Highly recommended for large and academic libraries." – **Library Journal**

Neither a guidebook or a history in the traditional sense, this book is about the Jewish face of Budapest from medieval times to the present. To get the broadest possible perspective, this book is not only about the Hungarian capital as a Jewish city but, as befits a cosmopolitan metropolis, delves into its myriad elements.

Here is a book at once personal and universal. It is about everyday Jewish life, the humor, the pathos, the human condition, which is the same or very similar anywhere in the Diaspora. Every image and incident, every happening is filtered through the strong sensibilities of the key citizens of the city throughout the past few centuries. Remarkable citizens personified by the likes of Theodor Herzl and Joseph Pulitzer.

The book includes a section of detailed comments on the illustrations with an explanation of the abbreviations throughout as well as a bibliography, an index of personal names, an index of cities and towns, and an index of Budapest street addresses.

A Selection of the Jewish Book Club

598 pages, 553 halftones, 89 color illustrations,
200mm × 280mm (7.8' × 11'), 1999
963-9116-38-6 cloth $69.95 / £45.00
963-9116-37-8 paperback $26.95 / £16.95

**AVAILABLE TO ORDER AT ALL GOOD BOOKSHOPS
OR CHECK OUT OUR WEBSITE WWW.CEUPRESS.COM
FOR FULL ORDERING DETAILS**